THE RICH ARE DIFFERENT

For one thing, they have a great deal of money.

For another, they have had the vision and the nerve to recognize and seize the many opportunities for wealth that the modern world offers.

Their methods differ widely. They may borrow money they don't have to pay back and lend money they don't happen to have. They may build a better mousetrap, or at least buy up the patent on one dirt cheap. They may gamble in a money game rigged so that they cannot lose. They may legally not only avoid paying taxes but have the government actually give funds to them. They may sell things that are not only unneeded but unwanted. They may even wind up in jail, but with their millions in safe deposit boxes waiting for them when they're released.

Here are their true stories.

Here are the many different ways and means to make a million in the world today.

HOW
TO MAKE
A MILLION

*(formerly, The Common Millionaire
and How To Get That Way)*

ROBERT HELLER

A DELL BOOK

Published by
DELL PUBLISHING CO., INC.
1 Dag Hammarskjold Plaza
New York, New York 10017
Originally published under the title *The Common Millionaire*
Copyright © 1974 by Robert Heller
Dell ® TM 681510, Dell Publishing Co., Inc.
Reprinted by arrangement with
Delacorte Press

Printed in Canada

First Dell printing—March 1976

It's no trick to make a lot of money,
if all you want is to make a lot of money.

—Mr. Bernstein in *Citizen Kane*

FOREWORD

THIS BOOK sprang from an obsession, not with wealth as such, but with the contrast between its public and private faces. Journalism led me to the desks, sometimes into the homes, of men whose fame rested less on their achievements, which varied from the great to the disgraceful, than on the results of those deeds—the accumulation of either wealth or the appearance of wealth. Riches had changed all these men in different ways, some for the better, some for the worse. But their careers and behavior as they strutted their stages seemed, the more I studied them, to conform to some unwritten body of economic laws: and these laws are my subject.

Like other legal systems, this one has been modified by time: today's rich are different from yesterday's. But their names are often the same as, and the sources of their fortunes similar to, those of the past. The first act in this theater of wealth describes the inheritance, protection, and preservation of such fortunes, including those of the aristocracy of money. The second act introduces shadier characters, because its theme is illusion: the practice of deceit, honest and otherwise. Whatever origins wealth has, however, big money tends to breed more millions still— and the theme of the third act is how the rich get richer.

The fourth act stresses the vital importance, in creating a lasting cornucopia, of waiting for it: of letting time get on your side. The fifth deals with the phenomenon which is usually only recognized in one form: the incidence of pure luck. But chance is not the only benefactor who thrusts wealth on the deserving and undeserving alike: there is, for instance, the government, any government. The final act includes many of my favorite millionaires—men who have persevered with the one genuine talent which marks them out from the rest of the world, and from which the world truly benefits.

There are four entr'actes, or intermissions: cautionary tales. One describes the perilous divide between excessive conservatism and overzealous change; the second the penalties of lack of concentration; another the meaning of "minginess" and the hazard of uncontrol; the fourth the dangers of gluttony. It is often only when the rich man has been incautious that the private and public images suddenly coincide, and the reality emerges. The reality is that riches and true human achievement bear only a tenuous relationship to each other: but that, if only you are rich enough, nobody will ever notice the truth.

I owe a special debt of gratitude to Felicity Krish, an invaluable assistant in every way; to Jeanne Bernkopf for her admirable editing; to Ross Claiborne (also of Delacorte) and Hilary Rubinstein for unfailing support and ideas; to others who have helped me directly and indirectly, including my excellent colleagues on *Management Today;* to Simon Dally at Weidenfeld & Nicolson; to John Thackray; and to the authors of the works quoted in the bibliography. But this book is above all dedicated to my children, for making it all worthwhile.

CONTENTS

big game, yachts, women, and gambling

PROLOGUE

The Rich Are Different

Making a million is easier than it used to be; it never was very hard—which is why the trick has been managed down the ages by so many from the ranks of the untalented, the uninspired, and the forgettable. In this age, however, thanks to the blessings of inflation, the points total for winning players, while seemingly the same, is far lower. It's as if, in the game of financial baseball, the strike zone has been widened almost to the full width of the diamond.

To match a million in the dollars of 1914, when a world war ended the golden age of plutocracy, requires $4.8 million today. A million in 1928, before a cataclysmic depression robbed some silver age plutocrats of their riches, is the equivalent nowadays of $3.2 million. A million in 1948, when the rebuilders of the postwar economy began to reap their rewards, equals $2.2 million in the currency of the early 1970s—deep in a new era, the Age of the Common Millionaire.

Inflation has not only belittled the score; it has made scoring easier. The apparent or monetary value of assets has steadily risen, so that a man buying any treasure, from a cider press to a car plant, has an overwhelming chance of reselling at a profit, which is the basic activity of every Croesus who ever cashed a check.

The rackets of the rich cover a range of real-life fairy tales that even Scheherazade, given another thousand and one nights, could not exhaust. Ballpoint pens, ball bearings, demolition, construction, shipbuilding, shipowning, broking, breaking, farming, not farming, molybdenum, milling, holes in the ground, filling holes in the ground, stealing, borrowing, lending, foreclosing, carpets, convertibles, soup, soupcans, pictures of soupcans, salad oil, nonexistent salad oil, betting, taking bets, extortion, exemption, Chinese money, Chinese food—the catalogue rolls on endlessly and with as much variation as the names and backgrounds of the blessed.

It's not exactly a roll of honor; nearer, somewhat, to a roll of dishonor since, in a significant bevy of cases, the basic wealth-creating activity has been augmented, if not by fraud, by tricks, devices, stratagems; all variants of the conjuror's game of doing it with mirrors. The basic activity, however, never changes. The millionaire earns his title by selling, or being able to sell, some property, some product, some service, some idea, for more than cost. The wider the gulf between the cost and realized value, the more rapidly the player gets to his ultimate reward. There have always been the two extremes of technique. The player can choose between selling to myriad customers at low profits (10 million customers at a dime apiece) or to a select clientele at high profits (ten suckers at $100,000 a throw).

In the golden and silver ages, there were no shortcuts: the resultant wealth was measured certifiably in cash, negotiable gilt-edged securities, and real property, all of which took time to accumulate. That measure was only natural in a time of low or no taxes, of minimal inheritance tax, and of a political dispensation which enshrined inequality. The truly kingly fortunes all stem from this golden age—the Rockefellers (put at 5 American billions today), the Rothschilds (weighed in collectively at 100 billion), the Du Ponts (worth over 7.5 billion in the mid-1960s), and the Mellons (supposedly neck-and-neck with the Rockies, thanks to heavy holdings in the Mellon National Bank, Gulf Oil, Alcoa, *et al.*).

No calculations have been made of the proportion of the world's wealth which, right here and now, is held by the three hundred richest families. Their share is plainly that of a particularly voracious lion. The combined total of a few outstanding American nest eggs alone—Mellons, Du Ponts, Rockefellers, Getty, Rosenwald, Land, Hughes, Mayer—must handsomely exceed $20 billion. That is equal to about the total end-1972 market worth of General Motors—and there is, of course, always the chance that these mighty aggregations, which are only the chapter headings, so to speak, in the golden book of international wealth, are under-, not over-, estimated. In most cases, if the concept of a man's wealth is widened to include all assets that he can enjoy exclusively, all business interests that he can influence while holding only a proportion (or none) of the shares, he emerges as richer by far than even an expert optimist can guess.

Land probably still constitutes or lies behind many of the greatest fortunes—although aristocrats, because of their touching faith in primogeniture and distrust of new-fangled financial devices, have often frittered away their wealth in estate taxes. The Duke of Westminster, who died in 1953, bequeathed a tax liability of £15-20 million. That this bill could be met, without touching 270 acres in two fashionable little villages, Belgravia and Mayfair, is some measure of the mighty iceberg of aristocratic fortunes.

The predominance of imperial, old-line families led one careful researcher, Ferdinand Lundberg, to conclude that "there is less and less room for new millionaires." But an old-new billionaire contradicted him. "Large fortunes will be made," wrote J. P. Getty, "in the next two decades by men who are beginners today." As usual in money matters the thinker was wrong, the Midas right.

In 1973 a minor British retailer of Iraqi family origin, Albert Gubay, created a headline sensation. Gubay, while cashing in £7.4 million of shares in his discount grocery chain, had sworn solemnly to keep his remaining £4 million stake as a long-term investment; in fact, he off-loaded the latter shares on the quiet, making a total cash take of possibly £14 million from all his sales, and then skipped the country. He had been in business for only a decade. He operated only thirty-eight stores around Wales and its borders. Had Gubay never existed, neither the gross national product nor the general welfare would have been affected one whit. Yet this one small grocer's snatch leaves any salary in the world limping.

Few men, no matter how distinguished, powerful, or valuable, earn £100,000 a year. To match the egregious Gubay, even before tax, they would have to labor for 140 years, or more than three working lifetimes. To match his joys after tax, the figures should probably be doubled, and that takes no account of the interest on Gubay's dollop of dubious reward—and the annual interest would also handily exceed £100,000.

The aristo-plutocrats may stay atop some lofty reserved Olympus. But on the lower slopes (and not so much farther down) a new and different breed has been climbing fast, propelled in part by the natural force of mass. The millionaire gets rich by creaming off part of the general pool of wealth. The deeper and wider the pool, the smaller the amount of skimming required to fill the same size money pot.

Thanks to the sheer abundance of natural resources and stupendously lax political control, the United States has spawned the bulk of the world's millionaires, from the gold and silver kings to the stock option fat-cats of today. Between 1914 and 1972 the gross national product of America—the annual stream of real wealth—has multiplied nearly five and three-quarter times. In real terms, with no benefit of inflation, $100 million in 1914 currency was 0.2% of American gross national product, whereas in 1972, measured in 1914 dollars, it was only 0.04%. Despite all the supposed efforts of politicians to curb and spread the wealth, the share of property and income held by the few has, according to several studies, remained more or less constant. Possibly there is some natural law, like that of water finding its own level, which constantly forces a given ratio of the national income into the hands of those who already have more than their per capita share or are burning to do so.

But the simple, mathematical growth of the pool of wealth is only the start of the story. Equally important has been the discovery of the modern philosopher's stone, the authentic way of creating thick wealth out of thin air.

An heir to many millions and creator of a fair few himself once observed that people "confuse wealth and money." He was, it turns out, distinguishing between the wealths of the mint and of the mind, but his remark holds the key to the Age of the Common Millionaire. For the Common Millionaire has succeeded in divorcing real wealth—property, the creation of new resources—from money.

In the first Rockefeller's day, to create money, you had to create an equivalent amount of assets. True, Wall Street in those days had no hesitation about multiplying such real objects by unreal accretions of paper, a pastime known agriculturally as "watering the stock." J. Pierpont Morgan in 1901 poured forth "securities" (an interesting euphemism in the circumstances) to a face value of over a billion dollars in launching US Steel on a gullible world; on the offi-

cial count he printed $726.8 million more in paper than
the company, in visible material form, was worth. In 1929
by similar zealous work at the printing press Goldman
Sachs issued one-quarter of a billion in securities in a mere
month.

But the day of the old pirate has gone; now is the time
of the new piranha. His sharp-toothed discovery is that the
wealth represented by real assets, or by no assets at all, can
still be transmogrified by the paper multiplier, with perfect
legality.

The new Open Sesame is the phrase "discounting of
growth." The Common Millionaire sells not what he owns,
but what (God willing) he *will* own one fine day. The
buyers purchase not today, but a tomorrow that sometimes
never comes. The cardinal invention of capitalism, the
joint stock company, was carried in the 1960s to what may
be its final form, an engine for the creation of endless
wealth unsupported by any concrete foundation.

Under this newest of dispensations, the company promoter doesn't have to water stock: the public dilutes it for
him. Suiting the technique to the times, the piranha promoter doesn't issue vastly excessive quantities of the same
paper but instead issues shares which are not shares (warrants, convertibles, letter stocks, etc.) in the promise that
by the time they become real, live equity, the real values
will have caught up.

The Age of the Common Millionaire made possible,
with perfect honesty, a trick of which J. P. Morgan himself
would have been proud. In the more extreme cases, a man
could sell an overjoyed public a fraction of his shares for a
price which, on a traditional basis of valuation, would purchase the entire caboose. He would retain total control of
the company through paper valued at several times the
cash fortune now safely in his pocket, which could be used
as currency to purchase more assets, to which a similar
multiplier could be applied, and so on, not quite *ad infinitum*.

In actuality, such operations reverse the historical
process of capitalism. Instead of the equity holder taking
all the risk, and consequently all the rewards, he now
partly off-loads his risk for the highest price the market
will bear and takes his reward in advance.

Bear traps aplenty lie along such paths. But the essential
truth remains unchanged. The market capitalization of ma-

jor companies has risen to such unthinkably large sums that possession of a tithe of a tithe of the stock equals a monumental fortune, even by Morgan standards. At the end of 1972 there were 161 US companies where a one percent holding was worth $10 million, ranging from IBM ($468 million) to Merrill Lynch, and 339 more, from Dun and Bradstreet ($9.9 million) to McCormick, where a similar stake produced a clear $3.3 million.

Market capitalization, however, is an entirely hypothetical figure obtained by multiplying the number of shares in issue, only a small proportion of which are actually on the loose, by the market price of the day; that, of course, would drop like a quarry-full of stones if even a quarter of the shares came on offer.

But one percent of Shell Transport and Trading in May 1974 was still notionally worth some £10 million; and the Samuel family, heirs to the founder, presumably have many of those percentage points. The family holding of Julius Rosenwald, who made Sears Roebuck the world's richest retailer, was put at 12.5%: that modest-sounding stake was in theory worth over 2 billions as the 1970s unfolded.

The rich today can thus achieve via the stock market the condition which their predecessors contrived by paying no tax: the combination of massive real assets with maximum personal liquidity. To put it crudely, you can't take your cash out in income, because the government grabs it; so you take the booty in stock, which the government touches either lightly or not at all. It's a sweet paradox. The efforts of governments to restore equality by soaking the rich have led directly to the development of methods which have created far more rich—and efforts to inundate these with taxes will probably make still more millionaires.

And the rich today *are* different. Not just because (as Hemingway correctly argued against Scott Fitzgerald) they have more money; but because they are a different breed of furry cat. The millionaires and billionaires of the golden age were would-be princes. Deprived by fate of royal stature, they outspent those who had it. But in the mid-1960s it was noted with astonishment that one spectacularly successful Texas oilman, Algur H. Meadows, with $55 million to his name, had shelled out only half a million on his dream house; less than the first Rockefeller, most parsimonious of all the billionaires, spent in a single year on the upkeep of one family estate, his $30 million Tarrytown pad.

The Common Millionaire lives the same way as the good bourgeois citizen, only more so—and even the Common Billionaire may do much the same. J. P. Getty bought his splendid mansion, Sutton Place, from the third Duke of Sutherland for a supposed half million in sterling. A Vanderbilt would have regarded that kind of money as a decorator's bill. (Cornelius Vanderbilt spent $5 million on a Newport cottage which he used for only ten weeks a year.) Almost the only lavish similarity between the ultrarich of the golden and silver ages is the passion for paying great prices for art; even then, demand for a greatly diminished supply of Old Masters waned so markedly that it took over a generation before the Duveen prices charged to the earlier merchant princes were seen again—and that was in depreciated money. *The Mall in St. James's Park* by Gainsborough cost Frick $300,000; the same artist's *Mr. and Mrs. Andrews,* at 1973 exchange rates, fetched only $357,000.

Mostly, today's new millionaires come from the amorphous mass of the middle classes and bear the stamp of their origin. Even the titled exceptions start about their millions in a down-to-earth or déclassé way. Baron Marcel Bich, for example, is a French aristo whose cash in hand of over $40 million was accumulated on the humble base of the disposable ballpoint pen. Bich launched this after the war on $1,000. From sales of 1.5 billion Bic pens a year, the good Baron in 1971 gleaned $10 million of profit (which comes to 0.0066666 cent per Bic and is thus a perfect example of the multitudinous small profit approach).

The foresight of the rich is their prime justification. Although nearly all owners of big, middling, and small money owe much of it to multiplication by mirrors, many derived their riches originally from some flash of true inspiration, the equivalent in the material world of Nijinsky's leap, Picasso's Cubism, Proust's memory, Land's instant camera, Getty's Kuwait oil, even Bich's ballpoints represent breakthroughs from which millions of people have had real benefit, and from which, therefore, millions in currency have naturally flowed.

The breakthrough, the searing stroke of genius, lies in spotting a demand, latent or blatant, and simultaneously noting how that demand can be satisfied at the necessary

premium over the cost of supply. Characters like David
Sarnoff, the genius of RCA, are in this sense great philosophers and artists. In 1916, almost alone in his faith, Sarnoff wrote, "I have in mind a plan of development which
would make radio a household utility." In 1922-25 sales of
his "radio music boxes" came to $83 million. In 1923, he
wrote, "I believe that television . . . will come to pass in
due course," a belief that cost him $50 million before a
pay-off of incalculable size. He then pumped another $130
million into his final bonanza, color TV.

Whether the return is proportionate to the contribution
is another matter. In the overpowering majority of cases,
there can't be any argument. The balance between capital
and income has been tilted grossly in favor of capital; and
the capital gains of the capitalists often bear only the
slightest relation to the social or even economic value of
their work.

In the Age of the Common Millionaire, the possession
of 50 millions as opposed to 500 of them has a primarily
social connotation. The billionaire is an uncrowned monarch; the multimillionaire is a global potentate; even the
Common Millionaire is a welcome, highly placed courtier
(like Bebe Rebozo at the court of Richard Nixon) and a
potential folk-hero. At each of these three levels, there is a
common denominator: the affirmation by the rich that
money means nothing to them. They are telling the truth
and lying in their Sulka socks at one and the same time,
because the possession of money bestows the ineffable
power to make more money still; and power, for most of
the rich, new or old, is the name of their game.

All wealth equates with power, which has as many
forms as there are Rolls-Royces. To Andrew Carnegie, once
he was through with giving steel rivals and steelworkers
hell, wealth equated with the power to establish free public
libraries; to George Armstrong, a Southern millionaire,
wealth meant the ability to offer a staggering sum to a
small military college in Mississippi if its curriculum would
stress the racial superiority of the white man (the college,
to its undying credit, refused); to a legion of rich men, it
means the power to dominate the corporations which they
have created.

Antony Jay, the management writer, once asked a
tycoon wherein lay his own contribution, given all the bril-

liant and forceful men who labored in his employ. "I'll tell you," said the Croesus, "I own 67.5%."

For the mass of millionaires, the loot is a by-product of achieving some other end, although the objective and its results get mysteriously intertwined. That doesn't matter; the clue is still that the budding Baruch or Bluhdorn has to decide what he wants. That is the first step along the yellow-brick road, and most businessmen—9,999 out of 10,-000—never get even that far. But lack of focused intention, of truly moving motivation, is only part of the story. While nearly everybody vaguely "wants" a million, few are prepared to work for it. Lack of knack is equally crippling. Tall Texan stories abound with accounts of the brilliant men who drilled on land known to be stiff with oil, but found nothing but dry holes.

There are also hundreds of millionaires who have only one gift—making money. In this they resemble the master chess player who is good at nothing else. Making money resembles chess in other ways, not least in its cozy relationship with mathematics, still more in its abundance of traps, ploys, gambits, stratagems, variations, even its recognized offensive and defensive openings. As in chess, the moneymaker gains more through his opponent's mistakes than through his own immaculate brilliance; and for every winner there must be at least one loser.

The First Law of Millions states that "every millionaire creates his wealth at somebody else's expense," and it is this law which the new techniques for divorcing capital from income and taxes have exploited to such wondrous effect. The sale of shares to the public to guard against estate taxes or whatever has, almost inadvertently, created a new dimension of wealth; it has enlarged the number of those whose finances can be tapped by the resourceful few.

The new gimmicks reinforce the old maxim that money is its own best protection, a bulwark which gains further strength from the plutocratic habit of huddling together for added warmth. André L. Mayer, the driving force of Lazard Frères and reputedly worth $200 million on his own account, is said by Anthony Sampson, in his book on ITT, to run a syndicate for three well-heeled groups: the Rockefellers, a relatively obscure but immensely wealthy Belgian family named Boels, and the English Pearsons (better known as the Cowdrays). Sampson quotes an informed view that "Lazards isn't really a bank, it's a damned great moneymaking machine for a few very rich men."

As long ago as 1968, the Internal Revenue Service calculated that the total of American millionaires, having risen by 150% in a decade, had passed 100,000. One downy investment banker, sitting on nest eggs belonging to some of the choicest American clients, remarked that, for all his experience, he was constantly amazed by the number of unknown, substantial private fortunes: lump sums that lie forever protected in the giant investment portfolios of the banks (Morgan Guaranty, the champion in this arena, looks after $27 billion, not counting real estate); great lumps that often lie, silently sleeping and fructifying in their sleep, behind the anonymous nameplates in which banks rejoice.

Trusts and nominee (or dummy) companies are two of the more obvious ways in which the wealthy can squirrel their wealth away from view (and sometimes from their nearest and dearest). There are doubtless banks in the US still storing cash—reportedly a million—belonging to the bank-hating W. C. Fields, under names like Mahata Kane Jeeves and Otis Criblecoblis. Fields had hundreds of bank books and once claimed to have $50,000 in wartime Germany "in case that little bastard wins." For the same reason, many of the war rich put their money in Switzerland; and here, too, some of the famous numbered accounts doubtless contain wealth whose identification has passed into the grave.

Many of the rich, old or nouveau, have no more knowledge of three-dimensional monetary chess than the novice player—although the moves may be played for them brilliantly by some well-rewarded functionary. The novice, however, must make the moves himself, and knowledge of them is not enough to turn the graduate into a grandmaster. He needs, like a supreme player of real chess, an extra and indefinable quality which, in making money, manifests itself in different forms: as luck, as timing, as genius, as ruthlessness, as insight, as opportunism, as stubbornness. But increasingly, in the Age of the Common Millionaire, that star distinction has achieved a more common form: common craft. Which means that, even for assiduous evaders of millions, knowledge of the rules and the gambits is essential not for self-enrichment, but for self-protection.

ACT I

On the Permanence
of Money

or

You Can Take It
with You

SCENE 1

The Virtues of Inheritance
──────── or ────────
Nothing Licks a Silver Spoon

In the US there is the lone eagle Howard Hughes and the flock of Du Ponts. In Europe the financial powers cluster in tidy family groups: Peugeot and Michelin in France, Agnelli and Pirelli in Italy, Thyssen and Flick in Germany, Cowdray and Vestey in Britain, Rothschilds all over Europe (twenty-nine of fifty-eight weddings of the founding fathers' descendants united first cousins, which at least kept the money in the family), these are only odd summits of the vast, glistening mountain range of inherited wealth and power.

It's the simplest path to a million: inheriting the goods. Even in this age of people's capitalism, that is how most millionaires achieve their particular financial paradises—with the help of time and the magic of compound interest.

It works this way. By dint of luck, labor, and loose laws, an ancestor in some Midwest Bible Belt, or Midlands oasis, put together a million in 1920, when a dollar was a dollar, a pound was a pound, and a mark was a bad joke. It has never been especially difficult to achieve seven percent growth tax-free, which doubles your money every ten years, quadruples it every twenty, octuples it every thirty, multiplies it by sixteen in forty years, and in half a century turns that million into 32 millions. You have to be especially inspired in your choice of investment or adviser (and remember with a million you can afford advice) to do worse, although it's not impossible.

Sir Winston Churchill seems to have managed this discouraging feat. His Boer War escapades, journalism, and American lectures netted him £10,000 in his early manhood. The young Churchill, who had a shrewder eye for the main chance than for money, entrusted the lot to Sir

Ernest Cassel, an old family friend. That was his first mistake. The fact that somebody is on dining, golfing, or even advising terms with your parents is no qualification for employing him to mind your own money or (as Churchill put it in his instructions to Cassel) to "feed my sheep." Churchill himself ruefully admits that in a few years all the sheep had been roasted and devoured. Had the capital been preserved intact and grown by only eight percent per annum, Churchill would have died worth £1.3 million from that single source.

To revert to the lucky scion of a 1920 millionaire, if he survived his parent for fifty years, secured his seven percent growth, and spent only the income—then, from a starting point of a nice, steady rich income in the Roaring Twenties, he would now be pulling down 7,000 pounds or dollars a day for doing precisely nothing, and he would be in a position to make thirty-two further millionaires out of his lucky heirs. This story glosses over painful subjects like the Great Depression, inheritance taxes, and tax in general. But if the million was safely locked up in a sound private business with good marketing connections and tolerable growth (as many, many family millions were), the scenario is perfectly credible.

Some sagas far exceed this fictional rendering in their true fantasy. Clarence B. Mott, for instance, was a successful wheel and axle manufacturer, in days long before the motor industry had spawned its mega-millions. He sold his business to the infant General Motors for a parcel of shares in 1913. While Mott continued to labor sagely and well in the vineyard of the great corporation, the shares worked for him to so gratifying an extent—their total reached 2.5 million—that the Mott fortune, in the old man's nineties (he died at ninety-seven in 1973), was valued at some $800 million.

Great Depression or no, GM shares have fructified in a way that is characteristic of the huge concerns born in the age of affluence before the First World War. A few years back, a London stockjobber sold, to his pride, a £1.5 million line of shares in Shell Transport for a Scottish broker. Later he met the Scot, who told him their origin. Back in 1910, a canny father had left his sons £10,000. The jobber had just off-loaded the holding of one son.

Many sizable fortunes have turned into great piles of

shining gold by the same partly mathematical brick. Even a half-wit can reasonably hope to achieve the seven percent magic. But suppose the lad is actually bright, or, still better, lucky. Merely doubling the compound growth rate to fourteen percent turns a million into $32 million in only twenty-five years. In just forty years the family fortunes will stand at $250 million.

No matter what happens to the value of money in the next four decades, no matter how intensively the family breeds, that sum will still spell great riches. It will yield, with no trouble at all, an income of $12.5 million a year, and will grow at no less than $35 million annually. That mathematics explains how, despite heroic philanthropy, even on a Rockefeller scale, the surviving fortune is still enough to keep a large family in regal condition.

It also explains how vital philanthropy is simply to prevent the mushrooming of great private fortunes from undermining the economic foundations of the State. Indeed, the US government felt obliged to bring suit against one wealthy, dead eccentric, who left his fortune in perpetual trust; there his bread was to do nothing save breed compound interest, which would be plowed back to breed still more interest, compounding in its turn· within a perfectly foreseeable period, the trust would have cornered all the liquid wealth in the US ($100 million compounding at ten percent ends up after a century at over $2 trillion, or roughly double today's American gross national product). This lunatic scheme was not so far-out: in 1906 it was calculated that if John D. Rockefeller's wealth simply grew at the current rate of interest, he would own $90 trillion by 1936. The would-be perpetual trust was duly overthrown by the courts. But, more intelligently applied, geometric progression keeps personal fortunes marching on, seemingly forever.

There are, of course, several catches in this beneficent process. Fortunes can dissipate rapidly in the second generation, let alone the third and fourth, as family members (and the proportion of incompetents and wastrels) also multiply geometrically. It can be taken almost for granted that the money won't be thrown away in some harebrained manner, like actually paying the full inheritance taxes that the law lays down. But, for compounding to work its magic, reasonable time is required in the early stages. If the money has been made in a business, and is still invested there, it is dangerous for the scions to abandon all interests save their own enjoyment.

In some cases, the managers of the good old family firm would gladly pay the heir a million a year to keep clear of the office. No doubt, the satraps minding the A & P (the Great Atlantic and Pacific Tea Company) supermarkets for all Huntington Hartford and the other heirs were worth were delighted to see Hunt engaged in losing millions at a safe distance, on wild projects for establishing Shangri-La on Hog Island or, single-handed, reversing the remorseless flood of modern art with a fretwork museum (since abandoned by him) on Columbus Circle in New York.

But A & P hasn't benefited in any obvious way from Hunt Hartford's abstinence. The greatness has fled, even if the Atlantic and Pacific remain. In the 1961-71 decade, the company's earnings per share declined by 9.4% per annum, a lapse which was entirely owed to its own incompetence. If the family owns a store, or 1,000 stores, somebody in the family should mind it.

The management mafia at Du Pont likes to point out that Du Ponts play hardly any part in the company's affairs. Yet in 1973 there were three members of the family in the best observation place of all—the summit. Irénée Du Pont was a senior vice president, and a solid, dominating phalanx of Du Ponts sat on the finance committee, which is where they keep the money. (Apart from backsliders like Lammot Du Pont Copeland Jr., who ran up one of America's bonanza bankruptcies, keeping the money is something at which Du Ponts have always been good.)

Compounding has taken $36,000, the cost of the Du Ponts' original gunpowder plant on the Brandywine in 1802, to the estimated 7 billions plus of today. Even with a few hundred descendants putting their fingers in the pie— 632 of them sat down to celebrate the 150th anniversary—that leaves plenty of slices all around. As a mathematical curiosity, $36,000 to the magic $7 billion in 170 years is a compound growth of 7 percent a year, which accurately rubs in the truth that time is money.

The inheritor has alternatives to watching his pile from a close vantage point. He can manage the fortune directly himself, as, in one way or another, most heirs tend to do. Their fathers, powerful and puritanical about money (especially their own), inflict the work ethic on their children, imbue them in the business from early days, and persuade them, without much difficulty, that if you want to reach the top the easiest way is to start there.

Wealthy descendants like the grocer Sainsburys or retailer Simon Marks in Britain, Hughes and Getty in the US, or the Philips heirs in the Netherlands have developed their inheritances beyond the imaginative powers even of the family begetters. Yet folklore still has it that the rosiest path to managerial ruin is nepotism; that with each successive management generation the original impetus and talent get progressively weaker, until they disappear, usually in disaster.

This theory is hard to square with the facts of companies like Sainsbury, led by one Sainsbury after another; or Pilkingtons, which led the world in the invention and exploitation of glass made by the float process, despite the handicap of having half a dozen Pilkingtons on the premises; or S. C. Johnson, still literally waxing strong in Racine, Wisconsin, on a dose of fourth-generation management. When a British toy firm called Lines, once worth £17 million to its ruling family, dissolved into a worthless puddle, *The Guardian* newspaper observed smugly that "second and third generation managements are not usually the best"; and in truth it's hard not to sneer when somebody called Raymond C. Firestone is made chairman in a rubber company founded by somebody called Harvey S. Firestone—even if the press dutifully points out that Firestone Jr. "started work with the company in 1933 as a gas station attendant."

But such sneers are too facile, reminiscent of the cracks that Harold Wilson made at "the fourteenth Earl of Home" when the latter was elevated to Prime Minister: as Home reasonably replied, there was presumably a fourteenth Mr. Wilson. Everybody is second- or third-generation. The fact that pa or grandpa was a business genius doesn't mean that son or grandson must turn the former's silk purses into sow's ears.

In his *Up the Organization* that arch-antinepot Robert Townsend points out that "Gerry Eskow succeeded his father as president of Yale Express in 1960. Five years later the company went bankrupt." This merely proves not that son should never follow dad, but that Gerry Eskow should never have followed his progenitor. Nonfamily managements are just as capable of allowing events to drench their balance sheets.

For every weakness of family management there is an almost exact balance of strengths. Genetics is a bad management selection system, true: but you have to find managers somewhere—and the family does provide an immediate pool of men who should be deeply versed in, and deeply committed to, the business from birth. True, a nonfamily man of real talent will doubtless shy away from a company where his way to the top is barred or narrowed by birth; but the family provides a built-in focus of loyalty and continuity which can make even nonfamily managers work above their natural level.

True, the family develops a vested interest in the company as it was then, is now, and ever shall be, a fondness that can prove fatal if events (as they must one day) overtake the formula: but on the other hand the family manager—being proprietor, shareholder, and executive rolled into one—finds it easier to take the long view, while continuing to watch the short-term pennies (because they are his own).

Behind every failed family, moreover, there is a failed adviser—or an adviser who wasn't heeded, which amounts to the same thing. Bankers, accountants, and other well-paid courtiers were close to the Eskow elbow, as they were to the Lines toy family. The performance of the managing (or nonmanaging) kin, moreover, was sustained by the professional managers in the banks and institutions with cash belonging to their depositors, most of whom are far from being millionaires.

Between the end of 1960 (their last good year) and late 1971 (their last year, period) the Lines' borrowings from their friendly neighborhood bankers leapt from £270,000 to £9.5 million. The family went on paying out higher and higher dividends, and pouring more and more borrowed capital into the firm, despite the fact that profits only once, in 1966, crept past the 1960 level. Not content with this exhibition of speeding good money after bad, the City of London staved off the family's moment of truth for four more years by selling £4.2 million of securities to an innocent public in mid-1967.

Advisers, financial and otherwise, are indispensable to the owners of silver spoons. But they must be tested anew by each generation for their acumen, their effort, their results, and their toughness, and fired if they fail the test: it costs nothing to get a new lawyer. Social connections (remember Churchill and Sir Ernest Cassel) are neither here nor there. If their advice is ignorant, and their opposition either purblind or easily pushed aside, advisers are about as useful as the eminent physicians who, in the early centuries of medicine, resolutely bled their royal patients to death.

When the Lines' bankers finally came to their senses, no fewer than six directors, four of them named Lines, lost their managerial heads at one blow. It was far too late in the company's day. According to Peter Drucker, they organize things better in Japan, where the family fortunes are watched over implacably by the elder womenfolk (a much tougher breed than bankers). If any honorable nephew is no good, grandma gives him the chop.

Since this variety of Women's Lib is unlikely to wear well in the West, families have to exercise self-discipline in other ways—although Guinness may have a Western variation. For some decades now the magic stout, having brewed incomparable riches for the Guinnesses and transformed them into Earls of Iveagh, Viscounts of Kelvedon, and various other nobilities, has been managed by nontitled non-Guinnesses with such care and attention that in 1972 a French magazine, to Guinness' amusement, elected their company as the most dynamic in Europe. A watchful board festooned with Guinnesses includes a nub of titled ladies, representative of large family holdings, whose appearance at the annual general meeting has been likened to "a forest of cock's feathers and fur."

The rules of family discipline are easy enough to find—they are exactly the same as for firms of the nonfamily variety. Never appoint incompetents, related or unrelated, to any position of significance. Never allow the board to become overburdened with age, even if it means forcing the dominating father figure to retire at the same age as the lesser fry. Bring young talent into positions of real power while it is still young; but always ensure that wise, prudent, unambitious, and trusted elders watch what the young are getting up to, especially with money. (The Texan oil millionaire Tom Wagoner, chided by a barber for tipping less than his son, pointed out, "My boy's got a rich daddy, but I ain't.") Don't let indifferent performance drift by. The iron law is that stagnation leads to decline. The time to act to avert the former is when the signs of stagnation first appear, before huge deposits of inertia have had time to silt up the entire works.

The crunch comes when stagnation cannot be averted without severe discontinuity, and discontinuity is the process that heirs are worst at achieving. They can be superb at developing a great and soundly based business along more or less established lines, but never let heirs try to prove that they are better than good old dad, or granddad, by striking out in brave new directions.

That's what Gerry Eskow attempted at Yale Express and, in an even more bizarre episode, Herbert Hoover Jr. at Hoover. This would-be chip off the old block, dissatisfied with the narrowness of the view from North Canton, Ohio, set up an expensive international headquarters in New York, staffed by his own protégés, to revolutionize the company. Sadly, the only obvious focus for young Hoover's energies was the British subsidiary which Hoover neither wholly owned nor ever controlled to much effect.

The architect of Hoover's British upsurge retired, with an £83,000 pay-off, to make dishwashers; and Hoover's US and UK halves stewed together in so complete a mishmash that the suffering professional managers in North Canton finally mobilized the family and gave Herbert Jr. the old heave-ho. That is the only correct treatment for any descendant who rocks the family's solid silver boat, is rude to its servants, or wastes its compounding wherewithal.

There's nothing heinous in the rich heir who shuns the business (like most of the assembled Du Ponts): the only son of Lord Marks prefers painting to panties (Marks & Spencer sells forty percent of all ladies' briefs in Britain); the leading UK Rothschild, socially speaking, preferred biology to banking—and ended up in his sixties running the Prime Ministerial think tank in Downing Street. But dropouts should be discouraged from overspending their income or dissipating their capital in support of expensive hobbies—unless, that is, the family luck sticks to their fingers.

One sprig of a British fortune was having a boat built when he heard to his fury that the builder was going bankrupt. He thereupon told his factotum (good factota, stewards, or bailiffs are a privilege of the rich) to buy the business. On completion of the deal, the heirs found to their horror that the company also made nasty little wingless aircraft whose propellers were in the wrong place, whirling above the fuselage. They stuck with this unfortunate acquisition until one day a British government decided to merge the aircraft industry, helicopters and all, into fewer companies. In the reshuffle, the family found itself several millions better-to-do: all because originally one prince of the blood wanted his boat finished. There is justice in the world. But it tends to favor the rich.

SCENE 2

The Rewards of Exploration
or
Finding's Keeping

The clearest-cut way to new money is finding it, and always has been. The forty-niners after gold, the East Texas wildcatters pursuing oil, the Geiger counter gangs hunting uranium—all had the same, and the right, idea. Those who lack any other form of financial ability may still have just enough wit to find a pot of gold, and just enough strength to pick it up.

The shrewdest and strongest of them have founded the lasting empires. The truly interesting and powerful Hearst was not William Randolph, the Czar of San Simeon, for all his newspapers and noise, but his father, exploiter of the Comstock Lode, a hard, warm man whose interests expanded into most of the unmined metals and untracked deserts in which his day abounded. Hearst Sr. functioned in a more primitive age, when finding had an annoying drawback: the finder (unless he sold out smartly) had to wrest his mineral from the good earth; then he had to exchange the wrested rock for hard cash. He couldn't find it, sell it, and still keep it—a trick which modern Hearsts manage with prestidigitatory ease.

The truly modern and imaginative prospector sets forth on his mission armed with a bundle of share certificates, along with the more traditional tools. If he strikes it rich, the next stage is to engender enthusiasm for shares in his company. Mining shares can soar to more fantastic heights at faster speed than any other form of paper wealth, for investors all over the world, although personally unable to distinguish between nickel and molybdenum, or to separate geographically Wagga Wagga from Addis Ababa, flock for a piece of the finder's action.

Before long the momentum of the share price ceases to bear any relation to the prospective value of the new hoard. The shares themselves, though made of nothing but engraved paper, become the equivalent of the Comstock Lode: buyers desire and devour the stock because they find it so amazingly valuable—and it is valuable solely because buyers desire and devour it so avidly.

While this bubble swells to prodigious size, the finder and his friends can take generous reward in cash—and still retain total control of the claim and all that lies therein. Without an ounce of their metal on the market, they are already rich and they can get only richer when the wonder company actually comes to have some wonder earnings.

This convenient arrangement makes the methods of earlier prospectors, like Vernon Pick, seem positively self-abnegatory. Pick believed in both the "self-sustenance homestead" and the existence of uranium in the Four Corners area, where four of the United States come together. He was proved right, and was amply sustained by the $9.37 million handed over for the property by the Atlas Corporation. A whole army of would-be Picks promptly descended on the American deserts armed with Geiger and scintillation counters. But many years passed before other self-sustainers discovered the still greater surface riches lying around on the stock exchanges of the world.

In the good old days, before the Arab natives got restless, virtually the entire price of a barrel of oil extracted from the Middle East sand was pure (or, as J. P. Getty would put it, "clear") profit. The ineffable oil fortunes, like Getty's, are mostly private, despite the stock-market's multiplying charms, partly because their owners come from a past when a man's well was his castle, and what you had, you held, entirely and in perpetuity. Getty himself lovingly charts his own progress from the first $12,000 profit on a well in 1915, to the $6,387,946 clear profit on the Nordstrom Lease of 1921-37, with stopovers like the $400,000 plus "excess recovery" on the Athens Lease in 1924.

But what made these excess finds the foundation of an excessive share of America's wealth was not simply the initiative, intelligence, and industry of its finders: it is fine, old-fashioned freedom from tax. Not a single writer or thinker on taxes or oil has been able to explain precisely, let alone convincingly, why the oilmen of America should have received (as they still do) the blessing of an exemption which does for them by law what latter-day mineral explorers must achieve by dint of hard stock market graft.

The sovereign notion is not merely that, before getting around to paying any tax, oilmen should be free to deduct the cost of drilling all their wells, wet or dry. A beneficent state, noting that a barrel of oil, once removed from the ground for sale, cannot be replaced, decreed that its owners should be compensated by tax relief for this "depletion of their resources." It is as if a man finds a Ming vase buried in the woods, sells it for $10,000, and is then allowed to knock $2,000 off his tax because he no longer has Ming to market.

Until 1969, the oilmen got $2,750 in every ten grand knocked off their Ming equivalents. At that rate, an oilman had trouble getting into a tax-paying position, no matter how hard he tried—and most didn't try too hard. One of the least determined triers must have been Robert O. Anderson, chairman of Atlantic Richfield, which in four years paid no taxes on $465 million of profits—and ended up with the US government owing it money. Yet great was the outcry among oilmen when the depletion allowance was reduced from 27.5% to 22%.

What's sauce for the corporation is also spicy for the individual. If the finder can retain all his income free of tax, reinvest the surplus in still more properties that will yield even greater tax-free earnings, and borrow heavily against the security of the proved oil in his ground—his need to let the public, or anybody else, into his act is minimal.

This fiscal logic has enabled the oil barons to form a separate, politically powerful kingdom within the empire of the rich: their realm is as important, relatively speaking, as that of the Dukes of Burgundy in mediaeval France. Of the thirty-five richest men listed by *Fortune* in 1957, no less than fifteen were either oil-finders or entrepreneurs who had grown rich from tidbits from the oilmen's table: suppliers of services, bits and pieces, valuable odds and ends. H. L. Hunt, Sid Richardson, the Murchisons, John Mecom (who sold a mere fraction of his properties in the early 1960s for $27 million)—all these ducal figures of the new plutocracy owe their eminence and their fortunes primarily to the oil riches of Texas.

The supply of satrapies from this source, however, may be drying up, the result of greed outdoing itself. As the richer fields of the US were steadily sucked dry, new and lush finds became far harder to hit, and costs of production climbed closer to world prices: the latter were no longer determined in Texas but by the superabundant oil fields of the Middle East.

The reaction of the oil moguls, aided and abetted by all the political friends oil money could buy, was to get the oil out while the getting was good—at the highest possible price. President Eisenhower put on quotas to minimize imports of cheap foreign crude (selling at prices of, say, $2 compared to $3.75 for the Texas variety). How much money the quota system pumped into the oil industry's pockets nobody can ever calculate—one estimate runs between $40 billion and $70 billion over a decade. The cold certainty is that it rushed the day when the US would run short of energy. The Americans who found their oil supplies rationed in the winter of 1972, following which crisis the quota system was finally scrapped, were the direct victims of the brilliant deployment by the oil lobby of the millions which their previous lobbying had won. As the shortages of that winter developed into the Arab boycott of the next one, Americans had even more cause to regret their failure to grab all the Middle East oil that they could, when the sheikhs were quiescent and the price was four-fifths lower.

If there is any consolation, it lies in the fact that few of the Texas fat-cats had the sense or muscle to follow the oil trade's trend and head east. But for those who did—notably Nelson Bunker Hunt, a partner in British Petroleum's great Libyan fields until they were expropriated, and J. P. Getty in the Neutral Zone of Kuwait—the richest rewards of all were still to be made. In his advice to would-be executives, Getty stresses the pain of paying $12.5 million for the Kuwait concession, and of investing many times more before a drop of oil came to market. He fails to mention what financial pleasures he received in return for all that pain.

As a rough idea, British Petroleum sold under half—forty-five percent—its stake in Abu Dhabi, another lately developed gusher region of the Persian Gulf, to some eager Japanese in 1972. The price tag was $780 million. Getty was lucky, or wise. He got in early, when a sheikh was still a sheikh—and not the next victim of a nationalist, ex-military, revolutionary politician.

The Arab rulers, men like Ibn Saud or the Sheikh of Kuwait, were notably (although the competition for this title is stiff) the least deserving of all the multimillionaires. They became so loaded with unspendable loot that the simple process of investing their wealth itself generated new fortunes—the $12 billion that poured into Arab coffers in 1971 was expected to quintuple by 1980, even before, in late 1973, the Arabs craftily quadrupled the price. Well before that, as the sheikhs grew greedier and the Arabian political climate grew hotter, the tax take grew greater—and it has now become genuinely hard work to wrest a decent oil living (decent by oil standards, that is) from the desert.

Dr. Armand Hammer, for example, landed the industry's big fish when he gambled on Libyan crude. But the replacement of a compliant monarch by a cross colonel contributed mightily to the financial embarrassment of Hammer's Occidental Petroleum. Just as Texas has probably run out of future H. L. Hunts, and the West Coast of future Gettys, so the Middle East has probably seen its last big operator.

Big, lucrative plays remain in areas less politically tempestuous than the Middle East—in the North Sea, for example, where the British public discovered, to the chagrin of many citizens, that private oil firms, mainly American, had been allowed to gobble all the cream, and much of the milk, under tax conditions that the most stupid oil sheikh in old-time Araby would have considered generous. North Sea plays, however, require astronomical stakes: thirty-one drilling concessions sold at auction by Britain's government cost £37 million, and drilling one well can easily take $600,000. The action has therefore shifted to the giant corporations: the individual has had to look still further afield—for instance, to the wilds of Australia.

Here, a new generation of prospectors in the 1960s exploited the prime advantage of finding, as opposed to making, wealth. For, as we have seen, if the finder can prove (or get somebody to believe) that he has located a million tons of mineral-bearing mother earth, that find or purported find immediately has a value: not the price times the recoverable quantity—it cost money to get the stuff out—but a very reasonable proportion of what can be a staggering sum. Mining discoveries are thus the perfect material for a speculative share boom, as demonstrated by the movements of two linked Australian stocks, one heavy (Western Mining), one light (Hampton Areas). It was from Hampton that Western Mining acquired fourteen square miles near Kambalda, the seat of a spectacular rise in earnings. In 1966, the year before the deal, Western was earning twice as much as ever before—but that still meant only $692,323 in Australian money. By 1969, profits had almost trebled; the next year they were twenty times the 1966 figure; in 1971, at $22.7 million, the multiple was thirty.

In 1967, the shares paid to Hampton for the right to drill its land rose in worth nearly sixfold: at the peak, the stake was worth forty times the low price in the year of the big deal—showing how rosily a rise in profits can be magnified at the share price level. In later years, the bloom went off the rose somewhat, with dollar devaluation adding to the problems of nickel oversupply. But by then the harvest for Western Mining's insiders had already long been reaped.

This great Aussie boom had one peculiar economic characteristic. It was founded largely on finds of nickel, a metal which, at the start of the saga, was in short supply. With all those lovely new discoveries being announced, however, you didn't have to be a World Bank economist to forecast that before long—before, indeed, all the new mines could even open—the shortage would turn to glut. In the world of commodities, as many burnt-out speculators ruefully know, a little glut means a large price fall. Yet the shares of any company that had found, might find, or even thought of finding nickel in the outback went on upward as if the demand and price for nickel had been guaranteed by the US Treasury (a guarantee which in the days before several dollar devaluations had some value).

Fortune always favors somebody, including sometimes the brave. Two likely English lads, Richard King and Colin Forsyth, got into the Australian act. Their original idea was to launch a unit trust invested wholly in Australian shares. The launch was neatly timed for an Australian market slump, and the trust languished for an uncomfortable time.

But the duo's ears, close to the Australian ground, picked up the first nickel noises; largely because Forsyth, some time before, had picked up shares in Hampton Gold Mining Areas, which were then so much wallpaper. These purchases alone made Forsyth rich. But the trust, too, suddenly found itself the focus of the world's fastest stock market action and achieved wonders of supergrowth: its two founders finally sold out for seven figures, a reward which represented only their indirect gains—and even so they missed the best of the tide.

The phenomenal Poseidon ("the share of the century") was a share in which the Pan-Australian partners got interested early on, but after actually going to the Windarra nickel site, which explained all the excitement, Forsyth turned cool on the project. The trust's investment meeting nevertheless decided that the shares, then selling at £120, couldn't possibly fall below £80, which was still vastly above the trust's buying price. In fact, they crashed to £5: and nineteen percent of the fund was in this one stock.

It requires faith, as well as other people's money, to put trust in geologists' reports couched in meaningless technicalities and emanating from the back of beyond. For every honest prospector, there's always one who isn't above salting the mine—no salter ever swung the trick more daringly than one enterprising gentleman, who got hold of an insignificant British company and persuaded much of the populace, including normally shrewd financiers, that he had found a mine in the American West, which contained almost every valuable metal known to man (the claim stopped short of diamonds). A helpful scientist, according to report, had discovered a new secret extraction process which stopped short only of turning dirt into gold.

Visits by British pressmen to the Eldorado supposedly valued at £12.5 million discovered a ramshackle lab but no scientist, and a mine of uncertain title, more or less in the middle of a housing estate, but no gold and no mining. Even then there was a delayed reaction before the wizard decamped with his loot (the British government inspectors totted it up to well over £40,000), leaving the corporate wreck behind.

It pays to be skeptical. The catch, alas, is that it sometimes pays more to have faith. In 1961 an Irish-Canadian prospector named Pat Hughes, then thirty-seven, made a sentimental return to the old country bent on finding some mineral wealth. Now, the Republic of Ireland, as everybody knows, is good for cows, Guinness, Arran sweaters, and leprechauns; but the idea of a Klondike in those soft green hills was plainly the wildest Irish-Canadian blarney.

Hughes announced, however, that he had indeed made a find, of lead, zinc, silver, and copper to boot, and shares in his company, Northgate, began to move in the accustomed manner. In the bars of Dublin, where many wonders have been seen, the discoveries seemed perfectly acceptable. But elsewhere people were harder to convince.

Hughes even went to the extraordinary lengths of flying in journalists and investment men from all over Europe and the Americas to inspect his new mine. The inexpert saw Hughes, arm in sling after a recent accident and looking even more like the Pirate King than usual, observed a newly mined pile of dirt, noticed a few suspicious silvery twinkles in the heap, and went back to their Old Bushmills whisky as unconvinced as ever. But the silver was of sterling reality; and Hughes went on to discover yet another crock of gold called Silvermines.

Those who invested in these two companies, and Hughes in particular, did better than a lucky draw in the Irish Sweepstakes. By the end of 1970, Northgate was earning $6.3 million a year—and in 1972 Hughes sold just six percent of another find for $5.6 million.

There is no guide, no touchstone, to help the outsider to distinguish between the phony and, as here, the fruitful claim. You need the same tool as the prospector himself: a sensitive, quivering nose. Expertise in the geology, characteristics, and technology of whatever mineral you are hunting, and in whatever terrain the hunt has reached, is of course useful. As Getty tells it, he and his father spotted one of their most lucrative hauls by noticing a locomotive laboring uphill; this convinced them that they were looking at the top of a dome full of oil. Normally a prospector (provided he can afford the fee) turns to an academically equipped expert to tell him the good news. But experts have a disconcerting habit of being wrong—and you never know when.

Their failure is understandable. An expert is somebody

who has been taught all that is *already* known about a subject. But he doesn't know what *isn't* known, and he tends to dismiss any information or observation that contradicts his knowledge. The true prospector—indeed, the true business genius of any kind—listens carefully to the expert, and goes right ahead when instinct tells him that the expert may be wrong.

Rockefeller's Standard Oil was advised not to touch the area which held the great Spindletop gusher; the great D'Arcy was almost alone in believing that oil could be found under the sands of Arabia; Dr. Armand Hammer made one of his Libyan hits on a concession which Mobil Oil quit after drilling nothing but dry holes. British oil experts turned up their noses at Kuwait, the richest pool of them all. Two of the world's great oil companies, Shell and British Petroleum, are based in England, a country that for decades was believed to contain no oil or gas worth writing of; all that time these British moguls were sitting within seventy miles of some of the world's biggest untapped deposits beneath the North Sea.

True, the drilling and extraction of this bonanza would have presented insurmountable problems to the technology of an earlier age. But an American company even turned up a major field in Yorkshire, of all places. Geologists are not trained to look where they don't expect to find—but that is often where the true finder finds what is truly worth keeping.

As time goes by, however, the ignored and overlooked areas and chances get fewer and farther between, which has the unhappy result that the prospector has to try, try, and try again. Robert Anderson is said to have drilled two hundred dry wells before he made his first New Mexico strike. That kind of hitting and missing is a rich man's pastime. Without the possession of a small refinery, financed by a $50,000 loan from a banker father, Anderson could not have afforded the wells (nor, simultaneously, have built up a million acres of landholding).

Anderson was forty before his crude oil holdings were impressive—and even then a shrewd property-cum-oil deal with some California gas stations was his chief claim to industrial fame. Anderson bought the chain for some $4 million and sold it for $25 million eighteen months later to Gulf Oil. The big play, however, was again in the stock market. Anderson got 700,000 shares in Atlantic Refining for his oil business; the leverage he applied to this holding by merging Atlantic with Richfield and making the Big Strike in Alaska pushed his oil fortune, at its peak, to something like $100 million.

Like Bob Anderson, Joseph H. Hirshhorn, the richest of the Geiger men, went corporate, turning over his massive Canadian uranium interests to Rio Tinto-Zinc. As a miner and speculator, Hirshhorn was big in uranium by 1950; from this base he made the superstrike of 1952-53. He listened to a maverick expert, one Franc Joubin, who was almost alone in suspecting that the Algoma Basin of Ontario contained uranium. It cost Hirshhorn $30,000 to prove Joubin right—in return for which proof, Hirshhorn was transmuted into a mining giant worth over $130 million in 1961. He sold out his stake for Rio Tinto-Zinc shares, whereby hangs another story.

In the palmier days for the mining corporation, before the management ran into troubles with environmental pollution at a wildly uncontrolled plant investment in Wales, the shares boomed to a value of £640 million in April 1970 on the stock market, which subsequently dwindled to almost half. It must be galling for a gambler to see his winning chips dwindle in as mysterious a manner as they grew. Anderson had just this experience as Atlantic Richfield ran into the massive Alaskan pipeline roadblock and the general unhappiness of US oil in its degenerating phase. The owners of Western Mining, too, saw their shares plunge.

By playing finding's keeping, then, you can have your cake and eat it; the catch is that you can no longer control the size of the cake.

SCENE 3

The Prize of Privacy
— or —
The Grave's a Very Private Place

At regular intervals private companies that have deposited great wealth into the hands of their private owners yield their virginities and become public by selling a modest chunk of their shares. There is always some plausible explanation of this self-sacrifice: fear of death duties, difficulty in raising money for expansion, trouble in attracting or keeping smart-enough hired help. But none of these obstacles is insurmountable: the clear proof is that so much of the world's wealth is in wholly or largely private hands. The public has no more than a look-in, if that, at the fortunes of Howard Hughes, D. K. Ludwig, Forrest Mars, or H. L. Hunt in America, or of the meat-packing Vesteys, the mail order and football-betting Littlewoods, or the shipowning Sir John Ellerman of Britain. The latter died in 1973 with a £100 million fortune in ships alone—part of the proceeds of £37 million bequeathed by his father forty years before.

Few people outside Eire and Palm Beach, Florida, have heard of Mrs. Ambrose Congreve, for example. More have heard of Humphreys & Glasgow, a British chemical plant constructor that was founded by an American immigrant (the Glasgow of the title), using American know-how. The huge profits made over a long life—father died at ninety-six—were invested with high success in the US, and the entire fortune was bequeathed to Mrs. Congreve, putting her among the world's richest women. Her husband, Ambrose Congreve, did a sterling job in building up the value of the original business, controlling it from a legendary Irish estate, Mount Congreve. But of the shares in the firm, Mrs. Congreve owned 119,999 all to herself, and Mr. Congreve just one.

None of the standard excuses for selling shares to the public has any convincing validity; the only point in doing so is to exchange assets for real money at a time when the switch is advantageous. The advantage of publicity is clearest if the private owner has it in mind to take his money and run. But even if the private owner has every intention of staying put, going public has considerable financial benefit, simply because the parts can be made wondrously more than the whole. Nobody ever got richer faster than a former wizard IBM computer salesman named H. Ross Perot. But this wasn't simply because his computer software business grew like the giant mushroom (as it did). The American public fell over itself to buy the tiny amount of shares that Perot generously released—fifteen percent of the total equity. At its palmiest, this was valued at over one hundred times earnings. Nobody in his right mind would have paid that kind of multiple for the whole of Perot's company; if he was exceedingly lucky, it might have fetched a third of the market valuation.

Giving the public a piece of some desirable action not only multiplies its purported value in a delicious manner—it enables the owner, while grabbing some real money, to retain total control over the cornucopia. The mystery therefore isn't why so many wealthy citizens, on generally spurious grounds, give away part of their privacy, but why so many cling to absolute ownership of empires like the *Reader's Digest* or the Ellerman Line.

The practical advantages are minor compared to the loss of financial flexibility. Even Howard Hughes found the public route indispensable when he wanted several millions, presumably to cover his legal dispute with TWA. As it turned out, Hughes won his case, and needn't have bothered. But note that the crafty recluse hung on to all of Hughes Tool, except his daddy's former oil-drilling bit business; he got $140 million for that (off the stock market)—although its profits had dwindled for three years and three commercially significant patents were shortly expiring.

The Hughes case is self-explanatory: the private person avoids public ownership because of his very lust for privacy. This lust can be obsessional, blotting out common sense as well as financial self-interest. John Moores, the dictatorial boss of a Littlewoods empire that pulls in £300 million a year in retail sales and has an astronomical turnover in football pools, once explained his position in language worthy of a small shopkeeper. "If we were public," he said, "and I didn't make enough money, [the shareholders] would be after me."

Useless to tell such a Midas that a holding of well under fifty percent will yield absolute control, that shareholders don't even speak when they are spoken to, that large public firms have reported indifferent results for a decade without the directors attracting anything more than a unanimous vote of thanks at the annual general meeting.

The Midas is motivated by deep, inward fear: anxiety lest his personal control be weakened by dilution. The proprietor has a simple, all or nothing, approach to proprietorship; and this same attitude underlies the privacy of all other enclosed tycoons, though they range from men who all but keep their money under the bed to international jet-set sophisticates like Aristotle Onassis.

This private passion is no prerogative of the ultra-rich. One of the main causes of bankruptcy is the refusal of the infant entrepreneur to let others into his action at an early stage. The explanation is human enough. The man knows how wonderful his idea is, how irresistible his own managerial force, how dynamic his growth rate (if you start from zero, almost any growth looks marvelous). If he lets somebody else in on his ground floor, no matter what that person provides in capital or knowledge, the interloper is getting in dirt-cheap; cheap, that is, by the standards of the unrealized future supergrowth.

This denial leads straight to the dread condition known as overtrading or undercapitalization, in which the sufferer tries to cure his shortage of money by desperate means—like not paying his bills to suppliers, and praying that his customers pay theirs on the nail. If these makeshift means fail (they do, with depressing regularity), the proud and private independent casts around, at last, for outside money. Only, it's too late. The time to swallow private pride is when you are not forced to do so: diplomats call it negotiating from strength.

By all odds the craftiest exponent of this art was the wily Armenian Calouste Gulbenkian. Zen masters are rumored to teach pupils the essence of swordsmanship by striking at them with sticks when the student isn't watching. The Armenians in much the same way have acquired such dexterity from dodging their persecutors down the ages that only the foolhardy ever tangle with a businessman whose name ends in "ian" or "yan"—and that prohibition included Anastas Mikoyan, the craftiest trader and most professional survivor thrown up by Soviet Russia.

Gulbenkian's contribution to the world's welfare was to lay his hands on the rich oil concessions in Mesopotamia. His wiliness emerged in his readiness to give up all but five percent of this treasure trove to the mighty oil companies that were anxious to share the wealth. That five percent not only gave Gulbenkian his nickname; it generated, painlessly and annually, one of the world's great fortunes, and it demonstrated beyond a peradventure the truth of an unforgettable maxim—that a little of a lot is better than all of a little.

The small, would-be-big entrepreneur ignores Gulbenkian's gambit to his own detriment. In any event, giving away some equity early on isn't a final, fatal step. If the business flourishes like a green bay tree, the entrepreneur can always buy his partners out. That was the course favored by Henry Ford I, who began his rise with a motley crew of faithful supporters and devoted much of his time in later years to liquidating their interests.

By and large, despite Henry's appalling mismanagement in the 1930s, the other shareholders were wrong to sell out. Ford shares were worth more than dollar bills. But few people can resist the lure of cash, even in small amounts. The great majority of the oilmen who, at the point of John D. Rockefeller's economic gun, were forced to sell out either for cash or for Rockefeller shares took cash; it was a ludicrous error. Keeping a Gulbenkian-sized corner in somebody else's gold mine is one of the easiest ways to wealth, so long as, like Gulbenkian, you are in a position to safeguard your interests.

The private imperialist values his privacy partly just because there are nobody's interests to safeguard but his own. This enables him to build the company in his own image and for his own sake. Power, in these circumstances, is plainly more important than its full expression in money terms. Britain boasts one Quaker company that is kept resolutely private by the will of the family—or, to be more precise, the managing members thereof. As usual in these circumstances, a formula exists to put a price on the shares in the event of death or dissolution. It prices the holdings far below even a conservative estimate for the company's stock market value. This undervaluation robs the family of a cool £ 30 million: the price tag on allowing the few actively ruling family members to preserve totally untrammeled management control.

Why do the family outsiders suffer such penalties? Aunts may be intimidated by Cousin Eric; nephews may fear that, unless they comply dutifully with Uncle Al's wishes, he will up stakes and retire to the nearest tax-free island. Apart from paranoia, they are victims of ignorance. Almost as if they were uninterested in their money (which, in a sense, they are), they are happy to have the anxiety of its care lifted off their shoulders. Tell them that they are being defrauded of the odd million and you turn contentment into a state of acute anxiety. It is kissing cousin to the equally ill-founded apprehensions of private family managers that, without the protection of all-family ownership, their management grip will first be loosened, then contemptuously knocked away.

If their abilities are defective, so much the better for one and all—including themselves as shareholders. But managers of the blood are seldom anxious to recognize their own incompetence, no matter what it costs. The beauty (or horror) of privacy is that mistakes are more easily buried even than in big public corporations (where funerals can be fully as discreet as Mafia disposals in the East River). Only rarely does a scandal reach such dimensions that the veil is lifted, not merely from the management failure of a family business, but from the very facts of its life.

When Tino de Angelis, the great salad oil swindler, finally ran out of empty tanks, a company called Bunge discovered to its horror that $15 million of the nonexistent oil belonged to it, so to speak. Another $3 million had oozed away in a simple check fraud. To mislay $18 million, even to the second greatest swindle of all time, you have to be adequately rich—and Bunge was and is part of what may be the richest private kingdom of them all. At that time its sales were £ 800 million a year; it held one-fifth of the entire American trade in grain, oilseeds, oils, and fats; the whole Bunge y Born earthly paradise, known in its Latin American home as The Octopus, was in the ownership of two families, the Borns and the Hirsches.

Mario Hirsch was said at the time to know "if a typist blows her nose in São Paulo"—despite the fact that he had never visited Brazil. Yet here was a single suborned employee in New York waylaying checks to the value of $3 million—and nobody noticed. The family fury, when informed that of four tanks supposed to contain 160 million pounds of salad oil, three contained gasoline and the fourth was empty, epitomized the close-fisted, close-controlled approach typical of the private empire. Bunge y Born was, in fact, having a management overhaul by British consultants at the time, a process that inevitably took it further into the world of public exposure, with all the disadvantages of lost secrecy. As a family member complained, "The bigger you are, the more tax you pay. The smaller you are, the more tax you evade."

The quieter you are, what's more, the better your chance that nobody will notice your size: like Michelin, which in 1968 was still trying to pretend that its turnover, entirely privately owned, came to only £12 million a year; the true figure is now around $1.5 billion.

For many years the ace London property developer Harry Hyams concealed a £40 million fortune behind total inaccessibility: by a quirk of fate, his Oldham Estates had a few outside shareholders, which compelled Hyams to hold uncommunicative annual general meetings; at one AGM he turned up wearing a rubber face mask to protect his anonymity. By then it was too late, however. Hyams had blown his own cover by erecting Centre Point, for years the tallest, emptiest, and hence most notorious, office building in London's West End. From the publicity angle, Hyams would have done better to stick to bungalows.

Privacy not only protects the tender personality from bruising, but allows the truly gifted proprietor to practice management experiments without hindrance. Whether the subtleties of Howard Hughes count in this context is debatable, but in the age of passion for communicating, for man-to-man, eyeball-to-eyeball confrontation, Hughes has proved that a monster conglomerate can be managed via a Morman bodyguard, telephone kiosks, and a tame lawyer or two. Practically the only business that Hughes botched up, in fact, was the one to which he was nearest—in Las Vegas.

Possibly the most successful satisfiers of mass tastes in Britain are the D. C. Thomson family, which makes a very public mint from children's comics (Dandy, Beano, etc.), Dundee newspapers, women's magazines (My Weekly, Annabel, etc.), yet keeps one of the lowest profiles in world commerce. The reigning Thomsons had to be photographed covertly with long-focus lenses, like royalty sunbathing. A spokesman (something of a misnomer in the circumstances) told the *Sunday Times* that "we never give information about anything to anybody"—and he was telling the truth.

The law does force the revelation that the Thomson family, whose personal life-styles are no more conspicuous than their publicity, earned £3.2 million after taxes last year. That alone adds up to a stake worth at least £40 million, which takes no account of the sums piled up in investment trusts, commercial television, paper, and property in the years (many of them all but tax-free) since 1905, when three brothers and three wives initiated the saga.

Another equally secret tycoon has no head office at all (unless you count a Washington hotel suite), yet operates one of the most effective management machines: Forrest Mars of Mars, who has been photographed hardly more often than the Thomsons or Hughes.

Mars left a successful father behind in America and went to Britain to build a confectionery giant so rich that, reversing the usual compliment, Mars finally took over the original parental business back home. He provides his disciples with a management grounding that is direct, steeped in common sense, and founded on a simple notion, as expounded by another émigré to Britain, Canada's Roy Thomson, in an immortal phrase, "You make a dollar for me, I'll make a dollar for you." Within that scheme of things, Mars has felt free to experiment with marketing approaches, production methods, incentive ideas—knowing that, if they worked, he would benefit; if they failed, he would foot the bill.

The wholly private emperors always lose some money, certainly in cash terms, probably in borrowing power, by retaining their privacy. Only if they deal primarily in solid assets—ships as well as oil in the ground—does the problem become minimal. Any banker will gladly lend on such triple-barreled security.

The fix may become genuinely painful if, like the Sainsbury family in Britain, which pocketed over £14 million by going public in 1973 (and still had £103 million left on paper), the solid assets in the form of shops are small in relation to the volume of sales that pours through; or if, again like the Sainsburys, there is trouble earning large enough cash margins to finance further expansion. In contrast, the great shipping fortunes—like those of Onassis, or the shy Daniel K. Ludwig (who runs an empire worth $3.5 billion, or more than Howard Hughes' little lot, from locales like the thirty-fourth floor of Burlington House in Manhattan)—have remained almost entirely in private hands. Their owners have no incentive to share their assets, their borrowing power, their tax advantages, and their gigantic profits with the suckers.

But what the private business always lacks, unless the family is exceptionally gifted and the racket especially rich, is the ability to generate decades of unlimited growth and diversification. Exxon no longer even bears the Rockefellers' Standard Oil brand, though it still keeps plenty of Rockefellers and allied families in caviar: but its $21.6 billion assets leave even the wildest Texan fortunes in the minor leagues. Like Krupp in German industry, or the Rothschilds in finance, the private business gets inexorably overtaken by the public concern as the years roll by. Big-time corporate managers can create money out of the air by issuing shares. The big-time privateer, like his golden age exemplars, can create his loot only by some form of real economic achievement—and that is a harder trick.

SCENE 4

The Joys of Neo-Nepotism
or
Let Your Nephew Try

In business, as in genealogy, adoption has much the same effect as birth. The main difference is that sons mostly inherit the trappings of office, and its loot, by divine right. The adopted protégé—usually, but not always, the lucky fellow who married the right daughter—really has to work for his keep. Rich fathers-in-law are generally suspicious of sons-in-law, especially poor ones, until the nuptial acquisition proves himself in battle.

Like Tamino in *The Magic Flute*, the adoptee has to pass through ordeals by fire and water before receiving full initiation. Once accepted, however, the son-in-law has all the advantages of his rich protector, including cash and power, strengthened by his own drive and relative youth (girls tend to marry men younger than their fathers). Compared to a natural son, moreover, the daughter's loved one has an irreplaceable asset—the Old Man isn't his father.

This doesn't remove the possibility, even the inevitability, of conflict between generations; but with luck it subtracts from the brew the ingredients of inferiority complex, dark primal hatreds, and contemptuous love. Many a son-in-law has found that Tamino's trials don't cease with initiation. But many a father-in-law has had reason to bless his daughter's natural instincts.

The great Philips electrical business was run successively by two sons-in-law. When the founder of Matsushita, another wondrous electrical enterprise, retired to the position of "rear echelon chairman," he was succeeded by his son-in-law—who adopted Matsushita's name (in much the same way as the Krupp in-laws added that family's patronymic). Three of Britain's greatest postwar successes, too, owe much to the in-law strategem—and, by strange electrical coincidence, the country's huge power station-to-plugs combine, the £1 billion General Electric Company, is among them.

In British retailing, Simon Marks and Israel Sieff, the second generation that transformed Marks & Spencer, were brothers-in-law: and it was the Sieffs, not the Marks main line, who provided the management succession.

The £359 million chain of Tesco supermarkets is another admirable example of the son-in-law variation—in fact, Sir John Cohen, the Tesco founder, had no less than two specimens of the genus on the premises, a doubling-up which provided additional problems of how to avoid favoritism. Nobody knows whether Tesco would have completed its Darwinian evolution from barrows to open-fronted stores to lock-up shops to supermarkets (a ladder from which many others fell) without Hyman Kreitman. This son-in-law, after a visit to the States, became enthused with the supermarket notion and is credited with imposing orderly business ideas on the "pile 'em high and sell 'em cheap" philosophy which Jack Cohen had trundled along in his original barrow.

Another moot question, however, is whether it's always comfortable for a son-in-law to have his wife's father hanging around the shop when the latter's day is officially done. It takes more than the honorary and empty title of president to keep a self-made family superboss quiet. In his pugnacious seventies, Cohen defined his role succinctly: "I'm a nagger. All I do is find fault." Performed tactfully, that's almost as valuable, in business terms, as finding gold. One slip on the wrong side of discretion, however, and the son-in-law can readily be driven to drink or hibernation—after all, the man has been made rich by his father-in-law's shares and his own efforts, and he doesn't actually *have* to work.

The most prominent son-in-law in British business, Weinstock of the General Electric Company, is good at giving the impression that he hardly works at all. "I've always got time," he has been known to say. No doubt, the pressure was greater in the days when his father-in-law's Sobell radio and TV business was stuttering along, and Weinstock's mind was the most valuable of its intangible assets. Weinstock finally took the firm out of the valley and into the broad uplands, where the old GEC paid a price for the Sobell business which gave the family and its friends fifteen percent of the entire, creaking GEC edifice.

Weinstock, as boss of the merged TV and radio side, was supposed to sit quietly on a small committee that, in theory, ran a group that, in reality, was marching inexorably toward £30 million of bank debt and beyond into the great hereafter. When the Sobell son-in-law (backed by his equity) announced that the committee was a waste of time, and that he would attend no more meetings, the thin red line that held GEC's top management together wavered, stretched, and finally parted completely. Within a couple of years, Weinstock and his Sobell sidekicks had the profits and the share price zooming upward.

In 1963-68, the shares advanced by ten times; and it followed, with gratifying reciprocity, that the Sobell family shareout rose in step. Each hundred percent hop in the shares, indeed, must have been worth several millions to the Weinstock entourage, taking Michael Sobell's gains far past his original fortune.

In truth, entrepreneurs are thrice blessed to have managerial talent visited on them by matrimony. Their luck lies in the essential difference between the creator and the critic. When Picasso died, the supply of Picassos (genuine ones, that is) ceased for all time; but the supply of critics of Picasso is timeless and inexhaustible. Business breakthroughs, too, are a form of creative art, and therefore often fail to conform to theoretical formulas.

The critic mentality and the son-in-law syndrome come in at the next stage: when the big idea has turned into reality, when the small holding has become a fertile, king-sized ranch of many acres, or has the chance to spread. At this point the creator finds himself in the additional, and often unwelcome, role of administrator. He needs a supply of managers, the artisans of business, to run his artistic shop. And he needs an analytical, understanding critical intelligence to run the artisans.

These henchmen, of course, are disposable and replaceable; but, then, so is the Picasso himself—in his new role of manager-in-chief. Very few masters are detached enough, or sufficiently interested in the wide world outside business, to recognize this reality—unless a son-in-law (real or metaphorical) fits naturally into the slot. The West Coast Croesus, Norton Simon, is a rare example of total abdication—maybe because this one-time scrap metal merchant had developed rare, expensive, and profitable tastes that absorbed more and more of his attention.

Simon progressed from metal to Old Masters on the unlikely back of the tomato, becoming the dominant force in American ketchup with scarcely a false step—except, notably, for an ill-judged venture into nonscrap metal, when he bought a big steel firm. The house that Norton Simon built had in its rooms the usual batch of misfit investments that the Croesus type always collects: all collectors, even of businesses, are magpies.

Simon found the man to tidy up the collection in a hard-jawed former advertising agent, David J. Mahoney. Quickly satisfied by the latter's performance, Simon sold virtually all his stock and quit his own board—leaving little behind but his name. Mahoney minded the store, while the retired Simon devoted himself profitably to paying (and at times getting) the world's highest prices for paintings.

Few founding fathers have the forbearance, or the sense, to retire from the scene so completely. But the logic is immutable. If a Weinstock or a Mahoney appears, by matrimony or by management selection, the elderly magician should retire to the wings and leave the sorcerer's apprentice free to multiply the brooms.

This policy has never worked better than for a British miller named J. Arthur Rank, whose flour had already earned him more sterling than he could conveniently spend. An ardent Methodist, Rank wanted to make good, wholesome films to counteract the insidious evil which he saw creeping over the screen. Making films was one thing; getting them shown was another. Rank ended up owning the largest cinema chain in the country, plus virtually all of the local Hollywood (a midget, hand-me-down copy of the real thing).

Rank found, inevitably, that movies weren't like mills, or film stars like flour bags. He came to rely on a young professional man named John Davis, to whom fell the investment opportunity of several lifetimes.

As Hollywood's moguls foundered before TV and the death of the star system, the Rank Organization shared their sinking, until a small Rochester, New York, company, desperate to exploit the expensive new invention on which its survival depended, made Davis an offer he could easily have refused. For $600,000, however, Davis bought half the world rights outside North America in the unwieldy document copier which the boys from Rochester had humbly lugged over to London's Piccadilly Hotel.

In no time at all, from that unlikely start, Rank found itself riding the biggest bonanza that British business has ever seen. Profits from Rank Xerox, less than half a million pounds in 1963, blossomed to £55.5 million in a decade. As Americans seeking a backdoor into Xerox bought the shares heavily, the Rank Organization was worth around £840 million in the stock market early in 1973.

Note, moreover, who has profited most lavishly from the arrangement. Davis then had half a million pounds in Rank shares alone, and another £1 million elsewhere in the group. Yet that hardly compares with the nest egg of £400 million odd in the various Rank trusts at the 1973 peak that Davis did most to create. (Any more than Dave Mahoney's holdings in Norton Simon Inc., after four years in which its earnings were boosted by seventy-five percent, would have bought him too many Rembrandts. Still, $300,-000 a year in salary, $50,000 in bonus, $6 million in largely company-financed preferred stock and a wedge of stock options took Mahoney to a net worth of $14 million, which is enough, even at today's prices, to cover the odd wall.)

Protégés who are unrelated are most unlikely to make the Olympian financial grade achieved by many relatives by marriage or birth. In 1966, Charles Bassine, chairman of Spartans Industries, merged his clothing conglomerate with E. J. Korvette, the fading and undermanaged discount store chain pioneered by Eugene Ferkauf. It was a mistake. Spartans not only mishandled Korvette—just as badly as its founding fathers had—but Bassine also lost business for his own clothes: his customers disliked being undersold by Korvette on the Spartans clothes lines. But son-in-law help was at hand.

The relative in question, Arthur Cohen, had done business with Bassine and with Ferkauf for many years in the process of building Arlen Realty into America's biggest property chain, with $2 billion of real estate. Worth a million in 1955, this boy wonder, who had started with $25,-000, rose to $5 million in five further years. Cohen now merged with Spartans-Korvette, saving its management from paying tax (property depreciation keeps Arlen from this horror), getting the benefit of $100 million cash (obtained partly by selling Spartans' money-losing factories) and grabbing management responsibility. Armed in return with a stock exchange quote on the Big Board in New York, Cohen could then call for a recount of the family stake: it came to thirty percent of the entire caboodle, which contained a shareholders' equity of $160 million.

This was an achievement almost fit to rank with that of Philip Graham, who turned his father-in-law's newspaper, the *Washington Post*, from the $20 million loss item Eugene Meyer had made it, into a gold mine. Of course, to lose $20 million you have to be reasonably rich to start with.

To him that hath, much shall be given, remains the golden law, even in enlightened nepotism. Where the nepot should look for a surrogate son, if neither genetics nor matrimony has obliged, is a tricky question. Selecting some stalwart who has risen from the ranks seems the safest step. But there are a couple of hurdles (not counting the first of all, the fact that those struggling for the crown prince's diadem will waste much energy that is better dedicated to the care of the founder's fortune).

One high barrier is that the prince will have served so long at his master's feet that he may find it difficult to stand up straight, even if the master does a Simon-like abnegation (which he probably won't). The other main disadvantage is that tycoons are often unwilling to put total, unquestioning trust in a man whom they have ordered about for many years. The logic is akin to the inability of fathers to have uncompromising faith in their sons.

One such overlord, having finally been persuaded that his newly named, loyal, and able president was underpaid, reluctantly told him to put through a salary increase. After deep thought, the man gave himself $25,000 more. The aggrieved chairman promptly summoned him and demanded an explanation. "You've only been in the job a few weeks," he expostulated, "and you've already cost me $25,000 profit."

If the tycoon looks outside for a protégé, he is less likely to show contempt and is certain not to get his man cheap. But unless he stumbles on a Davis or Mahoney by chance (Mahoney was working in a Simon acquisition, Canada Dry, and climbed to the top over the recumbent body of an adversary), the tycoon is apt to be terribly disappointed—and it's usually all his own fault.

He draws up an ideal blueprint, a job specification, for which the combined skills of Napoleon, Henry Ford I, and Winston Churchill are required—along with the humility and sweetness of Little Nell—and then is terribly disappointed when his choice turns out to be merely human. One such visionary was always discovering a new *Wunderkind*, who never had time to don the purple before he was being shown to the door marked exit.

Harold Ross, the editor of the *The New Yorker*, was a perfect example of this kind of proprietor. He wore out managing editors at a depressing rate in his endless search for perfection (the choice even fell, in one spate of inspired lunacy, on James Thurber).

Consultants or ex-consultants are especially vulnerable to this treatment. They come, armed with a reputation in modern management, into the camp of a general whose own ideas date back to the business Punic Wars. The general's natural attitude is a skeptical "show me"; and he often lacks the patience or forbearance to let his adopted nephew do just that.

In one case, the private vehicle of Sir David Brown, which included gears, tractors, and Aston Martins, was bouncing off the road at a pace that alarmed even its bankers. (A major indication of trouble, since even the sight of a £20 million overdraft doesn't normally seem to raise bankers' eyebrows—maybe because it isn't their money.) Brown's natural son was apparently not fully equipped by nature to handle the variegated problems bundled together by his sire. A properly selected professional manager, an ex-management consultant, was duly imported. In the battle between manager and proprietor, the former gained the support of the anxious banks. They theoretically bounced Sir David out of all executive power and put their trust in the pro: he lasted only a few more months, after which the knight of industry was revealed sitting once again firmly in his saddle.

Brown paid a palpable price, however: three of his businesses, including Aston Martin and the tractor enterprise, were sold to help clear the liquidity mess and the massive mountain of bank debt, over £45 million at the end of 1971. All in all, the affair was a nasty shock, which could have been avoided had the tycoon put his trust earlier in a nephew of nontycoon propensities.

A contrasting and better example is another private outfit whose owner, anticipating a move to noncommercial pastures, carefully nursed his unofficial nephew through two or three years of sometimes painful preparation. The family future was then, in effect, placed entirely in the nephew's hands. Within a year, he had made his benefactor a paper multimillionaire.

There is one magnate of notable capacity who, by great good fortune, conceived a natural son possessed of every necessary virtue: a calm, methodical, intelligent manager, with none of his father's passion for the big deal (of the double or single variety). The son quickly and sensibly developed the business, while his father prowled about looking for whom he might devour. Every now and again, seemingly as a tease for the good son, the father would fall for some simulacrum of his own young self; a fast-draw gunslinger who had made millions while still (in business terms) in short pants.

The father's favor would be publicly blazoned forth, often by the new nephew; this new love was cemented by details which were once or twice even semipublicly criticized by the good son. The implication was that Big Daddy, disappointed with his son's lack of adventure, might shift some of the inheritance to the dashing shoulders of Little Nephew.

In all the excitement, few people, even the nephews, noted that the terms of their business relationship were unduly favorable to the old maestro. His favor, suddenly and warmingly given, could be just as abruptly withdrawn; at which point the ex-nephew would find himself clutching the short end of the deal. A sound policy when dealing with wealthy veterans is to assume that the wiliness and power that propelled them to their wealth has in no wise been dissipated by age. Their favor, like that of any absolute monarch, is fickle: the sane courtier protects his front at all times and never turns his back.

That's why the most successful nephews are the heroes of reverse takeovers, those paradoxical corporate devices whereby the sprat swallows the mackerel. The General Electric Company big deal, while a perfect example of the son-in-law gambit, also worked out as a reverse operation: the much smaller Radio and Allied battle cruiser in effect took command of the entire GEC fleet.

In these cases, the nephew, the boss of the smaller concern, is backed up by his shareholdings, by his wealth (he is usually smart enough to extort a heavyweight price from the purchaser), and by his reputation.

Pliable nephews can be found almost anywhere. One mail order king, a relaxed fellow who likes time to count his money, picked on his old commanding officer, hiring him for £950 a year. The ex-colonel had built a business worth £36 million just twenty years later.

If the paragon can be found among kin, so much the better: it keeps all, instead of nearly all, the money in the family. But the remoter reaches of nepotism are probably a mistake in businesses that have already adopted all the standard corporate characteristics, including the routine defense mechanisms. The Du Ponts may just have got away with naming Crawford H. Greenewalt, a Du Pont by marriage, as president, although the results, the start of a long Du Pont profit stagnation, don't fully support their case.

Where professional, hired managers will accept a son, especially if they have been schooled to do so, they may jib at seeing nephews, cousins, and sons-in-law stepping on to all the top rungs. Nepotists try to get around this by adopting the odd henchman as "almost one of the family": in one case, where the blood line was strongly Sicilian, the few solid Wasps who had been admitted to the inner councils were forced to become honorary Italians. One even grew a Godfather moustache.

The acid test is whether there is any chance of a non-family insider being promoted over the head of a family member, as happened after 131 years at the F & M Schaefer brewing giant: a seventy-two-year-old father plucked a management expert-cum-academic from outside to replace himself as chief executive, passing over a forty-two-year-old son. If family boss follows family boss for-evermore, the non-kin will never be better than faithful family retainers—and some other, brusque solution, à la Schaefer, will have to be found, one day, to the inevitable succession problems.

The childless or effectively childless emperor is luckier than he knows. If he can stumble across the right protégé, the man who can make sense out of success, he can leave a lasting monument and enjoy his own last years. If he can't, or if it falls into the hands of feckless sons, the empire will eventually dissolve.

Men seldom toil to create gold alone: the business itself, their creation and dearest child, is the name of their game. Rather than lose its glory, it's far better to "let your nephew try."

ENTR'ACTE

The Crisis of Conservatism

or

What's Bad Enough for Grandpa

Every business has to tread a frayed tightrope between conservatism and change. Theoretically, it's a toss-up which course is more dangerous, sticking too long to the old or shifting too zealously to the new. But more once-great companies have vanished from sight through being swamped by the tides of history than through swimming too hard in an effort to keep up with the Marxist dialectic. That famous news photograph of the aged Sewell Avery being carried, chair and all, out of the Montgomery Ward offices, to end his resistance to President Truman's price control, symbolizes the fate of all firms and financial heroes who resist history. They get beaten: Montgomery Ward, once a name to mention in the same breath as Sears Roebuck, became but a shadow of that mighty shape.

The issue isn't only that what's good enough for Grandpa can't be equally good for every succeeding generation. Often it's the old boy himself who is the purblind villain. All great entrepreneurs have grave weaknesses, the blindest of spots, both in their business attitudes and in their treatment of other people. As they grow older, and more hallowed, and even wealthier, the partial blindness tends to become more severe and to affect the way in which the company does its business.

The natural belief of the rich, shared by their publicists and their public, is that the methods which brought them their yachts, mansions, and Monets are not only right, brilliant, and socially desirable, but everlasting. The heirs of founding fathers and grandfathers usually share this pious delusion, but worse damage may well be done by the old gentleman himself as he pursues his star to the illogical conclusion.

The postwar history of European business contains some ripe examples. A devastated Continent catching up on American standards of living, with the aid of American finance, offered inordinate opportunities to men of courage, men who often, because of the lost wartime years, came into their glory late in life. They were older in years and in background than the men who ran US business, and the concepts of public ownership or what passes for modern management were as far removed from their minds as Mars is from Earth.

Cornelis Verolme, once the czar of European shipbuilders, began his career in his later forties. Verolme entered a small shipyard near Rotterdam at sixteen; he spent most of his working life with a machinery firm, and broke out only after a monumental row. He then conceived the notion that, since 5,700 Allied ships totaling 23 million tons had gone down during the war, an insatiable replacement market must exist—which he set out to feed first by reconditioning old marine engines.

Verolme made fast enough profits in four years to buy an old shipyard, demolish it, and build a new, modern yard—much to the disgust of established Rotterdam shipbuilders, who blackballed the upstart from membership of the exclusive Rowing and Sailing Club De Maas. Blackballs notwithstanding, Verolme built over a hundred ships in under two decades to a value of more than £230 million. His was the archetypal cry of the victorious grandfather: "Never have any doubts about your own ability. Never ask, can I do it? No, do it!"

The catch was that, like most powerful self-made men, Verolme not only did it, but sought to do it all himself. Virtually all that anybody except Verolme knew about profits was that they were mostly plowed back. (As for capital and reserves, they were as secret as earnings.) At this point, the twin grandparental diseases of inordinate ambition and overweening self-confidence overran the system. Verolme got caught with an uncompleted monster shipbuilding dock, a difficult merger with a loss-making partner, and a pile of supertanker orders taken at unfunny prices.

The old man, turned 70, had to be bailed out by the government from a desperately leaky situation: total losses in 1969, the new regime reckoned, came to £14.7 million. An ex-Philips manager, called in to man the pumps, put his finger on the nub of the problem: "I warned him several times that in the end he would not be thanked if he went on running the show himself as long as possible . . . it is nonsense for a man of almost seventy to travel around the world personally to win orders."

But Verolme knew no other way of life: even from his big yacht, he had kept constantly in touch with his office on shore; even with his group virtually bankrupt, he kept on fighting to regain control of the £100 million empire which he had created and all but destroyed. The Greeks would have loved this epic of the old king who pulled down his kingdom about his ears by clinging too long to the methods that had originally raised him to the throne.

Similar doomed kings abound in business history. The Italian appliance industry had one of the sharpest rises and falls. After the war, consumer durables in Italy lacked both a market and manufacturers: the future lords of this slice of creation had begun by making iron-age products like wood-burning stoves, the original speciality of the Zanussi family. Another future giant, Ignis, began in 1943, when Guido Borghi, with sons Gaetano, Giovanni, and Giuseppe, started making electric stoves.

As Italian housewives began to clamor for more electric labor-saving, the manufacturers expanded at a furious pace, built the most efficient and productive plants in the world, and barged so heavily into other European markets (they had to, to keep the productive monster satiated) that they virtually destroyed much of the competition. In the process they so saturated their own market that the Italian boom in refrigerators was over by the mid-1960s; that in washing machines ended by 1967-68. The rest of Europe peaked out only slightly later, and the Italian tycoons were left with a tortuous management problem—and no managers to solve it.

Fortuitously, the families were hit by dynastic and business disaster simultaneously. Lino Zanussi, the entrepreneur nearest to managerial stature and builder of the strongest group, died in an air crash with his heir apparent. Only one Borghi survived to take Ignis into the all-enveloping embrace of Philips. The three Zoppas brothers died within twelve months of each other, leaving £50 million odd of bank debts and a company, taken over *in extremis* by Zanussi, losing about two-thirds of a million each month.

Another Zanussi buy, Triplex, was losing only marginally fewer millions, as the workers, the original beneficiaries of the appliance boom, acted as the final wreckers by staging a spate of strikes, staved off only by ruinous wage increases. Accidents aside, the families paved the way for their own dissolution by continuing to manage businesses of international scale with methods insufficiently remote from the old wood-burning days.

The appearance of simultaneous dynastic disasters emphasizes the chief danger of family enterprise: a bad genealogical run can ruin the act. In Lancashire textiles, where the heredity seems to have been no great shakes, the saying used to be clogs to clogs in four generations. These days it's far harder to return to square one: tycoons may lose their businesses, but seldom all their baksheesh.

There are cases of yacht to dinghy, triplex apartment to farm, Rolls-Royce to Rover or Pontiac in one generation, more often in one lifetime. In the Age of the Common Millionaire, few families are foolish enough to leave all their eggs in one locked-in basket, and few husbands imprudently forget to set up their wives in the manner to which they have both been accustomed. The two devices which have created and perpetuated the Common Millionaire, the partial sale of equity to the doting public and the "provision for family" in a man's lifetime by the formation of trusts, also serve to keep the family in bread and butter in the event of failure, by Grandpa or his heirs. You wouldn't know, from his style of living, that Bill Zeckendorf's Webb and Knapp property empire had ever gone bankrupt—he even preserves the same once-famous, circular office in Manhattan.

Following the Draconian law of business, that incompetence breeds more incompetence, few sights are more awe-inspiring, however, than the completion by heirs of the crumbling begun by the progenitor. Had William Randolph Hearst possessed less megalomania, less talent as a newspaperman, and more business acumen, the Hearst empire today would be fit to share the same paragraph as Ford or possibly even Mellon. But Hearst's dictatorial methods and disdain for economics left his two sons a dwindling empire with a managerial heritage which they proceeded to dissipate by squabbling violently with the managers.

The thirty papers which remained at the old man's death, still a formidable collection, shrank to eight. Unheard-of and relatively diminutive figures like Samuel I. Newhouse overtook the giant with stupefying ease. In one generation, it was almost as if WR had never rejected an editorial: after two generations, there was even less evidence that WR's father had ever exploited the Comstock Lode.

The Hearst money was big, the biggest, and it's this size of accumulation which was thought all but impossible to destroy: as Henry Ford I proved by the survival of a colossal family inheritance through a decade of grotesque mismanagement and inept financial provision. But modest money takes a good deal of destruction, too: witness Britain's postwar proletarian passion for taking holidays en masse, in holiday camps that recreated something of the atmosphere of the wartime services.

Campers were wakened at military hours with screams of "Wakey! Wakey!"; dragooned into enjoying themselves

by staff actually called "Redcoats," a name strikingly reminiscent of the "Redcaps" or Military Police; fed in gigantic
refectories with food which the Army Catering Corps
wouldn't have been ashamed to own. But the holidays were
cheap, matey, fun for the kids—and a Canadian named
Billy Butlin (who became Sir William for his pains) made
many millions from the game.

Departing for the Bahamas, he handed over to his son at
a time when the business clearly needed new ideas even
more than new blood. Other fortunes were being created
from shipping the same masses by the million to Spain,
where the cost was comparable, the sun actually shone, the
food was edible, the booze was cheap, and the atmos...
was not para-military. But Butlin's management p...
able to solve the problem, partly because it persist...
lieving that the British public still wanted Sir Billy's holiday camps with undimmed passion.

In this conviction, the heirs failed to see that, from being
a majority taste, camps had become a minority trade—and
serving a cheap minority market is a poor financial risk.
From profits of £5 million at the peak, the chain sank
steadily to £3.4 million at its worst; even the turnover slid
slowly downward. The camps were finally sold to the Rank
Organization after Sir Billy had made a last-minute,
dramatic reappearance on the scene.

Rematerialization was also managed by W. Maxey Jarman, the prodigious apparel acquirer, whose buying had
lifted Genesco from $360 million of sales to $1.2 billion.
Just like Butlin, Jarman handed on the mantle to his son;
and Jarman's son proved unable to wear it. When profits
more than halved, and then went on downward, the terrified directors simply called Maxey back. He took one look
at his own purchases and concluded tersely that about a
quarter of them were no good—no wonder his heir, who
then had to wage a bruising war to get his father demateri-
alized again, hit even worse trouble than Sir William's.

Billy's own shares went when their going value was £2.2
million; they had been twice as high. In the same way, a
young man, Geoffrey Kaye, who on his father's death so
mismanaged the Pricerite supermarket chain that the company's own internal accounts could show nonexistent
profits, cleared nearly £7 million from the eventual bid:
this family's stake had once been worth nearer £13 million.

The incidents demonstrate how, even in an undistinguished, one-product company in a declining, shabby market, a family can grow poorer, while still staying rich enough to take care of every need of subsequent generations—provided that the generations are neither excessively prolific nor overfond of disputation.

In the 1920s the German family of Stinnes possessed one of Europe's premier fortunes, fit to vie with Krupp and the like. A nineteenth-century shipping and coal Stinnes had founded the fortune; a third generation, Hugo, known as the King of Assyria for his stern black beard, added steel, oil, and papermaking to the mix. Within two years of Hugo's death, the family had to turn to American banks for $25 million of salvage money for his widow.

The family kept half the American company, which now held most of the Stinnes assets, but lost these (as enemy property) in the war. Through all this period, and thereafter, the main problem was the total inability of Hugo's three sons to abide each other. One was bought out; the other two had to be forcibly parted by the widow, who sacked the second son. This Stinnes, Hugo Jr., went off to found his own empire in engineering and plastics. When that came unstuck in 1963, the rest of the family interests, still presided over by the King of Assyria's widow at the age of ninety-three, were also on the rocks.

A not so incidental fact is that the final manager of the widow's truncated empire was Franz von Papen, the last German Chancellor before Adolf Hitler. It's nearly always a fatal sign when proprietors bring in a political or similarly distinguished figure to heal family divisions or to mend family fortunes. The latter task is always beyond his powers, ability, and experience; as for the divided sets of kin, the poor man must either side with one or the other, or be torn apart.

An equally unpleasant and faster fate overtook the heirs of Sir Frederick Handley-Page, one of the great aviation pioneers, who made a bomb out of wartime and postwar bombers. HP's planes were the spearhead of Britain's erstwhile nuclear strike force. He was an autocrat of striking independence and considerable age, who, alone among the aviation overlords, refused to accept the government's forceful wish that the industry should merge into larger units. His reluctance failed to endear the company to those who doled out public contracts, without which a defense company is as well placed as a footballer with two broken legs.

When the great man died, in 1962, he left this dubious inheritance to three daughters, and too many females, in Western society as at present organized, make a distinct drawback. One of the husbands took over: Handley-Page, still wedded to the old man's dreams of independence, started looking desperately for some non- or para-military business. It came up with the Jetstream, an airliner which, had it been able to pack in as many passengers for the price as the specification suggested, would undoubtedly have beaten the world. In fact, it could do neither, and all it beat was the company—plus Bernie Cornfeld's Investors Overseas Services. Three of his sales sidekicks had bought unsalable Jetstreams at $530,000 a throw, all financed by IOS banks.

Contemplation of such cases reinforces the belief that fathers and grandfathers, however brilliant, should be compelled to retire from executive action at the ripe young age of sixty-five, and should be succeeded only by sons on somebody else's decision—even though this contradicts the fact, equally well established in this work, that many lasting fortunes have been supervised day to day to a great age by their progenitors.

The clue lies somewhere along that dangerous tightrope between continuity and change. If the progenitor possesses some instinct, even if only the desire to maximize a profit, which keeps him flexible into his dotage, he may do more good than harm. Once he gets glued into his ideas and ways, however, disaster is likely to follow: not least because his successors, lacking his genius, will be heavily indoctrinated in his rigidity.

It used to be a matter for marvel how superbly the successor generations at Pirelli, Fiat, and Olivetti had carried on the founder's good work. Men like Leopoldo Pirelli or Giovanni Agnelli had heroic reputations. The consequent temptation has been to blame not the sons, but their circumstances, for the disasters of the last few years. Nevertheless, in the third management upheaval visited on Olivetti in seven hard years, Roberto was retired to a nonexecutive position—even though the family had 22.9% of the company.

Managements which suffer such monumental reverses

can't have been doing everything right. Fiat was, after all, forced to omit its dividend. The Agnellis, whose tentacles spread into every corner of Italian business life, can manage without the money. But could their main company have done better without the one-man Agnelli pinnacle? If your father and grandfather dominated the show, you are unlikely to settle for less. This is rarely a source of strength —the exceptions prove a different rule.

Four successive Johnsons have headed S. C. Johnson, the private wax and polish royalty of Racine, Wisconsin, with world sales of over a billion dollars. According to one admiring executive, there's "not a dropout, not a lemon, among them. Each one has been more aggressive than his father in business terms. They've all had different ideas about what could and should be done, and each seems to have had the very strong feeling that anything the old man could do, he could do a lot better."

The Johnsons, in addition to inculcating business sense into their sons, have indoctrinated their scions in a social ethic of good works. This has given the company a frame of reference more specific than the general Italian paternalism, as practiced at Fiat *et al.* But Fiat is still run in an autocratic manner that the old Agnelli, and his strong-man successor, Professor Valletta, would have recognized. The reasons are not just Italian (although from mediaeval and Renaissance times dynasties have wielded most of the country's real power). The autocracy also reflects a curious internal logic of car companies the world over.

Historical accident produced car companies which were structured around one man, largely because the successful car companies were built around one automotive hit; and a wonder car almost always springs from one man's instinct and inspiration. The Ford company under Henry II, though perforce utterly different in most ways from the creation Henry I left behind, still bows its collective head to the reigning Mr. Ford, who is less a *primus inter pares* than a king among courtiers.

Showing, say, the British company's new models to "Mr. Ford" for prior approval is a futile exercise in the management sense—this one American's opinion on what will sell in Europe is almost certainly not worth having. But the trundling up for pats or kicks makes perfect sense in the atmosphere of a court. And if the dynastic firms lag behind in adapting their management styles to changed days and ways—including the irritating wish of the workers to have some say about their work—the fortunes of the dynasties are sure to suffer: as they have done in Italy. Leopoldo Pirelli, returning to work in 1973 after a car crash which killed his brother, had to face the hard fact that management autocracy, coupled with technical failure, had laid his company appallingly low.

Another strange case of ossified attitudes overtaken by change afflicted the one-time focus of the crowned wealth of the world, Monte Carlo. Prince Rainier III, though substantially bolstered by the money Princess Grace made from movies and from being an Irish-American builder's daughter, can't be indifferent to the fortunes of a casino in which his state owns a seventy-two percent controlling interest—a stake dating back to the creation, in 1966, of enough new shares in the Société des Bains de Mer to deprive Aristotle Onassis of the control he sought.

Once upon a time, the SBM was one of the world's great money mines. One François Blanc in 1863 paid $366,000 for the casino concession. He died fourteen years later worth over $14 million. Those were the years when kings and grand dukes rubbed shoulders and chips; that was when the expensive favors of the "Great Horizontals," courtesans like Liane de Pougy, Emilienne d'Alençon, and Cleo de Merode, could be had for the paying. (They were also known as the "Ladies Who Cushion.") Today amateurs have ousted the professional ladies, and other haunts are attracting the gambling money of a lower class of clientele. But the men who ran the bank at Monte Carlo continued to act as if Edward VII were still arriving for his nightly diversion.

SBM actually started losing money: a state of affairs roughly akin to Kuwait having a gasoline shortage. The year before they reported their first loss, the old guard resorted to the ancient maneuver of cashing in some assets (blue chip securities) to cover up the falling profits, and raise the dividend. The next year misfortune, as it usually does, followed on deception. Gambling income dropped to less than half the normal take.

Rainier had to install his cousin, Prince Louis de Polignac, as president and to find, of all things, a Harvard Business School graduate as managing director. Even then, the 1972 net of some 7.5 million francs is a long way short of M. Blanc's mountainous standards. What goes up, says the law of nature, must come down. And the history of all monarchies, tiny ones like that of the Grimaldis in Monaco or lay monarchies like that of the Agnellis in Turin, demonstrates the working of that natural law in human institutions.

The wreckage a truly determined family can wreak on Grandpa's legacy is demonstrated in reverse by the work done on Waterman by the unlikely Mme. Francine Gomez. Waterman once enjoyed all but a tithe of US fountain pen sales; but the US company, battered by ballpoints, had been sold in 1958, while the French company, which had the European rights, struggled steadily toward the grave. Mme. Gomez, taking control of the inheritance from her mother, had to sack nine out of ten top executives, cut the labor force by 485 persons, reduce the head office to a quarter of its former size, move it, buy back the American company, and refurbish everything in sight—thus converting a half a million loss into a $1.5 million profit.

If Grandpa and his heirs are to hang on to their hats, again the ideal balance has to be struck between conservatism and radicalism. The principles are quite easy. First, no cow can be sacred: anything can be changed, and anybody can be put out to grass, if change or grassing appear necessary. Second, there's an obvious distinction between those traditions which are material to the business and those which are merely nice to have around—like a clump of mistletoe at Christmas. Leave the latter alone, so long as they don't cost much and people like them. As for the former, meticulously question every one; and if the answers come out wrong, found a new tradition.

Finally, suppose that the business is running quite beautifully; don't succumb completely to the correct urge to leave well alone. Search for one area of inadequately exploited opportunity; find one function or part of the company which isn't running with the same degree of smooth beauty as the rest. Concentrate on these two fields—good Grandpas always do, before their arteries begin to harden.

But that leads to the hardest trick of all: removing or immobilizing the old boy (or boys) before he (they) starts costing the rest of the family a deal of money. Short of parricide, which isn't legal, there is no sure method. The older the family incubus gets, the harder it becomes to insult him, to intimate that he is no longer wanted. There is only one gun that his juniors can level at his head—a threat that, if he doesn't go, they will. But heirs are generally too intimidated (and too scared, often with good reason, of their chances of finding acceptable employment elsewhere) to fire that weapon. They prefer, unwittingly but surely, to go down with the captain—and the ship.

ACT II

On the Delights
of Deception

or

Honesty Is the Worst
Policy

SCENE 1

The Fortunes in Fraud

— or —

You Can Fool All the People

You can fool all the people—not all the time, but enough of it to steal their money. The definitions of theft range from criminal dishonesty to false bills of goods, and the penalties range from mere business failure to moderate prison terms. But the punishment seldom ever fits the crime: somehow or other, the thief nearly always ends in possession of enough loot to line a gilded cage for his retirement or future activities, even if he is caught.

Mythologists of crime dream of a Mr. Big, the Mephistophelean brain behind the £2 million Great Train Robbery in Britain, the $2.75 million Brinks caper in the US, the removal of the Nazi gold reserves at the end of the Second World War, the wave of art robberies that have run curators and collectors ragged all over Europe. But only a pervert would suffer the possible prison penalties, the logistic difficulties, the dangerous and incompetent colleagues, and the other risks attendant on robbing even a small bank—when he can start his own bank, and rob the depositors in comfort.

People deposit their hard-earned dollars, pounds, marks, francs, lire, yen, or zloty; the bank pays most of them no interest at all (if it's a Swiss bank, the depositor pays for the privilege; yet so profoundly do the rich trust the Swiss that they place their loot in non-interest-bearing accounts); then the same bank lends out that same money at rates of up to sixteen percent. If you are borrowing £1,000 for nothing and lending it for £160 a year, you don't need much else to wax rich: even after paying for the marble halls and marble-headed managers with which banks are traditionally oversupplied.

The principal species of millionaire-making fraud is a

variation on the banking theme. The gambit is to persuade people to give their money to you, rather than to the bank, by the childish expedient of offering them a return that is higher than nothing. The recorded annals of deception (probably there were variations in ancient Egypt) include the Apple Miracle, the Pig Pay-off, the Casino Caper, the Pyramid Ploy, and many, many others: as soon as one con is destroyed, another (often the same one) rears its head.

With apples, the idea was that the city dweller should buy himself a piece of the action in an orchard, because (as everybody knows) one little seed will grow into a big tree, showering apples and wealth on its owners forevermore. Pigs were another form of armchair farming: these noble animals have enormous litters, at great speed, so that possession of just one sow, cared for you by the promoter, would confer the benefits of compound breeding and interest for all eternity.

Casinos were for armchair gamblers. You turned over your money to a wizard who had an infallible system for winning at the tables: he creamed off a commission for his pains, and paid all the rest, at stupendous rates of interest, to his happy backers. One such scheme in 1962 offered the suckers a 360% return, in theory: in practice, none of the backers (there were 20,000 of them) got more than a fifth of their money back.

The oldest ploy, possibly older even than apples, is the pyramid, adopted with unstoppable enthusiasm in the early 1970s by American promoters like Glenn Turner of Dare-To-Be-Great, a motivational marvel, and Koscot Interplanetary cosmetics, if you please; or the late, unlamented William Penn Patrick, under whom Turner learned the trade, and whom the Securities and Exchange Commission accused of taking 80,000 investors for more than $250 million of Holiday Magic—which sold soap as well as cosmetics. These US wonders were exported gleefully to the British, who have always been fools for a quick buck.

In its origins the pyramid possessed perfect simplicity—best shown by the chain letter idea. Each participant is supposed to find a fixed number of other kindred spirits, who in turn each find the same number, until by the laws of geometrical progression a sum of money vastly greater than the original small amount comes in turn to each link in the chain. The logical defect is that no money is coming into the scheme from outside. Even if the chain doesn't break, the first come are the first served—but break it must. The mathematical fact is that, with each person recruiting four people, it takes only a relatively few stages before the entire population of the United Kingdom, men, women, children, and possibly even a few dogs, will be in the pyramid.

Precisely the same objection applied to schemes like Koscot. The gimmick of the Koscot-style pyramid is that its structure is linked to the sale of the wonder product: cosmetics, or liquid cleaner, or whatever. Each link in the pyramid recruits other links to sell the goodies in a carefully constructed hierarchy of regional bosses, distributors, and salesmen.

The subscription is a purchase of the wonder stock, offset by bonuses for each new link recruited into the chain. It looks absolutely safe: the money has gone for goods you can see, feel, count—and sell at a satisfyingly high profit margin. The mathematics are impossible: according to the SEC, if each Holiday Magic distributor signed up as many others as he was supposed to, 305,175,780 people would be hustling the junk (presumably to each other) within twelve months. The existence of the stuff appears to make the pyramid more plausible; but it actually makes the whole scheme incredible.

The combined profit margins add up to several times the exfactory cost at the start of the chain—a price which presumably includes a profit. What the pyramided suckers should wonder is why, if the product is truly salable at such gigantic mark-ups, its proprietor should want to let so many others into so lucrative an act. This is the self-same question that should be asked by those tempted by piggies, apples, casinos, and so on: if the profits are truly so great, why does the man need my money?

Even when the promised returns work out at an annual rate of over three hundred percent, the victims still wonder not. Their own urge to get rich quick blinds them. Actually, if you could invest £250 at three hundred percent, you would be a millionaire in six years. What is more pathetic, however, is that millions of people down the years have been tempted to part with their cash by quite small rates of interest, or (which comes to the same thing) small savings of money.

Two firms that crashed in Britain, for instance, regularly offered interest on deposits two or three percent above the going rate. There was no obvious way in which they could earn enough on the deposits to cover the interest: actually, there was no way at all. One firm, called Pinnock Finance, was Australian-based and was vaguely supposed to be in sewing machines. After its presiding genius had vanished with the boodle, it appeared that Pinnock had worked the oldest trick in the game, as faithfully practiced by the pig, apple, and pyramid boys.

You pay off the first suckers from the money generously provided by the next set, and so on *ad infinitum*. Just as the pig scheme contained only a third of the happily breeding pigs promised to investors, so much of the Pinnock money went nowhere except into the Pinnock money. The crunch comes when the flow of new money dries up, and the owners of the old money start wanting it back.

This painful conjunction caught a slippery specialist named Dr. Emil Savundra. Savundra's speciality was offering motorists insurance on their cars at premiums well below the going rate. Note that phrase again: if a rate is going, there's a *prima facie* case that it's the correct rate. Unable to resist the bargain, drivers earnestly loaded their cash into the hands of Savundra's own Fire, Auto and Marine, where the proprietor off-loaded as much of the proceeds as possible into his own pockets (located mostly in overseas bank accounts). When the inevitable collapse came, as accident claims by motorists exceeded the amount of money left in Savundra's kitty, the cops followed fast— and so did his conviction.

Savundra's fraud thus had a serious defect, shared with the devices of even greater removal experts, Tino De Angelis, the salad oil magician, and Billy Sol Estes, the silo wizard. All three men made, or conjured up, personal profits running into several millions. Both De Angelis and Sol Estes preyed on the Achilles' heel of the modern economy, which is its total dependence on bits of paper. If a man waves a document which says there is grain in a silo or oil in a storage tank, banks are wont to lend money on that security just as readily as a Savundra customer, having purchased a policy, believed that his car was safely insured.

If trust in paper broke down and bankers checked every individual paper transaction for its underlying reality, the log jam would reach intolerable proportions by noon of the first day. De Angelis fattened on this fact (just as, in an earlier era, Ivar Kreuger issued $500 millions in fictitious bonds) to the grand total of $120 million. Nobody knows how much of these sums—$167 million zoomed out of the De Angelis company in its last six months of life—was stashed away awaiting his exit from jail. But there's the catch: the convicted con has to face the inconvenience of a spell behind bars before he can enjoy his proceeds.

De Angelis caught a ten-year sentence, meaning seven years with parole. If the estimates of his take are correct and he hung on to half, that works out at $100 per hour of maximum captivity. In fact, that's not a great rate of return. And however you look at it, going to prison is a bad technical lapse, a blotch on the escutcheon of an alleged expert in the business of parting customers from their money.

It took another American to elevate this craft to the status of a higher art: Bernie Cornfeld, caliph and court jester of Investors Overseas Services. At its peak this mega-mishmash contained $2.5 billion of the suckers' money. How much of it ended in the maw of Bernie and his no less eager cohorts will never be known. But the public flotation of IOS Ltd. alone, the final act in its *Götter-dammerung*, made the Cornfeld and Co. stake worth $52 million—and that is competitive even with De Angelis.

Cornfeld's advantage over Savundra and Sol Estes was that, while holding out the self-same bait of riches, he actually offered *less* than the going rate. His idea, a stroke of pure genius, was to sell people dollar bills for $2. Any IOS customer in the US Armed Forces, where Bernie started business, could have bought mutual funds direct. The disadvantage of these investments, especially those of the "front-end load" genus, is that a major part of the investors' money goes straight to the salesman and the management, not into the investment.

With front-end load, the investor loses half of his initial outlay in this wildly unproductive way. On one calculation, the load and the continuing management charges meant that if an investment doubled in ten years, the investor would have had to wait for six of them to get back on speaking terms with his own money. In Bernie Cornfeld's case the investors paid his Fund of Funds to put their money into the same mutual funds which the overseas Americans whom he first tapped could easily have bought for themselves; the funds paid Bernie, and also exacted their own toll, before finally depositing the cash into some kind of investment.

The set-up was so glorious that eventually IOS couldn't stand seeing any of the money going into somebody else's wallet. So it set up its own internal mutual funds. The customer still paid twice for the same service, but he now paid Cornfeld twice. What's more, the internal funds were not confined to staid, quoted investments whose market value could be ascertained in a trice by reading the *Wall Street Journal.*

This made it easier to deliver what the customers thought they were buying—which was capital gain on (it was implied, advertised, and blazoned forth) a phenomenal scale. With funds so large as those of IOS, however, it was impossible to generate this kind of performance. The sheer weight of so much money was bound to bring down the funds if world stock markets fell, and Cornfeld could not suspend this law of financial gravity. Hence his ventures into dubious areas like the oil land operations of John M. King.

King's bait was oil for the masses. Working on the mutual fund principle, including that of heavy compensation for his pains, King was supposed to invest the money in oil wells, drilled by his own corporation—which also provided all other services required, at a price. The beauty of this scheme defied imitation: investors naturally had to accept that some oil wells came up dry. If King failed to deliver the bounty, it was an act of God rather than man, deductible (what was more) as a tax loss.

The King of Denver truly delivered for his friend Bernie Cornfeld. IOS invested in some territory found by King: a sale of a fraction of the tract was arranged at a staggering price that, when applied to all of the IOS holding (actually a bauble of dubious worth), amounted to a $145 million capital gain, prudently whittled down to a mere $91 million.

This was the purest fairy gold. But in practical terms, it hardly matters whether a value is fictitious or real, so long as the fiction is believed.

This lovable fact spawned an entire new branch of the money-lifting industry. Devoted students of Cornfeld's success plugged the main weakness in his operation; its ultimate dependence on stock markets, which by their very nature fluctuate. Property, on the other hand, is popularly supposed to go up and up as it goes up. A real estate mutual fund could therefore offer an investment paradise on earth—absolute security with everlasting growth, and good income to boot.

The investors (milked from the front end, as usual) were therefore offered little pieces of large buildings in the lush United States. Gramco, the most successful of these operations, would run the properties (at a substantial fee) and would periodically announce how much they had increased in value. In fact, the real value of this real estate was purely putative: you can sell shares at any time, but off-loading a portfolio of upvalued skyscrapers is no easier than selling your house at your own top price.

In other words, the investors who flocked to Gramco (and to even more obviously fraudulent imitators like Jerome Hoffman of the Real Estate Fund of America) were unwittingly burying their money in the most illiquid form of investment possible. The whole credibility of the edifice depended on the suckers continuing to believe it. If too many of them simultaneously wanted their money back, even in a completely honest operation, their Comstock Lode would have to sell its fairy gold—and if the fairy gold failed to fetch fairy prices, down would come the entire estate, buildings and all.

To illustrate, say that the suckers have paid $1 billion for their stake; you decide, after a time, that the buildings are worth $1.5 billion, when actually their realizable value is $1.2 billion. Any investor who thereupon takes his money out gets fifty percent more than he put in: it follows that if half the clients ask for the loot, you must pay out $750 million, leaving only $450 million to satisfy $750 million of claims.

Actually, crisis would be reached well before that point. As soon as schemes of this kind start, for whatever reason, to experience a net outflow of investors' funds, the jig is up, their days are numbered, and the vultures gather.

The Gramco fund, USIF, was eventually stuck with a billion in property, 20,000 anguished stockholders, and 1,700 salesmen running to keep a step ahead of the aforesaid investors. John Thackray reports that the El Salvador representative, on learning of the disaster, checked with an atlas to find the furthest spot on the globe from where he was and took a plane there forthwith. Many Gramco and IOS customers were Latin Americans bent on sending untaxed money to safer, less inflationary climes: it served them right. Gramco was caught in the IOS backwash—but it would have fallen, anyway.

But the Cornfeld gambit and its variations not only proved unprecedentedly efficient at putting greedy hands in investors' pockets; they generated so rich a cash flow that other, fatter fowls of the air came clustering: the brokers, the fund managers, the bankers, the underwriters—all clamoring for a piece of the action. Drexel Harriman & Ripley in the US, Hill Samuel in Britain, and the French Rothschilds (the English ones asked to be excused) were intimate actors in the final stages of building Bernie's Valhalla; and in the Twilight of the Gods that ensued, many were the respectable hands being washed.

Respectable front, back, or side names are no protection for the investor. His true defense is simple refusal to believe that money is subject to miracles. His true weakness is envy. Armchair farming, gambling in plush casinos for high stakes, wheeling and dealing on world stock markets, owning oil wells and skyscrapers—all these are hobbies for those who are already rich. Would-be millionaires fall for their own envy, and the Cornfelds of this world shrewdly exploit that temptation: so shrewdly, in fact, that there is no reason why, given self-restraint, they could not have lasted far longer. So much money was flowing into IOS at its peak that merely lending out the cash before it was invested produced a torrent of wealth: all of which would have belonged to the Cornfeld mob if they had known how to stop it streaming right out again.

But the expenses of running a worldwide door-to-door selling operation are also wondrous: the instincts of these entrepreneurs arise from their own weakness, which rules out any chance of retrenchment or caution; and, anyway, they are terrified of any fall-off in the money flow.

The writing on the wall for Gramco, in fact, appeared even before Bernie's blackout: the Gramco proprietors Keith Barish and Rafael Navarro, an unlikely pair of boy-wonder financiers, took over two dozen pages in a news magazine to discuss their financial and philanthropic virtues in full color. Those sufficiently unenthralled to seek details of the company's system for paying commission (a highly material subject) were cross-referred to number eighteen of the unnumbered pages; the eighteenth page contained no reference whatsoever to the commission system. But the customers for such schemes don't really want to know anything, except that they are getting richer. And they do not share the instinctive feeling of the experienced hand that if somebody has to buy two dozen pages of advertising to say how wonderful he is, he can't be.

There was, truth to tell, something terribly, appallingly wrong with all the great con artists of our time: something so abominably amiss that any reasonably shrewd child from the Brooklyn streets (where Bernie Cornfeld grew up) could be expected to spot the defect at once. They are not the obvious philanthropic types, these gentry. They are flashy, showy, greedy, conceited; they give themselves away by hiring expensive political names as window dressing; they act like exactly the kind of used car salesmen from whom you shouldn't buy, the type that has to accomplish only one trick to sell the jalopy which is to sell you themselves. If you can believe them, you can believe anything, including their unbelievable propositions.

As Cornfeld's sun sank painfully in the West, no less weighty a figure than John M. King, the Colorado Bull Elephant, made the early running at rescue. As King's empire melted in the glare of publicity, Robert M. Vesco appeared from nowhere like a jack-in-the-box. Within a remarkably short time, Vesco had disappeared in his private Boeing 707, into the welcoming arms of President José Figueres of Costa Rica, while the Securities and Exchange Commission sought, in high dudgeon, to discover the exact whereabouts of $224 million in IOS funds.

"We brought down our families," said Vesco, "enrolled our children in excellent schools, and started our new life in this American Arcadia." But there was no Arcadian resting place for either Vesco, caught up in the Watergate disaster and hounded by the authorities, or Bernie Cornfeld, arrested by the Swiss authorities on a visit to his aged mother, and popped into a Swiss jail where he pondered over the dwindling of his IOS fortune from $150 million to $5 million for a most uncomfortable length of time.

These Joe McCarthys of the business world live off the Big Lie, off the law that the more outrageous a proposition, the more likely its hearers are to suspend their critical faculties altogether. In this the ungodly are aided and abetted by the virtuous—not merely in the way the latter, too, fall for the Big Lie and the easy commissions it generates, but because the godly also make such hay out of the savings of the small.

Take the most popular form of investment, the thoroughly respectable industry of life insurance. In Britain the insurers take people's money year after year, with no firm undertaking to pay back more than the face value on expiry; if the investor wants his money back in midterm, he has to take a large loss. He has no information about what investments, in turn, the company is making on his behalf, or how well they have done. By and large, the results are no better than could have been achieved by investing in a mutual fund. And the profits to the company are so large that it can afford to pay very handsome commissions to the agent who merely books the business.

In the United States, by the same happy conjunction of circumstances, the men who sell insurance have profited so mightily that they account for a significant crop in the harvest of postwar millionaires. These are men like the tub-thumping supersalesman W. Clement Stone, practitioner of success through a Positive Mental Attitude, open-handed distributor of largesse to Richard M. Nixon and other positive political thinkers, and author of the ripe remark: "If a family has wealth in the neighborhood of $400 million, what's a million in gifts?"

The mainline insurers continue to collect their easy pickings. Returns of four percent a year on invested funds (which big insurance companies think decent) are well below recent rates of inflation; but the average investor has never had a respectable place for his money that would both defend its real value and return some income for his use.

When the decent, established, accepted forms of investment offer so poor a deal to investors, it's no surprise that a gigantic latent market exists for those who are less scrupulous, but who offer (or appear to) a better bargain. The fact that the offer is always some modern inverted version of the philosopher's stone, turning gold back to base metal, will never deter the unwary; so around that stone, coming out from under it if necessary, will cluster all those with a highly developed nose for the scent of other people's money.

But, at least, you could assume that regular insurance companies were honest—until Stanley Goldblum came along. Goldblum was the genius behind Equity Funding, the "blue-suede shoes, hipster type of outfit," in the posthumous words of one Wall Street observer, that made the immortal discovery that you don't actually need to sell people insurance policies to achieve $2 billion a year in sales. Far easier to invent the people—then you can invent the policies, too.

At the first count, Equity had 50,000 phantom policies, and sold the premiums to other insurance companies (so-called reinsurance) to create $25 million of far from phantom income. Not only were the purchasers fooled: so were the investment experts, which, as a matter of unpalatable fact, is their normal form. Equity's dishonesty was bred from the need to feed a stock price which had soared from $6 to $80 in five years, then had dribbled down to $13 a year later. Yet a group of analysts specializing in this area chose Equity Funding as their pet stock among all the finance and financial services bundles on the market. That was the beginning of 1972—about a year before the whistle blew on this people-fooler. The whistle always does blow, in the end; but too late to save the people's pelf.

SCENE 2

The Treasure in Statistics
or
Lies, Damned Lies, and Figures

The economic world is full of engaging, exploded ideas in which everybody believes: none more engaging or detonated than the notion that only governments can print money. Ever since the invention of the banking system, banks have been creating paper gold; and ever since some genius stumbled across the joint stock company, individuals have been free to engage in the same profoundly rewarding activity.

Printing money means producing a piece of your own paper that others will accept in exchange for the pieces of paper put out officially by the government. Just as the government's paper no longer has to be backed by solid gold, the paper spawned in streams by individuals and corporations need have no foundation, either. That is why the old, simple tests of millionairedom no longer apply—even though so seasoned and flush a hand as J. P. Getty still believes that a millionaire is someone whose assets are worth $1 million.

That depends on what you mean by worth. It can't mean that the man should be able to produce $1 million of his own cash, since a large proportion of the assets won't be readily negotiable and many of them may be covered by debt. Even if he can write a million dollar check, all that proves is that somebody will honor the paper. Getting the paper honored is the real necessity; and getting the maximum amount of honor is the real trick. It has nothing to do with the underlying economic assets that the paper pusher possesses, but everything to do with clever mathematical games.

Another of the obsolete, absurd ideas in which all men believe is that figures mean what they say. The double billionaire H. L. Hunt once remarked, "Money is nothing. It is just something to make bookkeeping more convenient." He had it the wrong way round. It's bookkeeping that's nothing—only something to make money more convenient.

For instance, a man purchases twenty garages for $50,-000 apiece, a price which represents five years' purchase of pretax profits; he has profits of $200,000 a year, and he is presumably worth neither more nor less than the million with which he started. That presumption, however, is demonstrably false. Suppose he takes the company to the stock market as Auto-Electronic Developments: he sells a quarter of the shares for $250,000, and the market thereupon values the firm, modestly enough, at seven times earnings. So his smaller stake is *still* worth a million; and he has $250,000 in cash to be getting on with.

Still not satisfied, however, he borrows $1 million at ten percent, buys another twenty similar garages, thus raising earnings by the $100,000 which represents the difference between $200,000 of profits and his interest costs. The stock market will be vastly impressed by this powerful growth rate: fifty percent per annum is the stuff that analysts' dreams are made of. So Auto-Electronic gets revalued to ten times earnings, at which point our hero is worth $2.5 million—representing his $250,000 in cash, plus three-quarters of the pile of Auto-Electronic paper, which is now valued at $3 million.

The uninitiated may marvel how a property with a market value of $2 million can suddenly, with no material change, generate a million of new wealth. Equally, just how has the hero deserved or managed to multiply his original million two and a half times? There is no good answer to these questions, merely an incontestable observation: that on this simple statistical foundation have been erected most new fortunes of our time.

Note that the figures in the fable were all uncooked. But suppose that the garage proprietor's expenses included a major Christmas advertising promotion that cost $50,000 just before the year-end; and suppose that his accountants were persuaded that this bundle should be treated as deferred expenditure. The logic is unassailable: after all, the bulk of the sales will occur in the next financial year, so shouldn't the cost more properly be apportioned to the year in which the sales will fall?

This change will have the not so incidental effect of producing $50,000 of extra profits. Instead of the fifty percent profits jump achieved by the merger, the proprietor can now boast a seventy-five percent advance. Even if the stock market sticks to the same price-earnings ratio of ten times pretax earnings, the company will magically become worth $3.5 million; and the delirious owner now weighs in at $2.9 million, stark naked.

The beautiful truth is that, if a company boasts a PE ratio of forty (after tax), each extra dollar in after-tax profits equals $40 in capital value. It follows that any device that maintains or enlarges the PE ratio, or which inflates the earnings per share, is worth more, by virtue of the multiplier effect, than any amount of honest toil. That is why profits are so rarely undercooked. The bias in accountancy is always toward producing the highest figure possible; and the possibility of bias exists (a) because accountancy is as imprecise as the music of the spheres and (b) because accountants know on which side their bread is buttered. If there are few millionaire accountants, it is partly because they expend so much nervous energy and time in making millionaires of their clients.

The deferring of the garage promotion, for example, is no farfetched joke. In 1972 a London evening paper actually commended a paint company for the *conservative* practice of costing its advertising expenditure in the year when it was incurred. That same year, American oil and gas men waxed indignant because the SEC turned thumbs down on an accounting method that allowed them to spread the cost of dry wells across several years, instead of taking it in the actual year of the expense; in one of the charming euphemisms that litter accountancy, the smellier, partial method was called "*full*-costing."

Equally partial were the habits of Britain's bankrupt Rolls twins (Razor and Royce): one deferred the commissions it paid to door-to-door salesmen, the other put off the costs of its massive research and development spending.

In each such case, a respectable—nay, an eminent auditor—was prepared to approve the approach; and if by any chance your auditor won't approve, the correct response is obvious—get another one.

Precisely that course was adopted by one US computer leasing outfit, whose profitability hinged on renting out its machines for seventy-eight months. Unfortunately, its customers obliged only to the extent of leases which averaged forty-eight months. If the outfit could manage to lease the machines for the missing thirty months or more at roughly the same terms and without much extra marketing cost, all would be well. If it didn't, however, heavy losses would stare it in the face.

When its auditors couldn't be convinced that the re-leasing would duly occur, the company found a more trusting set of accountants.

In such circumstances, the offended company usually takes the precaution of asking its prospective auditors their views on any contentious points. Surprisingly often, total harmony results. Maybe that divine music is connected with the fact that auditors' fees provide so much flavorsome food for thought—in 1972 one British company, for instance, shelled out £343,000 to its various accountants.

No wonder that Arthur Andersen, auditors to International Telephone & Telegraph, among other colossi, earns two-thirds of a stupendous income from audits. In the year ended March 31, 1973, its twenty-seven offices around the globe raked in $271.5 million: its 750 partners averaged $74,000 a year—and the twenty top partners, considerably more equal than the others, collected $215,000 apiece on the way home.

You don't pay that kind of money to get your profits shaved away. ITT is a case in much point. Originally its accountants wanted to include the paper profits made on unrealized capital gains in a newly acquired insurance company's investment portfolio. When this ingenious step was barred, ITT simply sold off enough of the portfolio to equal the unrealized gain, and took that into the profit instead. The object of this strange exercise, which has nothing to do with the trading of either ITT or the insurance managers, is "to maintain the continuous rise in earnings per share."

Now, just why would Harold S. Geneen, the millionaire boss of ITT, want to achieve that objective? Has it any connection with the fact that Geneen and his managerial cohorts are all, thanks to the wonders of the stock option, heavy holders of ITT stock? Remember that the rise in earnings is purest bunkum. The true, underlying earnings of the arch-conglomerate have not altered in any degree. All that has changed is their presentation—as approved by the distinguished auditors.

As a shrewdness test, ask yourself whether, should the value of the insurance portfolio drop, ITT would deduct an equivalent amount from its profits. You can bet *The Godfather's* profits against the proceeds of a piggy bank that few boards of directors would do any such thing. By an agreeable irony, ITT's auditors are advocates of a brave new accounting world in which accountants might "discard their exaggerated concern for conservatism and objectivity, which have too often resulted in irrelevant, unfair and imprudent information."

This statement can be tested against the case of Four Seasons Nursing Centers where, by disagreeable irony, Arthur Andersen was again the auditor—and where a couple of its own partners were accused by the US government for their part in the affair. In their search for millions, the Four Seasons founders had correctly diagnosed that untold wealth lay in wait on Wall Street if the nursing home idea could be successfully marketed. That in turn meant showing a suitably rich and fast-rising profit record. This was duly produced by devices that, so the accusation ran, included sales of nursing homes that never took place; and, still more imaginative, sales of the money-*losing* homes to a buyer secretly owned by Four Seasons itself. Since figures, not facts, sway markets, the multiplier took immediate and telling effect. The shares zoomed up from $11 in 1968 to $181, before plunging all the way back to the nothing from whence they came.

This wasn't even an isolated case of its time. National Student Marketing Corp. was an even wilder wow. This operation, headed by a hyper-salesman named Cortes Randell, was allegedly founded on marketing techniques developed by young marvels selling to the explosive young growth market on campus. As Andrew Tobias, an alumnus of NSMC, has revealed, this company too was a free-running machine for generating reported or projected rises in earnings per share.

On November 5, 1969, Randell dangled before the New York Society of Security Analysts a forecast that earnings would all but treble in the 1970 fiscal year, and even broke down the rise into seventy-eight percent from internal operations, five percent from recent acquisitions, seven percent from an extraordinary item, ten percent from acquisitions under consideration. According to Tobias, the paper value of Randell's stock jumped $6.5 million on such good news, backed by such precise—and utterly meaningless—figures.

More meaningful information would have included the fact, for example, that in 1968, NSMC reported perhaps $1.4 million of sales which were never actually made as "unbilled receivables"—in a year when its earnings came to $700,000. Another half million of expenses are deferred to the next fiscal year (there's that deferral trick again). Exactly the same tricks were worked in 1969, but with an extra twist—for, even after the tricks, NSMC had to count in $3.8 million of earnings from companies actually acquired after the end of its financial year simply to show any profit at all.

In 1970 the spiraling corporate overhead, the heavy loss-makers, and past accountancy strategems caught up with NSMC: it had to report a first quarter loss, and the shares promptly and properly collapsed. But in the long dizzy ride up from $6 to a peak of $143, how many nests had been feathered? When a twenty-point rise in the stock is worth over $6.5 million, you have a license to print money—and too many accountants will happily provide the rubber stamp.

Don't suppose that the reporting of unmade sales or the disposal of money losers to corporate insiders (both used by NSMC) are rarities. Not only did Four Seasons use the same devices, so did a company selling prefabricated houses; it counted in its turnover figures (approved by its accountants) letters of intent to purchase homes for which no sites existed. The key to many of these larks is the Material (or Immaterial) Gambit. If the accountants are satisfied that a proposed distortion of the corporate earnings won't affect them by as much as ten percent, many of the sharp-penciled gentry in the US will let it through as not "material."

In the case of the crashed Penn Central, use of the most liberal accounting interpretations (all properly detailed in five pages of footnotes) allowed it to report a profit of $0.18, before extraordinary items, when—according to analyst S. Scott Nicholls Jr.—the same figures, on conservative principles, added up to $1.18 of loss. Another company, AMK Corp., succeeded in turning a twenty-five cent per share decline in earnings into a forty-nine cent gain by no less than three accounting changes.

Or take General Dynamics, where bookkeeping changes produced a credit and a debit, both more or less for the same amounts, which were let through the net. The difference between them was a mere $900,000—but that immaterial amount equaled thirty-six percent of the net income duly reported to the happy shareholders. Then there's Memorex, which on its way to the junkyard of dead growth stocks included in its nine months' figures a sale worth $14 million, a fifth of its total revenues, to a wholly controlled leasing subsidiary of its own—which had not paid for the goods.

The difference that a piece of fast accounting can make is impressively shown by the case of Dr. Armand Hammer after he bought little Occidental Petroleum in 1957.

Occidental in 1963-72 multiplied its sales eighty-three times, one of the most extraordinary rises in the oil industry's history. Nevertheless, in 1969, according to the SEC, no less than $14 million of the $49 million profit reported for the first three quarters resulted from unrevealed changes in accounting methods. The same source charged that the same profit-inflating technique was used in Occidental's peak year of 1970.

The reason why so rich a man as Hammer should permit such practice is that Occidental wanted, wittingly or unwittingly, to conceal a negative trend: in 1971, it had to report a $67 million loss; 1972 was no great shakes, either; and Hammer had loaded $900 million of long-term debt on Occidental's back.

The beauty of the doing-it-with-figures approach is that it has infinite variations and can be repeated *ad infinitum*—not to say *ad nauseam*. The garage proprietor who miraculously turned $1 million into $2.5 million can carry on buying businesses on the same mathematical basis; each new business acquired, moreover, stands to offer new chances for rearranging its figures in a more profitable light. And if he gets tired of borrowing money to finance acquisitions, the figure man can always use his licensed paper money.

One conglomerator, Meshulam Riklis of Rapid American, while on his way to accumulating a rapid fortune, observed that "by the time the debentures (Russian rubles) or warrants (Castro pesos) became due, the company you acquire can generate more cash than they are worth." Even without the Soviet and Cuban capers, the game looks even more painless than debt. You can actually exchange pieces of paper printed by your own sweet self for the real-life assets of other companies, even for real cash. One paper counter valued at forty times earnings can buy two lumps of equal-sized earnings in two companies selling on a PE of twenty. The lure of this Riklis mathematics is so seductive that many a bright young thing has been led to his own destruction on the rocks of hard arithmetic.

Assume that you really do have a great $1 million business, growing at fifty percent per annum and commanding a PE of forty. You have a million shares in issue, so the firm is worth $40 million, of which you own half. You buy a few siblings for half a million shares, which produce profits, at a twenty times PE, of another $1 million. This raises your earnings per share to $1.33, boosting the capitalization to $80 million, of which you own a third—or nearly $27 million.

So far, so marvelous. The next year, however, your original activity produces its fifty percent, but your acquisitions stay put. The earnings per share rise again to $1.66, and the capitalization rises by another $20 million. A third of that, however, goes to the new shareholders whom you unhesitatingly bought in; and the lost $7 million or so is really a delayed cost of the original purchase.

The situation can get even worse. A progression from $1

to $1.33 to $1.66 looks like a slowdown, and that high PE
may wobble. So the new temptation is to make another set
of acquisitions, and buy another $1 million of earnings for
half a million shares. But that isn't enough—earnings per
share will rise only to $1.75. Try $2 million for a million
instead. That's $1.80 a share, representing another increase
of a third in earnings, and pushing the capitalization to
$180 million.

Your stake has now, after much huffing and puffing,
risen from $20 million to $36 million—but so has that of
the new shareholders, who brought in only $1 million of
profits. And what will you do for an encore? Another fifty
percent rise in the original business is now utterly
swamped. Even an acquisition program twice as large—$4
million of earnings for 2 million shares—won't do. You either have to engage in supercolossal buying, or somehow
get your 33⅓% growth rate from the existing businesses.

That is precisely why figure specialists (of whom the
conglomerators are the prize breed) are led into ludicrous
overstretching (like James P. Ling's purchase of Jones &
Laughlin) or into imaginative accountancy (like NSMC),
or both. The mathematical game all too easily turns into an
arithmetical treadmill, moving far too fast for the players
to stay on.

The beneficent rain of long multiplication, of course,
falls on the just and the unjust alike. *Time* magazine in
early 1973 printed a roll-call of families who had struck it
rich by the easy expedient of watching their shares rise.
There was, for instance, David Packard, who left President
Nixon's Defense Department in time to take his shares out
of their temporary resting place, dust them off, and count
the loot. It came to $260 million, or $77 million for every
year in which Packard didn't work at his Hewlett-Packard
company, founded in a garage just before World War II.
During Packard's Pentagon service, the shares sat peace-
fully in a trust. It is another perfect example of the total
untruth of the widely believed maxim: that you can't have
your cake and eat it. Packard's partner, in fact, ate even
more confectionery: his stock rose by $271 million—more
than ample reward, even for a sixty-one percent profit rise.

That multiplier, alas, has a nasty knack of working in
reverse. If the PE is forty, if the profits are $10 million,
and if you own half the shares, each $1 million of extra
profit is worth $20 million in your safe deposit box. Sup-

pose, however, that the profits fall by $1 million in one dull year; and that a disillusioned stock market consequently pushes down the PE to twenty. That one slight slip will cost your kitty no less than $110 million.

Now, being able to lose a fortune of that size may be gratifying in its way—H. Ross Perot lost almost half a billion on paper in a single day as his eighty-five percent of Electronic Data Services zoomed down from its high; but that is not how most millionaires like to be titillated. Indeed, the awful prospect of that slide is what keeps the millionaires and their ever loving accountants on the hunt not for bigger and better profits, but for something which looks just as good and even works as well, if only for a time: bigger and better figures.

SCENE 3

The Mirage of Turnarounds

or

It Can't Get Any Worse

The good reward can come more easily from a bad situation than a good. Quick and risk-free fortunes have been made by managers seduced into deadbeat and dying companies. They have cleaned up doubly, both for themselves and for the moribund corporation. Their rewards are out of decent proportion to their turnaround contribution—because it isn't easy to heave a corpse out of the industrial graveyard.

Still, the can't-get-any-worse artist has a saving grace or two. Bad needn't become best to produce the financial transformation he seeks. A mere improvement from murderous to moderate suffices, provided that the manager is prepared to use every trick for adjusting earnings per share sharply upward. If investors believe that a corporation is headed for the slaughterhouse, they will shed the shares like so much molt. The price will slump deeply below the physical value of the assets. (The one certainty of a deadbeat situation is that, in effect, dollar bills will be on sale cheap.)

More: since the company hasn't actually collapsed in a smelly heap of bad debts, the odds are that it won't. When the Chrysler Corporation was turned round from its mid-1950s slump, its market share was shot to ribbons, its earnings were barely visible, its debts were monstrous—but the company was still sufficiently intact for George M. Love (custodian of the Hanna heirlooms) and his protégé, Lynn A. Townsend, to mount a swift and enriching rescue operation.

The possibilities for swiftness are another virtue in the situation. Since the company is now down on the floor, probably the management that dumped it there lacked even the normal self-preserving executive attributes. Sweeping away the expensive cobwebs, a simple task for an educated manager, must produce an immediate and lush financial saving.

The Philips electrical giant, under financial duress, managed to cut its inventories from thirty-six percent of 1970's sales to twenty-seven percent of 1971's. If a relatively efficient firm can squeeze out that much juice, imagine what can flow from a rotten apple. And, again, any juice will be compounded by the mathematics of the fact that a stock set for a turnaround operation will be in the stock exchange discard.

Assume that the company used to earn $2 million a year, and earnings have collapsed to $200,000. The market may value the entire misfired shooting match at $2 million. In comes Sir Galahad with his team of trusty knights, throws out the old-line management, and buries the skeletons in their cupboards in the first year's accounts.

That year a thumping loss results. But the shares, buoyed up by Galahad's reputation and his press interviews, advance fifty percent to a $3 million capitalization. Galahad & Co. don't mind this at all—they have stock options at the old price. They push profits up to $1 million: only half the company's old earning power, true, but think of the steep rate and angle of climb. If the knight-errants merely return to $2 million, the next year round the course, that will mean doubled profits. No investment analyst can resist a proposition of this kind; so the shares go to twenty times the million dollar earnings, or $20 million, a tenfold rise; the knights cash in their options; and if they are lucky and keep their noses sharp and lances clean, there are years of pickings to come.

In Britain a whole squadron of raiders came galloping down on the deadbeat hulks of the country's industrial history in the 1960s—led by a master of business backgammon, Jim Slater. Slater moved into a metal window firm called Crittall-Hope (the hyphen was a euphemism for a merger that had never been consummated), sold off surplus and money-losing assets, and was left with £5 million of "liberated" cash, plus a business making half its old turnover. But Slater's personal vehicle, Slater Walker, had shot up from a fringe operator to a big-time conglomerate: in the Crittall-Hope year of 1968, the shares soared by 329%. Slater's empire marched on to more mergers and a market capitalization of £120 million.

Most Slater starlets failed to match these sudden millions. The imitators nevertheless lined their fur coats for life. In their hands, the game, basically the old conglomerate ploy, acquired a subtle difference, a new complexity.

The essence of conglomeration was, and is, the exchange of paper for earnings: achieved by the alleged creation of a new management world in which finely honed minds using razor-edged techniques ran diverse businesses much more brilliantly than did the unconglomerated, older generations. The snag was that the conglomerators, who (like all con men) believed their own publicity, in reality had to manage convoluted, complex, ill-assorted bundles of companies—at which they had no greater success than any previous generation of managers out of their depths.

The British mutants, however, produced a gentle twist. The conglomerator would manage the assets only to the point where, like the bear cub of mythology, they had been licked into shape. The cubs would then be sold off, preferably for cash, while the conglomerate, its coffers replenished, padded off in search of new cubs to nurture. Where the simple, straight turnaround artists concentrated on one desperate situation at a time, the Slater mutants could handle two, three, four: each time milking or stripping the surplus assets, revamping the businesses, selling them off.

But the lifespan of the conglomerating wholesale salvationist was brief. Most turnaround specialists in individual companies sooner or later run into the same roadblock that stopped the previous management in its faltering tracks:

the wholesaler simply runs out of road. This happened in spectacular fashion to an Old Etonian practitioner, John Bentley, whose Barclay Securities issued over 17 million pieces of paper as it corralled terrible, run-down companies in toys, media advertising, pharmaceuticals, even films. Over its four years of life Barclay's earnings per share rocketed as the awful companies were made tolerable; and the shares followed suit, shooting up by 852% before the dreadful truth dawned; the higher the shares rise, the less chance the take-your-money-and-run technique has of making a real profit.

Suppose you have a £1 million company with £1 million of assets that issues £1 million of shares for another million. Suppose that it then performs the standard revamp, cuts the unprofitable products, ceases to serve the unprofitable outlets, gets rid of the surplus offices, and gets profits back to a respectable height. At that point, a buyer appears ready to pay £6 million in cash for the revamped wonder. (If a buyer is not in evidence when wanted, a handy device is to have a captive customer, a good and true friend, or another company that you control yourself to take the baby off your hands.) On the face of it, your firm has a very nice £5 million profit; but that sum depends entirely on what has happened to your shares in the interim.

If they have multiplied tenfold, the effective price paid for the assets now being sold for £6 million is £10 million. Paradoxically, the worse the shares have performed, the better the deal. This basic, uncomfortable mathematics explains a great deal of what happened not only to Barclay Securities (which, in a bad case of biter bitten, got gobbled up by another financial conglomerate), but to the multimarket, share-sprouting companies as a whole. Their share prices ran far ahead of the real value of their wheels and deals.

The proprietors could, of course, say the mathematics be damned: if you can cash in on a tenfold share boom, who cares about fundamental realities? The promoters, however, were the chief cashers-in: Bentley pocketed the best part of £2 million from the last round-up. The whole game otherwise added up to another method of shifting wealth from the many weak to the few strong.

The prime example of the combined turnaround and conglomerate technique is the great and mighty International Telephone & Telegraph, the pride and the passion of the archetypal midcentury millionaire manager, Harold S. Geneen. When Geneen came to ITT, it was big, but its bigness was in dreary areas, such as communications utilities, with some brighter but neglected operations, such as manufacturing telecommunications gear in a booming Western Europe. The simple knowledge that Geneen, a man of miraculous reputation, was on the move from Raytheon forced down the price of the latter's and boosted that of ITT by several millions—and Geneen, with a single-minded devotion of awesome dimensions, proceeded to prove the stock market right.

In a decade the sales multiplied 6.7 times, the profits 10 times, the assets 6.3 times. Quarter after quarter the wreck that Geneen inherited waxed richer and richer, and Geneen waxed with it, in wealth and reputation. The waxing was accomplished primarily through a corporate acquisition program remarkable for its catholic, openminded nature. If it moved, ITT seemed to buy it: the collection eventually included old ITT items like Standard Telephones and Cables, new buys like Avis car rental, a hotel in Hammamet, Gwaltney Smithfield hams—and still the shopping went on. In 1970 alone ITT added $1.5 billion in assets and the next year put on a billion more in weight, as Geneen used what he himself modestly called ITT's "unusual abilities to follow a policy of diversified risks in selected fields of above-average opportunity."

All modesty aside, ITT is the world's all-time champion of the turnaround carried to its logical extreme. The 1972 sales were $8.5 billion. The original ITT, when Geneen moved in, couldn't have got very much worse without disappearing. The new ITT, so popular belief had it, couldn't get any better: it was the ultimate in modern management, as Geneen himself said. In terms of wealth creation, ITT's progress was broad and strong indeed: at the end of 1972 the former deadbeat was capitalized at a wondrous $5.8 billion.

Probably, any ITT fan told that earnings per share in the 1961-71 decade had grown only 7.84% annually would have refused to believe it; but that was the fact. What's more, 197 of the biggest American corporations listed by *Fortune* outgrew ITT in that decade (ITT looked better over the 1962-72 period, but only because earnings fell under Geneen between 1961 and 1962). What's still more, the ITT record resulted, again, in part from some elegant cookery of the books. In 1971 the gain in earnings was a worthy ten percent, from $3.14 to $3.45—save for the little matter of losing the Chilean business after a peculiarly inept attempt to overthrow the host government. Adding in (or taking out) this "extraordinary item" reduced the figure to $2.85, a 9.2% decline. But the essence of making a bad situation come good is that the impression created matters more than the reality; and the impression arises from assiduous public relations—and from assiduous accountancy. The latter art form is easier to use when a company is changing its shape and size almost weekly by merger, spreading itself from microwaves to insurance in the process. In fact, without the 1970 insurance acquisition, ITT's income in the next year (even without knocking Chili off the score) would have been down in 1969—despite a sales increase of $1.6 billion in the intervening period.

But in 1971, for all that fine timing, not only was ITT's growth record modest, so was its return on invested capital (194 large companies did better), and so was its industrial performance. In industrial and consumer products (3.8%), ITT earned hugely less on sales than 3M (11.5%). In food processing and services ITT could contrive only an abysmal 1.9%.

The conglomerate's best performance, to nobody's surprise, was in the business in which it started and which it knew best: 4.5% on telecommunications equipment, or slightly better than a rival like Western Electric. Nobody can take away from Geneen his amazing feat in turning a beat-up old telecomms company into the eighth largest company in the US. But equally astonishing to the inexpert in mass psychology is the easy acceptance by the outside world that creative accountancy allied to rapid acquisition equals magnificent performance.

As a textbook exercise in turnarounds, the ITT drama will never be matched, for the political and public mood has turned against this style of conglomeration. But there are plenty of hulks drifting in the rougher seas of commerce waiting for a boarding party that can achieve the kind of first take-off results that sent ITT on its way: in 1961-67, earnings per share doubled, long before the big takeovers. As to personal fortunes, in 1971 and 1972 alone Geneen collected options worth over $3 million.

Every situation, no matter how evil-smelling the egg, contains within it the possibility of a nice, fresh profit. One American operator, Harry Weinberg, once even made $100 million out of the most certain financial deathtraps in the big cities: bus lines. In his own accurate words, every urban bus company Weinberg bought was "a cow with no milk." But people still had to go to work; cities were still prepared to subsidize and otherwise assist any big-hearted citizen who would help his fellow citizens on their way; and Weinberg's squeezed-out cows yielded a surprising flood of cream. So long as the market demand is there, there is some device, some new approach, some scheme of rationalization that will convert the demand into dollars.

The Dictaphone Company, at the time of E. Lawrence Tabat's takeover, was running steadily downhill. It lost money in both 1970 and 1971; it suffered from a sick product line and from the best efforts of the most formidable competitor in American marketing, IBM. In the first nine months of the next year, Tabat got operating income up twenty-four percent on a six percent sales rise by certain simple changes. He sold off money-losing office furniture companies, brought in a new product named the Thought Tank, engaged in aggressive advertising that committed the lèse majesté of being rude to IBM—and shoved the share price up fifty percent in two months.

The moves were no less obvious than those of the Chad Valley toy company—where, out of 650 lines, about 100 provided eighty percent of the profits, and 250 could be erased almost overnight without doing anything but good. But another operation greatly enhanced the prizes from the Chad-style gambit: the now-you-see-it, now-you-don't shell game—a shell in this instance being a company so burned out that it has almost nothing left, except the crucial asset, its stock exchange quotation.

The British colonial past has left a particularly interesting set of relics, with names like Galaha Ceylon Tea Estates or Parit-Bruas (Malay) Rubber Co., whose shares sell at infinitesimal prices, when they sell at all. As of March 20, 1973, the last deal in Parit-Bruas had been reported on March 31, 1970, three years before, at the princely price of about one penny. The shell gamester buys control of such an outfit and, when he has a suitable stake, allows the word to leak to others—at the same time revealing that high-earning interests are about to be injected into the empty shell.

If a company is capitalized at £25,000, with hardly any earnings, the injection of £50,000 of net income must enhance the shares by moon-man leaps and bounds, even if the profits are valued conservatively in the market. In fact, a well-manipulated market will value the shares on the basis of their inexhaustible capacity for early spectacular growth.

The two outstanding performers in Britain in the 1970s, Jim Slater's Slater Walker and Ralli International, run by Slater protégé Malcolm Horsman, began life respectively as H. Lotery and Oriental Carpet Manufacturers; of the gains in their share prices over the 1962-72 decade (a respective 2,691% for Ralli and 2,986% for Slater), the bulk of the rise was recorded largely in this early miraculous transformation.

In 1968 Oriental Carpet employed £2.5 million of capital; from 1969 to 1970 the shares multiplied sixteen times as the capital soared to £33.4 million. The little H. Lotery employed a mere half million of capital in 1962. Between 1967 and 1968 the share price multiplied over tenfold as the assets jetted upward from £4.7 million to £94.3 million.

Again, though, the great danger is that the recovery, the upward thrust, will run out of acceleration, and even decelerate sharply: in the same dizzy style, and with the same desolating effect, as the share plunge in fallen conglomerates like Litton and Gulf + Western. Getting back up from poor to moderate is only the first stage of the battle; the distance from moderate to excellent is far longer.

The calamities of Chrysler are a cautionary tale: pulled up by the Love-Townsend team to $303 million of net income, then slumping back to an $8 million loss and a near desperate credit crisis. Stock options, cashed-in options, bonus schemes, and the like look painfully sick in such circumstances—unless, like Townsend, you have the ultimate turnaround gambit up your Ivy League sleeve. From 1968 onward Townsend and his president, John J. Riccardo, received not one cent of bonus. But in 1972 the famine ended. A payout of $413,660 to the chairman and $351,-400 to his number two raised their total takes to new company records of $638,600 and $551,400 respectively. The strangest fact about these peak pay slips was that Chrysler's 1972 earnings, while sharply up on 1971, actually fell short by some $93 million from the 1968 record. The directors had pushed down the profit level on which the bonus payments were calculated.

The Townsend-Riccardo gambit rubs in the point: that in this line of work, it's not how successfully you turn around that counts, it's how efficiently you exploit the angle of turn.

SCENE 4

The Miracle of Mergers
or
One's Company, Two's a Fortune

The one unassailable truth to emerge from an age in which every ambitious or half-ambitious corporation sought to improve its affairs by merger is that merging does not improve corporate affairs. When two Goliaths join in unholy wedlock, the general result is to produce simply a fatter target at which the Davids of business can aim their hard, round stones. When the fat company buys a small outfit, the chances are that the profitability of the buy, and still more the contentment of its people, will be squashed by the fat man's heavy tread.

No matter how the effects are measured—return on capital, growth in earnings per share, movement in the share price, share of new markets—the merging firms seldom outdo the corporate spinsters and bachelors, and often get undone themselves. And the unhappy record isn't just the result of an incurable corporate tendency to overpay for company purchases.

The rich individual runs the same financial and managerial risks, whether he is diversifying into some beckoning field of which he is wholly ignorant or merely eliminating some supine or rampant competitor. But the

risks are offset by one sovereign fact: unlike the corporation, which is theoretically bent on accumulating higher
earnings, the millionaire is predominantly interested in a
higher pile of assets—which, apart from other blessings,
carry no tax if they carry no visible earnings.

The relevant math is that thirty percent of £100 million
in company assets is worth more than fifty percent of £50
million—to be precise, £5 million more—and still gives
fully effective control of the operation, the cash box, and
the underlings. It therefore pays the accumulator to surrender part of his ownership for fresh piles of assets, so long
as the surrenders are always smaller than the piles.

Maxwell Joseph, who rose in the property world via
the promising routes of estate agency and marriage to a
property tycoon's daughter, probably accomplished more
by basic surrender than by any of his astute advances. As
recently as 1963 Joseph's hotel interests, consisting largely
of undersized properties in Mayfair, weighed in at a
measly £9.8 million of capital employed. Seven years later,
after he bought up hotels, dairies, dance halls, and a sizable brewery, all in exchange for a plethora of loan
stocks, shares, and other pieces of paper, Grand Metropolitan Hotels, the Joseph vehicle, was worth twenty-two
times that amount. After adding a vaster brewery, Watney
Mann, Joseph's personal share stake, only eighteen percent
of the equity, was worth £19 million—or twice as much as
the entire company's capital a decade before: that is, before the stock, bowed down by the sheer weight of the
mergers, took a dive.

But the cumulative effect is unlikely to be so overwhelming if the accumulator insists on keeping total and
absolute control. Friedrich Flick, a tenacious financial
genius who bridged the Nazi and Adenauer eras, had been
deprived of his fortune by the Allies after the war, and so
was not in a mood to surrender control of his rebuilt empire in the peace.

The rebuilding itself was a miracle within the wonder of
German resurgence. At his death at the age of 89 in 1972,
Flick possessed $1.7 billion worth of sales in steel, chemi-
cals, paper, and odds and ends (including the Leopard
tank); and that bundle, which earned $9 million in profit
in 1972, excluded the ripest fruit of all—a forty percent
holding in Daimler-Benz, with sales of $3.7 billion.

No one could argue that the Flick family plot was

tended with any evident management skill: 0.4% on sales (even allowing for the reluctance of German firms, especially family ones, to show more profits than they need) is not the standard preached by the Harvard Business School. But that is the profound advantage of the personal proprietor in the merger sport: so long as he covers his costs, in borrowings or any other out-of-pocket expenses, possession is nine-tenths of the game. It's the professional manager, or the proprietor with outside shareholders on his back, who must go for growth at all costs—including the costs of painful mergers.

This necessity in turn means that the professional corporate merger must be made to work. Either the deal has to be pitched on such glorious financial terms that the earnings come out ahead; or the managers must manage their heads off to achieve the hoped-for synergy. It often degenerates into a desperate race between the corporate earnings and the conversion date of the convertible stocks issued to finance the big deal. From the off to the finishing line, however, the corporate jockeys can never do one thing: sit back and relax. But then, most of them don't want to.

Acquisitions are a challenge to the professional manager's innate sense of order and neatness, his desire to subject the entire corporation to the same systems and discipline. Dorothy Parker had a poem for it: "They hail you as their morning star, They love you just the way you are. Then when they've got you safe and sound, They try to change you all around."

One British entrepreneur has never forgotten his shock when the full weight of ITT's planning descended on him. For his proportionately tiny morsel of the corporate feast, some three hundred man-days of planning were demanded. (As it happens, the effort turned up a potential seven-figure loss in one product, which was duly corrected; this discovery converted the Briton to planning, but later, in a very similar business, he found that three man-days did the planning trick; and the paperwork was the equivalent of *Jonathan Livingston Seagull*, rather than ITT's *War and Peace*.)

Many accumulative individual millionaires are just as incapable psychologically of leaving well alone. But, unlike the managers, the rich have the option. If they pile on $10 million of assets earning a beggarly million, it's a matter of some indifference—within reason—whether the earnings rise or fall (a millionaire's reason seldom extends to actual losses). The tycoon, if he wants, can afford to treat his interests, purchased or not, as they really are—a portfolio of investments, no different from a hand dealt in the stock market—except that the holder can call all the plays.

He can put up with large minority holdings which would greatly vex any conventionally managed or mismanaged company: like the Flick forty percent of Daimler-Benz. He can run every single company in a different manner, or have it run by somebody else: it's uneconomical for somebody whose time equals a fortune to fiddle when perfectly competent hands can be hired. Far better to sit, like Howard Hughes, in lofty isolation, communicating with your managers either not at all or by telephone, while they make millions on your behalf.

At the start of their consolidation, the Cowdray family, by some repute the richest in Britain, owned two public newspaper companies, one of which held the controlling interest in the other; a private newspaper company with no connection with the other two; a book publisher; the obligatory oil and gas; a merchant bank, Lazards; Châ-teau Latour, with its fine clarets; a sizable share of the potteries around Stoke-on-Trent, including Crown Derby; engineering firms—and so on. Not one of these appeared to be managed by any system common to the rest of the family holdings.

Not that the Cowdray group was ill-managed. Profits at £4.2 million in the year before Cowdray went public, at a total price of £100 million, rose to £10.5 million four years later. The point is rather that management to the Cowdrays and their able administrators bore no relation to the homogenizing, staff-breeding, interference-prone systems of the pros. That fact alone removes a great dose of malaise from mergers, on two conditions: that the merger millionaire must always be prepared to replace a bailiff who mismanages his acres of the estate; and that he be equally ready to sell.

The men who hold the sovereign advantage of personal wealth hate to sell, as a rule. They are acquisitive, and the act of acquisition lasts a lifetime. But, just as they are free to let a valuable investment accumulate more wealth, so they are at liberty to sell without exposing themselves to criticism as incompetents, either for buying the thing in the first place or for selling it. In big corporations, disinvestment is usually the pleasurable job left to the next incumbent: pleasurable, because the very deed proves him deft and his predecessor dull.

But even the most dexterous accumulator buys the occasional lemon, if only because what makes excellent sense for a free-lance financier may fit uneasily into a corporate blanc-mange mold: and most great free-lance fortunes become corporate one day. Norton Simon, in the process of extending his tomato-based empire, picked up not only extra tidbits in food, but also printing operations, trade books, magazines, and Talent Associates, the film and TV company: all of which his managerial successor refused to have in the shop.

Individual tycoons do not have the professional manager's love for tidiness. The lucrative lessons of tycoon mergers should not be lost on the professionals (although they usually are). Never buy dear. Manage what you do buy according to its internal logic, not yours. Don't try to manage the new crown jewel at all if some other custodian is already, by your standards, running it successfully. If the selling occasion arises—an offer you can't refuse in good financial conscience, a misfit, a need for resources elsewhere, plain and unadulterated boredom—sell without compunction.

The most unlikely of the conglomerates proved to be the biggest real winner partly because it followed the habits of its rich founder. No sane corporate planner would put his name to a scheme for combining sick textile companies with upholstery cushioning, radar antennae, and electronics, all as the base for an "acquisition of the month plan" designed to add forty companies in eight years. This incongruous outfit predictably ended up in a confusion of money spinners ranging from chain saws to upper-class stationery, from watch straps to power lawn mowers.

Yet from 1958 to 1963, sales piled up from $244 million to $1.4 billion: and in 1973, when Litton was showing a grisly loss and ITT a so-so gain of 1.58%, this company, Textron, was still boasting a ten-year return to its investors of an annual 9.9%. The founder, Royal Little, "didn't see how the textile business [in which he had started in 1928] could ever be good again in my lifetime." He did, however, see acutely how the intelligent use of tax losses in an acquisition program could create the good capitalist life all over again, provided he stuck to good capitalist rules.

His principles included keeping the head office down to a small number of bodies in an unglamorous locale in Providence, Rhode Island; Providence is a long way from rivaling Wilmington, Delaware, in sophistication, let alone Park Avenue, New York. That, by no means incidentally, is another asset of the rich empire-builder. His personal and corporate overheads are one and the same thing.

While Howard Hughes must pay a pretty dollar in private air transport and the hire of whole hotel floors, his costs don't begin to cover those of a truly ambitious multinational corporation. To get some idea, one scion of a dollar imperialist, Edgar Kaiser, had $14 million of his money saved in a year by the head office economies implemented by a newcomer at Kaiser Aluminum: which gives an inkling of the appalling burden that bigger companies still must carry on their backs.

Royal Little would never buy for Textron on less than a seven-year pay-back of his money, and would throw out with unsentimental dispatch any acquisition that sooner or later failed to come up to the corporate snuff. This set of policies by no means implies disinterest in the subsidiaries, their well-being, and their wherewithal. What gives the individual investor and his imitators such abnormal financial potency is the combination of passionate interest in the balance sheet and the bottom line (where the earnings are kept) with lack of passionate involvement in the mechanics of each individual enterprise. The large, managed company cannot in the nature of bureaucratic life sustain this potent combination for as long as the individual. So the corpocrats make rich men richer by paying overrich sums for their assets: and then proceed to make their corporations poorer by managing these expensive acquisitions into the ground.

ENTR'ACTE

The Error of Imitation

or

Anything You Can Do, I Can't Do Better

In spite of everything in his favor, the rich man's freedom to move how and where he likes with his loot is snare and delusion as well as opportunity: not least because so many mortals importune him to buy a slice of their real or imagined action. Tycoons are as capable as corpocrats of pursuing an inane ambition to the bitter end; and the danger sign, in both cases, often appears in one mantrap—the lust for somebody else's moneymaking market. When this passion takes over, the man's comptroller had better get used to signing checks.

The phenomenon occurred when Harry Ferguson, the tractor genius, decided that he could build a superior automotive transmission. So he could, but the effort took so many years that he died before the work was completed; even then, the cost of his system was so high in relation to its benefits that only one luxury car adopted the gadget, and not to much effect, either.

In his tractor system, Ferguson performed some tricks that couldn't be done at all previously and performed others at much lower cost than the then competition. But his automotive devices performed the same stunts only a little better—and far more expensively. That, as his own experience should have taught him, is no way to make money.

The identical phenomenon occurred when Henry J. Kaiser, supreme as a shipbuilder, thought that he could outdo Henry Ford in the automotive market. The Kaiser car is now a historical curiosity, more curious even than Henry Ford II's Edsel. The wisest move which Henry J. made in this connection was to get out before the Henry J. car ruined the family altogether.

Kaiser was quite right about the total market: by 1949

car production in the States had reached 5.1 million, passing the old pre-Crash record of twenty years before. Where the shipbuilder went wrong was in assuming that the American car buyer was as simple and direct in taste as a purchaser of Liberty ships.

Possibly there is some fatal seduction about the automobile, for not only Ferguson and Kaiser succumbed to this lure. Donald Lear got on a faster and happier transportation bandwagon with passenger jets selling at $750,000 or more per throw. Then he poured some of the mint made from executive aircraft into the steam car—a concept that went out while the Model T was enjoying its heyday.

These three men, though rich with the spoils of industries in which they had deployed revolutionary concepts, were not wealthy enough (because no individual could be) to buck the billions in resources and fixed assets of the car-makers. Even if they could have designed a supremely better car (which they couldn't, although it doesn't sound too hard), they could not also have financed the mass production and distribution without which a mass market, by definition, is impossible.

The notion of becoming a second Henry Ford (or, since there is a second, a third) is laughable: in fact, old auto families have been dropping out at a time when nobody much is dropping in. The Rootes males passed on their pains to Chrysler in Britain; Studebaker-Packard vanished from the American scene; on the Continent mergers have radically altered the motor map.

The truly lush pastures for big diversifiers are different in every respect. They don't demand great aggregations of capital; they are not dominated by a handful of well-founded giants; and they don't depend on the build-up of expensive consumer franchises.

The well-shod individual, like the stacked company, can reap a wild harvest only from a market in which the exploitation or the economics are wrong: that can eventuate. But while corporate leviathans have as many defects as leopards have spots, and change them about as often, these faults seldom extend to the basic products from which, over long years, their managers have earned their loaves of bread.

The legendary Canadian financier E. P. Taylor, with interests extending from the Argus giant, owner of stakes in companies like Massey-Ferguson, to personal dealings in the Bahamas, tackled the British brewers by buying up first one small chain of pubs and breweries, then another. The beer barons could taste a threat: they closed ranks, forced up the prices of independent breweries, mopped up most of them, entered into mergers and trading agreements that would have given the American antitrust authorities heart failure—and did it all so thoroughly that Taylor in effect sold out and retired from the scene for easier game.

Even the most able of businessmen, sooner or later, finds something that he can't do better than somebody else; that he does even worse. That, in a nutshell, is what happened to the conglomerate millionaires. Their collective ability was probably above average. But most of the conglomerators overbought, or bought bad companies, or took on more than their management abilities (such as they were) could cover.

Not that they recognized the fact. One bravado-rich fellow even stated, after a 38% earnings fall on a 4.3% sales increase, that "our performance last year was a positive answer to those who question the viability of the conglomerate form of business enterprise." That was the unsinkable Charlie Bluhdorn of Gulf + Western.

Martin Stone bought National Screw for his Monogram Industries: both purchase and new parent sank deep into losses. "The problems of modernizing a long-neglected company," admitted Stone, "are almost overpowering, the costs staggering."

Possibly the ghastliest example of all was the effort of Boise Cascade to turn itself into the "General Motors of the timber-products industry." Its executives had freedom to buy practically any operation that bore any relation, however far-fetched, to their traditional wooden business. In the process, they popped $600,000 into a construction company for minority housing back in 1967. Aggressive anything-you-can-do-I-can-do-better management rapidly turned that modest investment into a $37 million write-off, which contributed mightily to writing off the entire Boise Cascade effort at magical self-transformation.

The truth is that there is something to be said for one-product, one-market companies: that they are often blazing successes. In 1959-69, when the conglomerates were recording their crazy growth patterns, seven mainly single-market sagas made up the rest of the top ten for earnings per share growth, taken from *Fortune*'s top five hundred American companies.

The happy seven were Control Data (computers), Xerox, National Can (containers), American Petrofina (oil), Automation Industries (electronics), Pabst (brewery), and Monfort of Colorado. An easy family company, the biggest in beef, Monfort made its proprietors millionaires thirty times over, although its liberal-minded boss used to take only a $52,000 salary "because that's all I need." As for return on shareholders' equity that year, the top two were also in the one-product category: Skyline (mobile homes) and Avon Products (door-to-door cosmetics).

Much the same pattern is true of British business and of the Continent, where whopping fortunes have been made by men who strayed little or not at all from lines like chocolate (Ludwig), mail order (Quandt), ballpoints (Baron Bich), media (Springer). Of thirty-nine new multimillionaires counted by *Fortune* in September 1973, and ranging in riches from $50 million to $750 million, only a small handful were in varied lines of business and the variation was mostly into real estate. Otherwise, from the richest (petfood prince Leonard N. Stern) to the poorest (the Tropicana tycoon of orange juice, Anthony T. Rossi) these well-shod winners won big at one principal game.

By and large, then, the most successful financial cobblers stick to their lasts, and the most ruinous course is to mar the one you have in pursuit of other lasts you don't need. An inviolable maxim applies: never embark on a diversified activity if its prosecution (never mind its possible failure) will harm the existing golden eggs- and Mother Goose, for that matter.

Magnavox was once an enviable one-product company, built over thirty brilliant years of one-market application by Fred Freimann, who died in 1968. But Freimann's successors, heir to a superb TV distribution system that fed directly into the company's own dealers, were worried, even as the conglomerates cracked asunder, about their own dependence on their single market.

They began to buy: into furniture, mobile home components, musical instruments. They developed new devices in commercial navigation equipment, antiskid braking, facsimile (the latter lost a million year in, year out, culminating in a $3.1 million black eye). But all this time, Magnavox had made a crucial error in the TV market. The company didn't realize that consumers wanted the newfangled solid-state TVs.

Magnavox found itself floundering far behind a field of competitors. In 1972, Magnavox contrived to sell 36% fewer sets than it had four years previously when, in its one-market innocence, it had earned 29.5% on its stockholders' equity. Ah, yes, Freimann's successors could (and probably do) argue: but, thanks to our inspired policy of diversification, TV now represents only a third of Magnavox sales; think how dreadfully we would have fared if Magnavox were living by TV alone; at least we made a profit in 1972, even if it was the lowest since 1964.

The short answer to such apologias is that maybe, if Magnavox had kept its eye on the screen, the solid-state shambles would never have occurred. If you are simultaneously fussing over home furnishings and looking for other new marbles, there must be less attention to spare for the business in which you have genuinely been able to do something better. And there is surely a moral in the quote from a Magnavox executive, printed in *Business Week*, about Freimann's successor as president: "fundamentally a financial man [who] doesn't pretend to be a marketing man, and certainly not an engineer."

There you have it: the key to business success, as must be seen, is always in feel for the operation on which the attack is based. In the great majority of cases, it takes men who have a basic talent in one market, in one style of operation, sometimes in only one product. These men are often market geniuses; occasionally engineers of brilliance; never (unless money is their product) are they fundamentally financiers.

The Ronson Corporation was founded by an inventor who deployed substantial technical genius. The grandson who led this creation into the humiliation of a takeover bid from some Italians was an anything-you-can-do merchant. Faced by expiring patents on Ronson's lighters and by Japanese competition, Louis V. Aronson II put little electric motors on virtually everything in the home, from toothbrushes and carving knives to shavers and blenders. Despite all these efforts, and other ventures which ate more cash than they provided, lighters still remained Ronson's staple: and the new throwaway lighters thus loomed as a serious threat which all the Aronson II strategies failed to meet.

Ronson's diversifying caused major stress and slaughter in the executive ranks. Profits had slumped from $7.64 million in 1967 to $1.34 million. Even the Aronson stake, like the family's business ability, had been eroded over time, dropping to a mere nine percent.

Never overestimate your general business powers because you have been a screaming wow in one business; and never conclude, either, that, even in that one business, you have all the cards and always play them correctly. The unfair advantage of a Kaiser, a Ferguson, a Lear, or a Hughes, fortunately for them, is that they can afford their foibles. The Mafia, it turned out, ran Las Vegas more efficiently than Howard Hughes. But Hughes has always been fundamentally a hardware man; even his TWA involvement sprang from a technical fascination with airplanes. Las Vegas, in contrast, is nothing but a service industry, and the technology of one-armed bandits and roulette wheels isn't fascinating to anybody, unless they are being fixed. So Hughes chose the wrong home for his TWA proceeds. The richer the rake, true, the less likely his progress is to be critical, but, even so, the tragedy is best avoided by fearless answer to a frank question: what, if anything, makes me think I can do better?

ACT III

On the
**Multiplication
of Millions**

or

The Rich Get Richer

SCENE 1

_____

The Pile-up of Property
or
The Upside-Down Pyramid

The pyramid, the most elegant of geometrical shapes, has twice in history been associated with great wealth. In ancient Egypt the Pharaohs buried their treasure, the equivalent of Rockefeller or Rothschild-sized fortunes of today, in these imposing structures. There it lay waiting for the next generation of tomb robbers to pocket the proceeds: as neat a demonstration of the passage of wealth from weak hands to strong as history can offer.

Pyramids did not reappear until the halcyon days of free and untrammeled capitalism. But in this reincarnation the pyramids were made not of stone but of paper, and their construction served the opposite purpose: the transfer of money was still from the weak to the strong, but this time the weak were many and the strong were few. No device conceived in the Great Boom and destroyed in the Great Slump provided a more geometric multiplier of money.

If a promotor had a Twenties business which the stock market, roaring away, valued at $100 million, that sum rapidly ceased to seem adequate in the light of the still more rapturous paper values being created on all sides. But what if a second company were created whose principal asset was a major holding in the first? Bonanza No. 1 was still worth $100 million: Bonanza No. 2 could rapidly be run up to the same comforting figure. A third company could then be formed whose prime holding was a major share in Bonanza No. 2. If that, in turn, could be rushed up to $100 million, the entire paper fortune had been trebled without any commensurate improvement in the underlying assets.

The practitioners of the 1920s carried the device of the holding company to undreamed-of extremes: in his supreme deployment of the pyramid art form, Samuel Insull constructed an edifice in which, on one estimate, one dollar invested in a company called Middle West Utilities controlled $1,750 held by the public in the operating companies which actually produced the nation's electricity, or at least twelve percent of it.

But pyramids, for all their seeming solidity, have a basic weakness. If one lower layer starts to crumble, all those above must fall in on top. Insull's frantic efforts to protect part of his complex pyramid from the imagined depredations of a rival financier deposited a $20 million profit in the latter's lap and eventually deposited Insull in court, accused of using shareholders' funds for his own pyramidic ends. (He pleaded an "honest" accounting error of $10 million and got off scot-free.)

The wily outwitter of Insull was none other than Cyrus S. Eaton, later the capitalist friend of Khrushchev and the author of *Is the Globe Big Enough for Capitalism and Communism?* Eaton used his investment bank, Otis and Company of Cleveland, and his holding company with skill and daring—muscling in on Insull and on the territory of mightier forces still, the Mellons and the House of Morgan. As somebody remarked when Eaton was building up his huge holdings in Insull stocks, "Eaton wasn't really interested in running things. All he wanted was the money." For Insull, it was the other way round, even when in fifty days of the fatal summer of 1929 his securities were appreciating at $7,000 a minute, day in, day out—which must be some kind of record. He fell two years later for a very simple reason, as his market operator explained: "You can't go on buying your own stocks forever. Sooner or later you run out of money."

Insull's monument was just the most conspicuous of the structures erected by the latter-day Pharaohs. As for others, John Kenneth Galbraith has described the furious progress of outfits like the American Founders Group. It started in 1922 with two investment trusts, which shared a capital of $500 between them. By 1927 the two companies had become three, which between them had sold $70-80 million of securities to the thirsty public of the day. In 1928 and 1929 the sale of stock, in a group swollen to thir-

teen companies, reached epidemic proportions: its total
resources had enlarged gigantically to a clear billion. A
third of that, however, was accounted for by shares in the
American Founders Group itself.

The terrible result when the steps of the pyramid
crumbled away, and the laws of geometric progression
worked in reverse, are demonstrated by the performance of
Goldman Sachs. The Goldman Sachs Trading Company
was organized as the base of its pyramid. The public was
let in on this ground floor at $104 a throw. After the
débâcle, in 1932, the ground floor entrants were deep in
the basement: their shares were worth less than $2.

Small wonder that Insull or Goldman Sachs pyramids
have not been allowed to reappear. But the holding company is, as we have seen, alive, kicking, and capable of
generating profit at a most becoming rate. Indeed, holding
companies are still the prime medium for organizing corporations. Every big company has a pyramidic legal structure: the critical difference being that, with insignificant
exceptions, the apex of the pyramid holds one hundred
percent of each layer, a percentage that serves as an effective enough cement.

Every now and again, however, something suspiciously
like the old-style pyramid rears its head. The Welsh
financier Sir Julian Hodge created a company called An-
glo-Auto Finance, which handled installment purchases of
cars. He then formed another company, Gwent & West of
England, which owned a hefty stake in the finance firm.
When Hodge moved on to stage three, launching a third
firm, Hodge Group, which boasted ownership of a large
chunk in Gwent & West, hailstones of criticism showered
on his unrepentant head.

The critics were disturbed not only by the structure, but
by Hodge's enthusiasm for bringing small Welsh shareholders in on his act. Bringing the benefits of capitalism to
the masses has tended to leave the latter poorer and their
would-be benefactors considerably richer. The less money
the people have, the more they seem to be tempted by
low-priced shares: companies have been floated off, at
huge profits to the floaters, as shilling stocks in London or
penny stocks in Wall Street, that would have moldered into
dust at a heavier price.

True, Hodge let right be done in the end: when the empire began to come apart, he called in expert help to dismantle the pyramid and repair the cracks in its constituent bricks. But anybody who had invested in Hodge at the time of its launch had had a desperately bumpy ride. From a peak of 60.8p in 1963 they ended up in 1969 at one shilling, about as low as a stock can get without vanishing altogether.

Sir Julian had his reward for seeing the light. His holdings, both personal and through what the legal jargon describes as "the ultimate holding company," were worth £13.5 million five years after that one shilling bottom. And the Hodges had their last and richest round-up when a fat bank bought out their holdings for many fat millions in 1974.

Lurking behind most holding companies is a private company or trust in which the personal holdings are located. This is a handy device, used by many millionaires to provide more strings to their bows and to erect a decent distance between their dividend income and the taxman.

Some of these devices, like those run by the Rockefeller brothers, have achieved fame in their own right, although not necessarily profits. The International Basic Economy Corporation, for instance, was founded back in 1947 by Nelson Rockefeller and threw itself into worthy activities like food distribution, housing, marketing, and manufacture in various geographical spots, all in an attempt to stimulate the local economies. But in 1971, when Rodman C. (Nelson's son) took over the helm, IBEC had succeeded in making only $796,000 nine months' profit on sales of $213.1 million—which practically classified it as an outright charity.

The description would scarcely apply to the empire put together by Frank Lloyd, the past master at exchanging paintings for cash. He accumulated enough millions (reputedly 25, calculated in dollars) to buy a French holiday home from uranium king Joseph Hirshhorn (in exchange for art) and to finance a convoluted legal and fiscal structure. At its head is the Lloyd family trust, based in Liechtenstein; that useful principality is also conveniently the home of the master company, Marlborough AG, and of two associated firms, Art Finance and Kunst und Finanz (which means Art Finance in German).

Art Finance owns the two New York Marlborough galleries, while the master company owns directly the four businesses in Zurich and London, not to mention the four partnerships in Rome, Toronto, Montreal, and Tokyo. According to his partner in the latter business, quoted in *Time* magazine, "Lloyd-san almost seems to understand Zen." Be that as it may, Lloyd shows to a fine degree natural understanding of the process of financial self-preservation—which, in a sense, is why the Pharaohs built their pyramids, too.

But no family pyramid entombs more wealth than Christiana Securities, seventy-five percent owned by the Du Ponts, who have deposited therein the lion's share (twenty-nine percent) of their interest in the family gunpowder store. But as the clan's numbers have increased, so the usefulness of the structure has declined. The Du Ponts have been anxious to exchange Christiana for straight holdings in the family firm, but have run into legal obstacles. Their motive is to make it easier to sell the shares: the usual reason for family pyramids is to hang on to the contents. These family holding companies consequently rarely live and breathe: they are receptacles, legal conveniences, paper pigeonholes.

Nobody could say that of James P. Ling's Ling-Temco-Vought, which re-invented the pyramid in a most ingenious way and became the ultimate in holding companies. All conglomerates, partly because of their bad habit of buying companies too expensively, suffered through most of their lives from relatively low price-earnings ratios. This irritated their masters beyond reason: anybody who wanted to excite a flow of passion from Hal Geneen of ITT in 1972 merely had to ask his opinion of the company's PE. As Anthony Sampson said of ITT's type of construction, "The whole massive conglomerate, from Tokyo to Chile, from smoked hams to telephones, rested like a vast upside-down pyramid on a pinpoint—the share price on the New York Stock Exchange." If the price on the NYSE rocks, the pyramid sways in time; and if the bough breaks, the cradle may fall.

Ling was virtually alone among conglomerators in deciding to take this cradle by the rockers. If the NYSE price stuck at a point where the parts were worth more than the whole, he would float off part of the parts, thereby establishing a stock market value and simultaneously dispatching some needed public cash to the LTV coffers.

One of the news magazines published a map, rather like a game of chutes and ladders, which showed how Ling, through an intricate series of deals ending with the flotation of the Wilson companies (nicknamed on Wall Street "meat ball, golf ball, and goof ball"), paid for the original acquisition and was still left holding control of Wilson's meat-packing, sports, and chemical businesses—all for free.

But Ling's empire always sounded too good to be true—and it was. The poor boy from Oklahoma had built up the fourteenth largest company in the US by initially developing an electronics and aerospace business; he shot himself down with a sequence of careless and costly purchases.

The sad truth the pyramid-builders overlook is that the underlying value of the business, which resides in its operating and earning assets, is not changed one iota by all their financial architecture. The separate market quotations for meat ball, golf ball, and goof ball couldn't increase either their intrinsic value (whatever that was) or LTV's: and on the latter score, the market was perfectly right—the sprawling bloated body of LTV was worth less than its parts.

That was simply because the parts cost too much money, even if the money was funny, and because Ling could keep the balls rolling (meat, golf, goof, and the rest) only by smothering the consequences of each deal in the next. Hence the catastrophe of bidding for the Jones & Laughlin steel giant, hard on the heel of the purchase of Greatamerica Corp. from another loaded Dallas conglomerater. The sole point of offering $85 a share for J & L stock, which was on the market at $50, was to make certain of the buy. Even if the government trustbusters had not stomped all over the deal, Ling was venturing into an industry where, given its low profits and low-browed management, the bravest and brightest angels would presumably have feared to tread.

The holding company, with its heavy mass of subsidiary interests balanced on top, becomes like a pyramid inverted and balanced on its tip. The structure is inherently unstable, which is why its builders, like Ling, and like Insull before him, have to rush from side to side in the desperate effort to keep balance and control. As they rush, it becomes harder, even for them, to keep track of the hectic paths they trace from brick to brick.

Far better is the simpler, static life of a little British outfit called A. Kershaw & Sons. Back in 1948 this company sold all its assets, except for under £50,000 in cash, to what is now Rank Precision Industries. At the end of 1972 Kershaw held not quite forty percent of the latter company's ordinary shares, and rather more of the preferred. A pretty unexciting investment, you might think—until you inquired what Rank Precision Industries owned in turn. That second holding company owned 5.6 million assorted shares in Rank Xerox, not known to be a gold mine in 1948, or 1958 for that matter. Even in 1968 the dividends filtering through to Kershaw came to only £387,-822. In the 1970s they were running at over a million annually.

The bulk of Kershaw's shares, in turn, are held by the Rank Organization, which owns Rank Precision Industries. What point there is in this perfect circle is none too clear: although there is a clear benefit to the Rank directors who hold a few Kershaw shares, highly desirable pieces of paper that have dutifully soared along with the Xerox profits. Thus the chairman of Rank, Rank Precision Industries, and Kershaw is the same man—Sir John Davis, who holds only 58,722 Kershaw shares. But since these weighed in at a peak of £16.75 in 1973, that small holding was worth not quite a million pounds. Of such are the blessings of leverage—provided always that the underlying securities and profits are truly secure.

The guiding principle for the construction of a pyramid is not necessarily simplicity, but sense. If the pyramid is taken to pieces, as with Hodge or Insull after the crash, what's left must be sufficiently viable to make the innocent wonder why the pyramid was ever constructed in the first place.

The guileless should ponder the case of Jimmy Goldsmith, possibly the most flamboyantly effective financier of the New Europe. Goldsmith has put together, from a base in the free and easy financial atmosphere of Paris, one of the great New European fortunes. At a modest computation, Goldsmith was worth £40 million on the completion of his superdeal, the acquisition of a faded group of grocery shops that, with the openeyed but still amazing aid of a fat company, Unilever, cost him nothing at all.

Goldsmith first surfaced in France (his mother is French, but his education was Etonian) with a business called Laboratoires Cassenne, which allowed sales to bound ahead so wonderfully that it ran out of the money needed to finance that bounding level of activity. This condition, overtrading, leads to bankruptcy just as surely as if the turnover had been heading for the cellar. Moving on to a pharmacy chain, Goldsmith made two mistakes: he bought it from an established multimillionaire (Sir Charles Clore) and in partnership with another young man of wealth, Selim Zilkha, whose subsequent and brilliant career was in shops for expectant or recent mothers.

As Goldsmith later admitted, "I nearly lost my shirt" in the overpriced and undermanaged pharmacies. But he bought out Zilkha's interest in some diet biscuits—and, several brisk deals later, seemed to have the nucleus of a specialty food firm, with products ranging from chocolate biscuits to snuff. Snuff, however, is what Goldsmith's Cavenham Foods was not up to. In its second year, the loss was almost £1 million. Only some fast and fancy footwork saved Cavenham from extinction.

In the process, Goldsmith not only turned to the United States for rescue, linking up with a company he found in Memphis, but committed a serious breach of the millionaire club rules: he sent more of his own money, half a million, after bad, to plug the hole in the boat. But there was a method to Goldsmith's bad financial manners. Behind Cavenham, if it could be kept afloat, was the even more compelling raison d'être of Generale Occidentale, GO for short, and *go* for real.

Goldsmith and a French cousin, Baron Alexis de Gunzberg, are partners in interlocking enterprises of formidable complexity. For instance, in March 1968 the pair took control of a former Algerian tramway company, and pumped various interests, from a chunk of Cavenham to banking, into the shell. They also bought, quite separately, another bank, which controlled another group of firms under the abbreviated name of FIPP.

By the time FIPP had taken over the diet foods from UTP, and had then been merged with Cavenham, and had agreed to merge with a French food group, GASA, and UTF had been merged with SGF to form GO, almost nobody could keep pace with the initials, let alone the interlocking and unlocking—except presumably Goldsmith and Gunzberg.

At the end of the day the formula FIPP+UTP+GASA +SGF added up to around two-thirds of GO, half in Goldsmith hands: its one-third of Cavenham alone was worth £60 million at the 1972 peak, the share price having soared eightfold in a year, partly through the benefits of two acquisitions, the food business of Bovril and the Allied Suppliers food chain. The latter cost Goldsmith £86.3 million of Cavenham's money. But Unilever, a big Allied shareholder, obligingly bought the Lipton tea business back for £18.5 million, which reduced the net cost to £67.8 million, most of it covered by surplus and salable property: within a few months Goldsmith had got rid of two City office blocks for £11 million and was on his way to an even cheekier coup, the purchase of Grand Union supermarkets in the US.

All this had to compensate for Goldsmith's woes elsewhere. While Cavenham was booming, the French interests were dropping a packet on bras and lingerie. Goldsmith's attempt to build up a financial pyramid à la Cavenham with an obscure outfit called Anglo-Continental fell foul of a mistake made earlier in his career—buying from a fellow millionaire. In this case, Jim Slater, the arch-accumulator of holdings and cross-holdings, offloaded a mixed assortment on Goldsmith, whose share price promptly suffered a fearful fit.

Dealing inevitably complicates the dangers of the holding game, for the impact of a bad deal must be magnified in exactly the same way as that of a poor set of earnings; and the really appalling buy can throw in some wretched earnings at the same time. The Goldsmith career demonstrates the basic principles both positively and negatively.

Negatively, never buy from strong hands: positively, always buy from the weak, which means, generally speaking, large corporations. Positively, coalesce diverse interests to extract their maximum value: negatively, don't diffuse your activities over unrelated fields. Negatively, avoid backing the wrong business horse: positively, capitalize on your mistakes by learning from them. Positively, remember that the ultimate gain from the ultimate holding company resides in keeping its control in your own hands: negatively, don't allow your operating base to become so weak that it won't support the holding structure above.

The essence of the modern pyramid can be seen, as through an X-ray, by examining its opposite: the public company in which the ultimate holder does not personally own most of the shares. He is limited to the latter and to their possibilities. The law doesn't allow him to build vertically much beyond one layer. So he turns to horizontalism. The holding company owns the master stakes in all the subsidiary or associated companies, but the latter can own useful holdings in each other and can deal and wheel incestuously as much as the master likes. This is not only a convenient way of realizing investment profits, but of burying mistakes or the so-so performers with which all holding operators are afflicted.

No greater practitioner of this perfectly legitimate art has ever breathed than Jim Slater of Crittall-Hope, etc., fame. The investments held by his master company, Slater Walker Securities, varied so greatly in percentage of the equity and nature that keeping track of them was a task beyond even fast financial minds. The spoor became clear, however, when Slater launched an investment trust whose contents, as City cynics were quick to spot, consisted largely of Slater-held shares that had been making something less than the running in the stock market; and the cynicism became so overwhelming that, eventually, Slater had to buy the whole bundle back.

It's an old trick to hide less splendid assets in some more convenient disguise, as demonstrated by George Weston Holdings, the master company of Garfield Weston's empire. For a group so little known, Weston's pyramid is of stupefying spread, with powerful companies in Britain, Canada (Weston's home country), South Africa (a regime to which Weston is partial), and the US. In America, when National Tea lost money and omitted a dividend, the first such omission by a Weston company for half a century, the seventy-five-year-old patriarch whipped in one of his sons to repair the damage.

But he had troubles before: he had attempted to build the mammoth Fine Fare, a British supermarket chain, without adequate management. First he imported a flock of Canadian managers, who flopped; then he put the whole collection in the care of an ace Canadian whose supervision was hampered by his refusal to cross the Atlantic in airplanes. So Weston transferred ownership of the Fine Fare supermarkets (and their losses) to the Canadian wing of George Weston Holdings until such time as the losses had turned to sufficiently respectable profits.

That day duly arrived, thanks to the discovery of James Gulliver, a consultant who had unearthed and cleaned up a mess in a small part of the Fine Fare stables. At which point Weston had a business well on its way to a worth of something like £120 million—a wonderful profit on his original investment. Fine Fare's ownership was then repatriated across the Atlantic, where it became once again an ornament of Weston's British empire. What an astute millionaire holds, he has.

SCENE 2

The Diversity of Riches

or

Too Many Broths Don't Spoil the Cook

One irritating habit of the tycoon (irritating to non-tycoons, that is) is his ability to pick sidelines, often pure hobbies that prove even more lucrative, proportionately speaking, than his original nest egg. A high and handsome collection of the world's rich have variegated interests on the side and go on accumulating more, like so many thieving magpies. Corporation bosses, too, love to pop a few of the shareholders' eggs into a side basket, but they usually succeed in demonstrating that managing the big basket in which the corporate eggs had far better all be kept is the full extent, if that, of their powers.

The rich entrepreneur usually has his base load, just like the big company. But unlike the corpocrat, the entrepreneur has both flair and personal resources. Consequently, his hobby is for himself: he bears any loss (or, more accurately, offsets it against his taxes). The corpocrat is betting on other people, the underlings who formed or will execute the plan; the loss, in the event of failure, will hurt his profits, balance sheet, or both; but the gain of a million in a $300 million company won't even be noticed.

That same capital profit, however, will look clear and sweet to any individual. Take the case of Kemmons Wilson, a multimillionaire who made most of his money by housing the quick at Holiday Inns, but who turned a considerable number of extra dollars out of the dead.

Wilson bought into the cemetery plot business, but was put off by the low density of corpses. He bent to the question the same ingenuity that evolved his franchise system for motel multiplication. Bodies occupy so much ground, he observed, because they are stored horizontally; insert them vertically, and the entire dimensions of the problem will be changed. Wilson adapted an oil-field machine to bore the vertical holes, and made a special cylindrical coffin designed to fit the slots.

That combination of opportunism and technical innovation is not easily reproduced. But expert entrepreneurs down the ages never seem to have hesitated before a new possibility: they needed only to see that if the barriers between hope and realization could be removed, a rich margin would result. The rewards don't even have to be realized fast: again, the individual investor, as opposed to the corporate one, has the inside track.

Since income is a potential embarrassment to the individual, he can be content with an unrealized gain, so long as it is sufficiently gainful. Virtually all grades of the well-to-do have these sidelines, extramural activities that are bred by the very existence of their wealth. It acts as both magnet and propulsion unit. Their wealth attracts propositions, and the possibilities attract them to proceed—often in fields that bear no relation to the sources of their bread and butter.

But Kemmons Wilson's corpses are no farther apart from his Holiday Inns than Norton Simon's art collecting is from his tomato ketchup—though in Simon's case the sideline has become the mainline activity. Old Masters of the Simon quality or Impressionists of the foremost rank have been among the most purse-warming, as well as culturally rewarding, investments of the postwar period. Take the £798,000 price Simon paid for Rembrandt's *Titus* (after the auctioneer got tangled up in Simon's tortuous instructions—to the effect that when he was standing, he wasn't bidding; when he was sitting, he was, and so forth—the bidding had to start all over again). *Titus* has already begun to look like a bargain.

In a sense, Simon, like Duveen in the age of the supreme dealer, made his own market: his prices have been a major force propelling his own art values upward. This, again, is a privilege of the wealthiest dabbler. He can move sufficient resources to the chosen area to force his dreams to come true. (There are, alas, exceptions: times when a market is too big even for Croesus to corner—although that may not stop him from trying. Two offspring of H. L. Hunt, super-rich both from Daddy's oil and their own earnest endeavors, in 1973's silver rush cornered over 6% of the world's total stocks, worth in early 1974 a quarter of a billion dollars—close to half of which was the paper profit of Nelson Bunker and Herbert Hunt, enough to make even the Biggest Daddy proud.)

The nature and range of a man's understanding determine how far he can dabble, and in what ways. Many men of surpassing wealth feel uncomfortable more than a stone's throw away from their business hearths and think little of happier, luckier spirits who fool around with coffins or silver. The choice is truly a matter of temperament as much as ability. The diversifier has to regard himself as an investor, which is an utterly different role from that of the entrepreneur.

Those who are content to sit back and collect the money, however, have made some extraordinary extra piles. The oil-rich Texan Amon G. Carter, for instance, bankrolled American Airlines; the Murchison boys, also from Texas, engaged in some spirited forays into New York finance, notably a battle for control of the giant Investors Diversified Services mutual fund complex; but nothing so spectacular as the Hunts' silver caper.

The oil fortunes, in general, have had less impact outside Texas than might be expected. Part of the reason is that oilmen habitually put their profits right back into oil, which is increasingly capital-hungry these days. Another is that Texas is a large state with enormous tracts of land:

those oilmen who have invested in land have done nearly as nicely as those Texan land barons who went into oil.

There's a rueful story about Albert D. Lasker, the Lord and Thomas advertising genius, whose $115 million packet is alleged to be the greatest fortune anybody ever has taken out of advertising. Lasker off-loaded the Texas land bequeathed by his father. Had he kept that rich soil, Lasker would have died $500 million better off.

After all, even a millionaire must live somewhere; and while buying two or three houses, he might as well have a small patch of land to call his own in their vicinity. If that patch contains a farm, or trees, or various other conveniences, moreover, its acquisition will reduce his estate duties, his taxation, or both; and while performing its good deed of reduction, it will appreciate mightily. In 1961 Sir Charles Clore, seeking a suitable home for a couple of million pounds, bought 16,000 acres near Hereford from a London hospital. A dozen years later Clore's country *pied-à-terre* was worth, on a conservative estimate, £14 million. And such agricultural land bears only fifty-five percent of the estate duty payable on other assets.

When Clore paid £550,000 for the site of the London Hilton, the first building to upstage Buckingham Palace, he was widely thought to be pulling off a masterly coup. But the site vendor invested Clore's thousands in country land up in Scotland, where his capital multiplied five and a half times in a decade—handsomely beating the profit on the Hilton for much less trouble.

That kind of appreciation has been recorded by almost every member of the well-endowed classes who has put money into real estate—and in the US, where the investor can charge depreciation on the purchase price even of old buildings, this type of sideline is practically obligatory.

There is no doubt some screwy logic in allowing a millionaire to deduct from his taxes the supposed annual fall in the value of a building which, as everyone (even in the Internal Revenue Service) knows, is actually appreciating in worth. But the logic is so screwy that it set a trap for none other than Charles Clore.

In 1960, Clore was in shoes, shipbuilding, textile machinery, jewelry, but property in Britain had been among his most successful fields. So a lovely, high building in America was the most tempting present left for the mil-

lionaire who had everything else. In buying his Manhattan
status symbol, however, he broke the cardinal rule by buying from another tycoon, William Zeckendorf, the then
master of compounded debt. The bauble, 40 Wall Street,
was seventy stories high and forty-one years old.

By the time the aged building had been reconstructed,
Clore had nearly $20 million invested in Wall Street, a
quarter of it his own cash. And the final twist came when
the owners of the new Pan Am building, towering above
Grand Central Station, had to buy up leases in 40 Wall
Street to persuade their owners to become Pan Am tenants.
By then, after a deal back home, the part-owner of the Pan
Am temple was Charles Clore. According to Oliver Marriott's *The Property Boom*, Clore emerged with a feeble
$700,000 profit (feeble, that is, by Clore's standards), and
that much only because of a technicality in the foreign exchange transactions.

Every British tycoon who brushed up against Zeckendorf got crushed in his embrace. Those who emerged with
profit needed all the strength and skill of Davy Crockett
wrestling with a bear.

Millionaire investors are no more likely to avoid bear
hugs than anybody else. But they have a double-barreled
safety valve. First, they can afford the inconvenience of an
error. (Looked at in the worst light, "Charlie's bad egg," as
40 Wall Street was known, tied up some $5.5 million of
his capital in sterile manner for half a dozen years; that
might have broken a lesser fortune, but didn't even cause
Clore to break stride.) And second is the fact that the most
pressing considerations drive the tycoon into hobbies where
the pasture is likely to be greenest: not only into property,
but into American oil, where the tax breaks are worth having even if the drilled hole isn't.

Bing Crosby and Bob Hope have ample reason to sing
about the day when a Fort Worth friend put them into sixteen percent of an especially sumptuous deal: after one dry
hole, fifty-eight came good and wet in succession. If other
Hollywood wallets have been emptied by less benevolent
Texans, that's only fair recompense for the terrible damage
done to those brave Texan millionaires who have put their
silver dollars into Broadway plays and as angels have
ended up with dirty faces. (The angel, however, isn't truly
buying a stream of future income. Like the millionaire cus-

tomers for Duveen art in the silver age, he is buying cultural respectability, and the prestige is presumably worth the fee.)

There are, however, other soups which confer both kudos and riches: for instance, owning your own *grande luxe* restaurant. William Brock, one of the three founders of Automotive Products, owned not only the Mirabelle in Mayfair, but also a country restaurant near his home at Maidenhead. The Mirabelle's value alone must have exceeded £1 million; a rival London establishment, the Coq d'Or, was reported to have changed hands for a round seven figures. In New York, the great Henri Soulé, who became a millionaire himself as a result, was set up in Le Pavillon by rich men who had enjoyed his cooking at the 1939 World's Fair. It's the most charming of hobbies: quite literally having your food and eating it.

You can drink your bottle and keep it, too. When Lord Cowdray was persuaded to take control of Château Latour, it was a run-down vineyard that clung to its precious first-growth status by continuing to make great wine—even though the vines and winery were dilapidated. The richest private purse in England repaired the dilapidations with expert local help. By 1970 the stocks held at the château were said in Bordeaux to be worth more than the entire Cowdray outlay, on purchase, maintenance, and repair. That was before the atomic price explosion from 1971 onward. With 1972 first-growth clarets selling at £8,750 a barrel, a rise of fifty percent over 1970, Latour must rank as one of the happiest investments of all time.

C. Douglas Dillon, investment banker and former Secretary of the US Treasury, can't be any less happy with his possession of Château Haut Brion; as for Baron Philippe de Rothschild, the 100,000 bottles of rare vintages in his private cellar at Château Mouton must be worth well over a million in their own right—a five-bottle jeroboam of the 1929, after all, fetched $9,200 at auction.

Viticulture is too technical a game for most of the rich who prefer to indulge in armchair investing. For some, though, the armchair is jet-propelled. Sir Isaac Wolfson devoted most of his energies to building up his mail order and store chain, but on the side he pushed a posse of financial interests into a company separate from his main Great Universal Stores. On one estimate, although the total amount of family money invested in this sideline was never more than £39,000, the Wolfsons emerged from the enterprise with £28 million. A 1951 investment of £1,000 in Drages, a Wolfson vehicle, would have been worth over a million (to be precise, £1,080,000) eleven years later.

Wolfson followed an important rule for sideline interests: never dilute your equity. The joy of a good deal—and all sidelines are deals—is greatly lessened if the proceeds must be given away to every Tom, Dick, and Hermann who has climbed on the bandwagon. That doesn't mean the entire bowl of soup has to be in your private possession: that may be not only impossible but illogical. The lesson is rather to avoid, in financing, anything that will prevent the maximum benefit from accruing to the most important person in the operation—yourself. In a mainline operation, this may be impracticable. Acquisitions may necessitate cashing in some of your own chips, turning them over to others.

But since the sideline *is* on the side, you can afford to wait until the manna is ready to drop from heaven. Let the case of Dan Lufkin, who made most of a $35 million fortune from the Wall Street brokerage house of Donaldson, Lufkin and Jenrette, stand as an example. A friend, Louis Marx Jr. of the toy family, thought that DLJ was coming in with him on an oil play in Kansas. But the check turned out to be from Lufkin personally: his DLJ company had turned the proposition down. According to Marx, Lufkin "really had to dig down for that money"—which in short order came back tenfold and provided the nucleus of Pan Ocean Oil, which has a stake in many deep oil diggings, including the biggest dig of all—in the North Sea.

According to *Fortune*, Lufkin made "spur-of-the-moment, almost impetuous commitments . . . on the spot to people he had never met or knew only casually." The trouble with this method is that it tends to balance every hit with a miss: to match Pan Ocean with the Ontario Motor Speedway, a $27 million flop; to offset the hit show *Oh! Calcutta* with the *Saturday Review*, a perfectly good magazine massacred by a pair of assiduous promoters with their marvelous ideas for renovation.

Sidelines should never commit more than side-stakes. It defeats the definition if an extramural activity begins to eat up resources. History does, of course, record cases of spin-offs that have either outgrown the original activity or become great economic empires themselves. Thus two founders of American Express, Mr. Wells and Mr. Fargo, set up what has now become the West's second largest bank when their Amex partners turned down their proposal to extend the service to the gold of California. In the same state, the Safeway supermarket chain was promoted by Merrill Lynch Pierce Fenner & Smith (né Bean), the world's largest stockbrokers (and very possibly its most prolific spawner of millionaires: when Merrill Lynch went public in 1971, 175 employees reached that financial status overnight).

The many soup technique isn't confined to those whose bowls are already brimming over. It can be used in reverse: adding together many mites to make a nice, fat mint. Owning several small businesses is one route, but the scurrying about required is out of proportion to the payoff, and the chances of one egg in the basket turning horribly bad are just as great when the eggs are small as when they are dinosaur-sized.

A better technique is to have no real commitment to a multitude of businesses, so that it matters not whether they soar like swallows or subside into the swamp. This may sound difficult, but the invention of the nonexecutive director makes the trick exceedingly simple. The only obstacle is getting accepted as a man of good sense, breeding, and contacts, whose presence would ornament and dignify any board. The difficulty is more social than intellectual. But once the barrier has been crossed, multiplication can begin in earnest.

The odds are that, out of a dozen or so companies, one will prove to be a big winner. The betting is fair that in most such cases the holdings are not purchased out of the pennies saved from the wise man's salary; although a fee of £ 5,000 multiplied twenty times does work out at a more than useful pittance.

Those who provide the pittance are unaware of the obvious fact that the main reason which makes their multiple man a catch in their eyes—the fact that he sits on so many portentous boards—greatly reduces his value. The more jobs a man has, the less he can contribute to each; yet, by some strange reversal of logic, the more he is sought after, and the more money gets thrust into his hands by the clients.

The multiple director, however, is not in the same league as the rich collector of broths, either financially or in the one essential respect which should govern diversifying. The nonexecutive never actually has to like anything about the businesses that employ him; except the money. In contrast, nobody who already has the latter should put it into a side enterprise unless it is partly for a kind of loving. The pleasure he derives from, say, owning Château Latour enhances the chances that even though he has only a fraction of his mind to devote to the property, he will tend it well.

The pleasure, moreover, is a useful antidote when soups curdle, as they often will, even for more careful investors than Dan Lufkin. Take the Chicago financier Colonel Henry Crown. His involvement with General Dynamics, whose bad habits included losing $450 million on the Convair jetliner and running through presidents like a paper shredder, must have been soothed by other, more hospitable interests, like the Hilton hotel chain, and, still more, the Empire State Building. Owning that landmark should have been a matter of pride as much as property—like a Parisian buying the Eiffel Tower or a Londoner landing Buckingham Palace. Whether or not his ego was well massaged, the Colonel eventually sold his sideline in the sky to the Prudential Insurance Company—and massaged his wallet with a profit of $50 million.

SCENE 3

The Gold in Gambling

or

The One-Horse Race

The man who hasn't got everything suffers a fatal disadvantage in the effort to get rich the easiest way, which is in return for nothing—otherwise known as gambling. Apart from the British football pools or national lotteries in Latin countries, there are hardly any opportunities for sudden, lightning conversion of the poor.

The sad truth is that, if a 1,000 to 1 shot comes home with £10 on its nose, you pocket only £10,000; whereas if you can afford £1,000, the proceeds are a whole, round million. It is even sadder that 1,000 to 1 shots rarely return to the fireside, a fact of which those who can afford £1,000 bets are fully aware. Which is why the rich prefer to speculate only on stone-cold certainties.

The richer you are, the easier it becomes to arrange the necessary degree of certainty. At the extreme, the best way of profiting from gambling is to run it, as the Mafia long ago discovered. However, the techniques that piled up an alleged $150 million for the pursued waif Meyer Lansky have as much to do with banking as with gaming. Like a bank, the Mafia parts the masses from their cash and makes sure that, before any of the loot is actually paid out, the mob collects its unfair share. It's the latter-day version of Robin Hood: taking from the poor in order to give to the rich. (The gambit is far safer than fixing fights or horse races, where the fixed contestant can always defraud you by having a heart attack.)

The organizers of the Irish Sweepstake, the world's single greatest horse betting exercise, may have taken much the same lesson to their bosoms. According to the finds of an enterprising journalist, the lion's share of the many millions taken by the Sweep may not get paid out to the beneficiaries. A nourishing chunk, he claimed, went into a variety of pockets, the deepest being those of the McGrath family, who for years organized the event on behalf of the Irish hospitals, the supposed beneficiaries, and was alleged to collect £3 million a year for its trouble.

Behind every mass gamble, there stands a small family with a large fortune—even if it does no more than allow the odds to work in its favor. The essence of any book or gaming table is that, no matter what combination of winners comes in, the house comes out ahead. In running a book on horses, an element of risk remains; on a football pool, however, the promoter can never lose, since he pays out only a fixed proportion of what comes in.

The take has always been terrific. William Crockford, whose gaming club was the birthplace of London's postwar gambling renaissance, died in 1844, worth the equivalent of $5 million. By 1961, on the *Saturday Evening Post's* figures, profits from gambling in the Las Vegas area had topped $100 million. The mob's pay-offs—$2 million a year in police protection from one Philadelphia ring—gave some indication of the profit margins being protected.

In the legitimate end of the business, the losses are paradoxically a measure of the mighty sums made. Before the government ended the pastime, William Hill, Britain's most successful bookie, plunged heavily into fixed odds betting on football matches. One week he paid out £850,000 on winning bets. "That's not what we call a bad week," he said. "It only worked out at 9:8 against us on the stake." What Hill hailed as a good week must have been quite something.

The bettor, too, can turn speculation into certainty, if his stakes are high enough. Exact calculation of the odds, plus a deep bank, enabled the so-called Greek syndicate (actually three Greeks, one Frenchman, and one Armenian) to win consistent fortunes playing baccarat. They chose baccarat because the bank has a slight mathematical advantage and can stop play whenever it fancies.

An even more enterprising Frenchman succeeded in rigging the national, State-backed betting game in his favor by careful and massive placing of bets around the country. All these operations appear to be perfectly within the law, which cannot be said for the gang of Britons who substituted a horse in a minor race, suddenly inundated off-course bookmakers with bets on this "ringer," and defeated the anguished bookies' efforts to lay off their bets on the course by cutting the telephone wires. But even here an element of chance existed. The substituted horse, the ringer, might have fallen over its own feet.

Pure business offers the only sporting contest in which you can buck all the horses and still win. As with most millionaire ploys, the mysterious absurdity of the stock market contains the formula: witness the Company Raid Gambit Declined.

As everybody knows, Wall Street, London, and similar emporia of shares are risky casinos: what goes up always comes down, and you never know when or by how much. But everybody is wrong. For in this stratagem the player knows when the share is rising and himself determines how far it is going to rise—and even when the rise will stop.

The first move is to assemble a sizable quantity of shares in the selected victim. This is accomplished through a variety of dummy companies, nominee companies (conveniently organized by banks for the protection and benefit of their clients), obliging friends, trust funds, and what have you. There was even a halcyon period in Britain when the amasser could build up any size stake he liked in sublime secrecy; now he has to reveal all when the nibble has become a ten percent bite. That, however, compares very favorably with fifteen percent in the US, and is perfectly adequate for the launching of the next move, which is to make a bid for the rest of the company's shares—pitched well above the current market price and even further above the average cost of your collection.

On the "heads I win, tails you lose" principle, the bid must be realistic (*i.e.*, cheap) so that, if by any chance it succeeds, you have a bargain on your hands. But since it is cheap, the odds are that the stunned directors, reeling from one hastily arranged board meeting to another, will fight to the death in defense of their company's beloved freedom (not to mention their own jobs). This fight for liberty more often than not takes the form of finding some other bidder to deprive them of the same priceless possession, but never mind. (Though one victimized company, threatened with absorption by the octopus-like Litton Industries, defended itself more skillfully by buying a furniture company; since Litton also made furniture, that killed the bid on antitrust grounds.)

The gambit player welcomes the appearance of a rival bidder, or the arrival of anything else—a scrumptious profit forecast, a swift revaluation of properties—which forces up the victim's share. True, he may have to raise his own bid; but that costs nothing, whereas the market rise in his previously purchased shares is money in the bank.

If the bid succeeds, he pockets the company; if it fails, he pockets the capital gain. An early demonstration of this beautiful truth came in the battle for the Savoy Hotel, that chromium-plated pride of London. Attacked by a mystery bidder, it also attracted the attention of Charles Clore, who in the days before his knighthood (and his construction of the London Hilton) was regarded by the Establishment much as Philip of Spain fancied Captain Blood; in face of this onslaught the Savoy board closed ranks with such adamant fervor that Clore and the mystery bidder, revealed as Sir Harold Samuel, must have come out of the fracas with over half a million between them.

There's no shortage of other targets. Oliver Jessel, an ebullient descendant of the Samuel millions (oil of the Shell variety and banking of the merchant blend), made a determined foray for an oil distributor, William Cory. Jessel lost the war, but won the prize—a brisk, seven-figure capital gain, which lent conviction to his saying that "at last my business is making more than my private income." The business making a raid may even be smaller than its intended victim. That fact contains two important principles of business chess. In this type of gambit, relative smallness is an asset, making it easier for the raider to maintain a sky-high value for his own shares. (A common double move in the game is to get a friend or friends to buy your own shares during the vital maneuvers, thus keeping up their price.)

The bigness of the target also has rich implications. Not only are large companies the ones most likely to stuff their cupboards with underrealized assets and their executive suites with managerial dodos; there also will be enormous numbers of shares around the place, thus making it possible for cloak and dagger merchants to buy them in relative secrecy. F. W. Woolworth has 378 million shares on the market in Britain, while A & P in the US has 24.8 million little pieces of paper: the once great A & P chain was thus a sitting duck for the gambit essayed by Charles Bluhdorn of Gulf + Western.

After a Bluhdorn pal made a blistering attack on A & P's grocery price tactics, Bluhdorn steadily bought shares in the sagging supermarket chain. (It had sagged to a $50 million loss in nine months, on rising sales, by the infallible expedient of giving away its goods to customers at less than true cost.) Market purchases of a million-odd shares by G + W were followed by a tender offer to buy another 3.75 million at $20—a price usefully higher than the $16 at which they stood at the start of Bluhdorn's gambit. The existence of his interest in itself supported the A & P price; and in this situation the player can always expect his opponent to work his hide off to repel the raid.

The ultimate beauty of such gambits is that the purchase money can easily be borrowed from some friendly neighborhood bank. The dealing creates automatic collateral for the loan, in the shape of the victor's shares; and the bank gets what bankers love best of all, fast turnover of their money and, if it's an investment bank, a nice slice of the action.

For the extremely rich, however, a little cash can go a wonderfully long way. One past master at this art can stimulate enthusiasm for a share by picking up a few and allowing word to get around that he might splurge on many more shares; that he might inject some of his own interests; that he might make the company the vehicle for any future empires he might choose to build.

As the shares bound up, this master takes his first profit: he next sells short, and the word gets around that none of the deals will materialize; the maestro then takes his second profit, and so on, until no more flesh is left on the picked-over bones.

In another variation, the deal was actually consummated. The tycoon concerned took shares in exchange for one of his companies, amid scenes of great rejoicing. With those shares in hand, he proceeded to control the market, mounting a bear raid of swift and stunning success. The very word that he proposed to off-load his newly acquired shares sent shudders down the collective spine of the stock market; and if you can move markets by a word, money is only a useful secondary tool. The combination of word and wealth is utterly irresistible.

But the essence of the Company Raid Gambit Declined and its variations is that the same player cannot make the same move more than once every few years; otherwise he loses the essential element of credibility. That would break a prime rule of making millions, which is that what people believe to be real is more important than reality itself.

Playing the market this way has the virtue of being completely honest, or (to be more accurate) entirely legal. However, the players are in a minefield of rules and temptations, any of which can blow up in their faces. The first of America's postwar company raiders, Louis E. Wolfson, who assaulted the heaving mail order bulk of Montgomery Ward, had some $210 million of assets under his control at one point, but ended up in prison uniform.

The same risks of falling foul of the law are run in another millionaire-generating game: the Inside Straight, in which the moves come straight from the horse's mouth. In theory, no insider of a public company is supposed to profit personally from information which has been kept from the shareholders at large. In practice, insiders are fixing themselves with this information all the time—and their crime, being difficult to detect, is seldom punished with anything save money.

The fatal error is greed. The more shares insiders buy of a stock that is heading for Cloud Nine, the more likely it is that some interfering busybody will notice. The more shares that insiders off-load in a company that is heading for the tomb, the higher the chance that somebody will compare before-and-after holdings in the shares. Once upon a time, indeed until recently in Britain, directors were under no obligation to reveal their interests; they still don't have to on most of the Continent.

Even today in the UK well over a year can elapse between a sale or purchase and its revelation—by which time the insider can have closed the deal and taken his profit, without anybody being wiser or sadder. Once again, however, the leverage of money is needed to make real money. The insider may know that a bid is coming at double the market price; but to reap a million from his coup, he needs a million first—and raising that kind of loot renders the necessary concealment even harder.

And when the stakes are high enough, caution gives way to avarice. Back in the early 1960s, an observant Canadian living in a town called Timmins in Ontario noticed that a certain aircraft used by an American company was flying the same route every day to a prospecting site. Being shrewd as well as long-sighted, he bought any land he could find in the area, which proved to bear silver, zinc, lead, and other such baubles in delectable quantities.

Back at the ranch, however, the Americans who controlled the exploration, executives of Texas Gulf Sulphur, had far more precise information than the plane spotter, and far earlier. Their public statements played down the value of the finds while their private dealings built up their stakes in a stock that was bound to multiply gloriously. When the true glory was finally unveiled, Timmons was swamped by a minor gold rush—and the Texas Gulf Sulphur insiders reached for their piggy banks.

After due delay, alas, the sheriffs of the Securities and Exchange Commission hauled the insiders off to the courts. They had offended not simply by getting caught, but by being too obvious.

Time and again before a bid is announced or a company

crashes, UK shares mysteriously either rise or fall in due season. The Stock Exchange duly investigates for the leak; only to find, time and time again, that the plug has been so neatly inserted that not a trace remains. Actually, you don't even need a leak. The safest honest way of making money known to man is to buy shares in elephantine companies that are receiving bids from determined raiders. The bidder is invariably forced to raise his offer, and the gap between opening shot and closing salvo can be huge. Watney Mann, trying to defend its brewing empire from Maxwell Joseph's Grand Metropolitan Hotels, saw its share price nearly treble before the day was narrowly lost. The outsider gets a free ride on the insider's bank.

Max Joseph is a grandmaster in the art of sure things. For example, at the time of the 1964 election he put a massive bet on a Labour victory, not because of any loyalty to that party, but on grounds of impeccable logic. If the Conservatives won, all his shareholdings would soar. If Labour won (as it did), he stood to collect a tax-free fortune on the bet. Joseph also showed that he had the correct idea about gambling by putting his money on the best chip of all: he bought up casinos.

The right side of the tables has always been where they keep the money. But the casinos of England have received a rich extra lining of plush from the unwitting munificence of the government. After gaming was legalized, clubs proliferated to an extent that bothered the puritans and affronted the police. And the Mafia regarded it as only proper that its members should take their share of this expanding market.

No doubt, no person in the entire apparatus of British government foresaw that gaming controls would inevitably create gaming gold miles. Few bureaucrats or politicians in central government do foresee the private results of their public decisions, which often require superhuman efforts of self-control from insiders. There's the famous incident of Lord Kindersley, who as a director of the Bank of England knew that a "swinging" rise in interest rates was on the way. By selling gilt-edged government stock, his bank (Lazards) could make or avoid losing great fortunes. An unwitting bank colleague, at this untimely juncture, approached Kindersley for his views on selling gilts; at which the latter looked "extremely po-faced."

A later government, by a decision on gilt-edged stock, made it easy for anybody with access to millions to make still more. The introduction of capital gains tax in 1965 applied to these securities; but some had been sold to the long-suffering public in the days before the tax at prices well below par. It was pointed out to the politicians that this was sharp practice, denying the purchasers part of a reward that had, in effect, been guaranteed by Her Majesty's Government.

So the bonds concerned were exempted from the tax, with the following unintended result. You buy £1 million of bonds, borrowing the money at ten percent: the security, gilt-edged stock, is watertight; the interest can all be offset against investment income, which is taxed at rates of up to ninety percent and more. The stock stands at eighty, but in a couple of years must be redeemed at one hundred, thus yielding £250,000 for the outlay of less than £10,000 a year.

As usual, it was mainly the already rich who reaped the fruits, although one Socialist millionaire, among the first to spot the wholesome opportunity, used the chance to set up his old professors and friends with some extra nest eggs before his political colleagues put an end to the caper.

The Socialists' addiction to defending the pound sterling created wonderful openings for international currency speculators. At one point, on a careful estimate, the official regulations had created eighty-nine varieties of sterling, a profusion which offered endless opportunities for switching profitably from one to another. What the politicians damned as speculation, and attributed to people unpleasantly nicknamed "gnomes of Zurich," was actually intelligent action on reasoned anticipation of inevitable events. The pound's devaluation was made certain by the incompetent financial policies of Her Majesty's Ministers, not by the machinations of astute men playing the international money market.

Harold Wilson was constantly boasting how these fiends would get their fingers burnt. In truth, those fingers were tastefully licked as the speculators cashed in on the fact that sterling's ability to rise (the upside risk) was limited by international agreement to a small percentage shift, while its downside potential was of mouth-watering size. In the event, the price slumped from $2.80 to $2.40, a killing matched only by the final collapse of the even longer American defense of the dollar.

In two weeks' heavy speculation in February 1973, at least $600 million was cleaned up entirely by those who were betting on D-marks, on the fact that the dollar had nowhere to go save down. Probably the majority of this take was cleared by corporations, but a goodly number of clever individuals were along for a free ride, which was financed by others and entailed (like all good speculation) a minimal degree of risk.

In mythology, risk is the way to millions, on the general assumption that "the higher the risk, the higher the potential reward." It's true that "the higher the interest, the higher the risk," but between interest (which is income) and a dealing profit (which is a capital gain) there is a great canyon fixed. Where the odds are 100 to 1, it is because the chances of the bet succeeding are small. The true speculator, however, is concerned not with the percentage of his pay-off, but with its degree of certainty. The surer the thing, the more heavily he invests. True and high risks are for the suckers—for those, in other words, from whom the true speculator makes his true rewards.

SCENE 4

The Bliss of Backing
or
You Can Count On Me

Once upon a time, in a real-life fairy story, there was a wise old general who spotted a bright little computer engineer and gave him both blessing and backing. Within eleven years that good old military man had seen his investment multiply to a quarter of a billion dollars. The cost of his initial backing?—$70,000 of the engineer's computer shares.

The investor was General Doriot, whose American

Research and Development became an international by-word for the astute backing of advanced technology. Backing successful outsiders is as rare in business as on the track, but picking winners in advanced scientific wonder gadgets is approximately as easy as drawing a royal flush at poker.

Doriot's record in this field was exceptionally good, even without his investment in Ken Norris' Digital Equipment. But exceptional achievement in this minefield means avoiding detonation. While ARD made some other lucky investments, none compared with the DE gold mine. And the net result, when ARD was finally sold out to the Textron conglomerate, was not the kind of capital gain to make a mutual fund manager jealous.

Doriot would have done better to place every egg in the DE basket—if only, that is, he could have foreseen its future. This is one variety of foresight not given to man, even to a man of such surpassing shrewdness as the General. A possibly apocryphal story tells of the General's being offered an ingenious plan for selling hardwood trees and bringing the valuable timber downriver to the sawmills. The General listened carefully to the details, the extrapolations of hardwood demand, the behavior of prices in the key markets, the increasing proportion of expensive veneers in furniture, and what not. He then killed the project stone dead with one simple question: will the logs float?

Successful backers need to ask log-floating questions. This demands some instinct about where the project is most liable to sink. The instincts of laymen confronted with technologists, especially technologists of advanced breed, are unreliable and tend to be overwhelmed by modesty. Backers of technological wonders usually come unstuck not because of failure to understand quantum theory of the significance of the Second Law of Thermodynamics, but because, hornswoggled by the bewildering magic of the unknown, they ignore the simple rules that they should know by heart and by common sense.

If an investor fails to keep a watchful eye on how his money is being spent, or fails to force his pet technologists to give him meaningful progress reports on the latest wonder of the world, he has only himself to blame when the logs sink (as, in such circumstances, they always do). One set of bemused bankers allowed their technical playboys to pile up monstrous extravagances on complex equipment like Rolls-Royce motor cars and interior decoration, completely ignoring the fact, which the simplest of checks would have unveiled, that there were hardly any customers in the whole wide world (only one finally turned up) for the particular magic being peddled.

In contrast, the potential clients for an instant camera were numbered in the multimillions; and it is a law of wealth that the bigger the market, the greater the chances of achieving financial greatness. The early backers of Dr. Edwin Land can congratulate themselves on following this elementary rule with conspicuous reward; they were, as it happens, a conspicuous group, financially and socially. Averell Harriman, James P. Warburg, and Lewis Strauss put up $375,000: family wealth never sowed more fertile seed.

The small sum of $1,000 invested in Polaroid in 1938 would have been worth $4 million within a quarter of a century. Plainly, backing will more often than not come from the rich—after all, they have the money. But it does not follow that the rich killings, the creation of the new fortunes of Polaroid dimensions, will inevitably also fall to the wealthy. If you have twice as many shots as the next man, you have twice his chance of hitting the target, and striking in the center (or the gold, as archers appropriately call it). But the man with fewer shots may still strike gold with his first aim; and the annals of golden backing contain many proofs of this satisfying truth.

John James is a Bristol millionaire who began to build up a chain of radio and TV shops on the strength of a postwar service gratuity. While rising to the giddy heights of three hundred outlets in fourteen years, James had trouble getting sets supplied by the orthodox, established manufacturers. He was forced to look elsewhere, and his gaze lighted on Radio and Allied, whose fortunes were in the tight grip of the then unknown Arnold Weinstock.

James ended up as the largest investor in Radio and Allied outside Weinstock's family. When Weinstock led his company into the General Electric Company, James became one of that company's biggest holders, too; when Weinstock led GEC into Valhalla, James cashed in on the richest transformation ever wrought on a major European company. His stake in GEC became worth a lusty sum, even compared with the £6 million that he made by selling his store chain. His first chain, that is; in a second incarnation, James made some less inspired moves, including the financial support of a chain of furniture discount stores of quite spectacular lack of viability.

Where Weinstock is (or was) a sharp and hungry man, the disappointing furniture king was heavy on the hoof, which is a useful, though not invariable, guide for off-track bettors. There are exceptions, of course, in both directions. But men who are big, fat, and sleep o' nights seem in general to lack the energy, insatiable drive, and self-made success of the true tycoon. The latter tends, rather, to be short, thick-set, small; like David Sarnoff, the genius of RCA, or Lord Marks, the creator of the modern Marks & Spencer; Samuel I. Newhouse, the newspaper, TV, and magazine tycoon, checks out at 5'3"; Meyer Lansky, the Jewish Mafioso, is 5'1"; neither Sir Issac Wolfson, the British mail order king, nor Sir Jules Thorn, the British Sarnoff, would be much use, physically speaking, on a basketball team.

In contrast, the truly disastrous receptacles for other people's cash often float high in water—like the salad oil swindler, Tino de Angelis, who, while only 5'5", weighed in at 240 pounds; like John King, the would-be ruler of Investors Overseas Services, or William Zeckendorf Sr., the real estate tycoon who took several of Britain's overambitious property men for a ride around the city centers of the Americas; or Marion Harper, the advertising man who created both the biggest and the brokest group of advertising agencies in the world. Most such men are terrific talkers, which is another uneasy augury.

One clearly identifiable characteristic of the supermanager is that he talks as little as possible, especially in public. This is partly because words waste time, and most men of true action are deeply, instinctively conscious of the way in which time, which is also money, runs through the fingers. They are also acutely aware that the more you say, the more you are liable to commit yourself—and commitment, unless you are exceedingly careful, also costs money. As in poker, so in business, part of the art is to keep the opposition guessing, because they will more often guess wrong than right.

Preference for the short, strong, and silent is a good start along the critical road of making a personal assessment. In the end, this is the nature of the backing decision. No matter how developed the nose for a good idea, no matter how careful the checking to ensure that the logs will float, no matter how quick and comprehensive the financial controls over the loved one, in the end everything comes down to the man himself.

There is no such thing, however, as the right man in the wrong opportunity; if you are backing somebody in ventures like tuna fishing, deveined shrimp, and frozen apple juice (to name three of General Doriot's failed brainwaves) you by definition have the wrong man. The right one, like Ken Olsen at Digital Equipment, does the right thing: and usually, like Olsen, has eccentric characteristics that stamp him as an unusual creature, a man unlikely to get diverted from the important business of making your money grow at the most urgent possible speed.

In 1972, when worth some $90 million, Olsen still worked out of a deserted woolen mill in Maynard, Massachusetts. He still had a paramount interest in the pure, unadulterated beauty of computer circuits. "I still keep my hand in at engineering," he said once, "for fear that I might one day be out of a job. I do it some Saturday mornings." Between 1965 and 1972 the sales presided over by this curiously indifferent capitalist shot up from $15 million to $180 million as Olsen survived a ghastly catalogue of errors in shipping out the PDP-6 computer. That, maybe, is the hardest thing to predict about an entrepreneur: how he will react in the all but inevitable crisis. Toughness alone won't see the man through; he requires the ability to stick like a leech to the essentials of his job—which, in Olsen's case, was to produce ingenious small computers that actually worked; like the PDP-8, which promptly sold over 10,000 units.

Among several moments of painful truth, the most agonizing for Henry Ford I was the year the Model T, thrashed by the ritzier models of Chevrolet, ran out of road. Ford closed the plants for a year, came out with the Model A, and drove on to a greater fortune than ever. This, admittedly, was an eccentric procedure. But Ford conformed so perfectly to the entrepreneurial stereotype as to define it: secretive, taciturn, passionate about engineering, eccentric to the point of lunacy, but crazy (most of the time) like a fox.

No backers of talent in history ever reaped what they sowed more richly than the few who climbed onto Ford's running board. When Ford bought them out, there was one little old lady whose $100 had come back to her 3,550-fold: $95,000 in dividends and $260,000 in the final pay-off. Another, bigger Ford backer cleaned up $17.4 million tax-free on an initial stake of $5,000. The surpassing loveliness of such returns is that they involve little or no effort on the part of the backer, while the backed one works himself to near the bone.

General Doriot, in fact, got sixty percent of Ken Olsen's equity for his $70,000; and although the General's firm provided a lesser amount in loan capital, along with doubtless excellent advice on money matters, there is a certain disproportion in the rewards of the backer (whose bundle was worth $350 million at the apogee) and the backed (even though $90 million, the Olson stake, is enough to keep a Siberia full of wolves from the door for several generations).

In most cases it is dangerous policy for the backer to control the stock—otherwise he may get to think of it as a subsidiary and interfere with the management—or for the backed entrepreneur to hold the thin end—otherwise he may get miffed and move to plusher pastures. When a South African, Mark Weinberg, spotted that the British life insurance industry's selling methods were circa 1817, he also saw how to exploit a delicious opportunity. Weinberg got backing from two American combines, Georgia-Pacific and the ubiquitus ITT, selling his own stake for what proved, in hindsight, to be peanuts. When ITT bought out its partner, the deal cost $38 million. Weinberg's take had been in the thousands; so it surprised nobody when he promptly stepped off to open a rival shop dealing in much the same line of goods.

The odds are heavily stacked against finding a trustee who is both vigorous and self-assertive enough to deliver a big bundle of goods and yet sufficiently mild to tolerate interference from on high. Preferably, high partners should sleep; and the entrepreneur should let sleeping partners lie, unless, that is, he needs their help. Rich, well-connected and self-interested men make excellent advisers; what's more, their counsel comes free.

The disadvantages of the partner who is awake, or thinks he is, can be seen in the saga of Fairchild Camera. Sherman M. Fairchild's inheritance of several noggins of IBM stock did not stop him from showing a marvelous eye for an opportunity. The discovery of a semiconductor group working out of a garage in Palo Alto was perfectly handled. (Another demonstration of the fact that truly rewarding enterprises have an affinity for beginning life in garages, lofts, and workshops in the garden.) Fairchild financed the electronic pioneers, led by William Noyce, to the modest extent that they required, taking an option on their locks, stocks, and barrels. When Noyce's team delivered the semiconductor goods, Fairchild took up its option for $3.5 million—one of the decade's most outright bargains. In just the first of the good, soft years, Fairchild earned as much as $8.4 million from Noyce's inventions.

But under Fairchild in person, as chairman of the board, the growing pains of the semiconductor market were compounded by the upheavals in Fairchild management. The stock gyrated, the managerial *Wunderkinder* came and went.

Although Texas Instruments had its full share of the market troubles, its rise in the same fiendishly clever trade worked out far more impressively. The Texans whose little instrument company found itself sitting on a fortune in silicon chips allowed it to develop its own life. The net result was that every worthy connected with TI, the two original partners, the executives who ran their show, and the Texan watchers who spotted the electronic oil well, eventually sported fortunes worthy of the Spindletop gusher.

The hyperactive partner, along with getting in the way, is prone to the most debilitating disease of the off-track bettor: impatience. The full, fair, and fine reward takes time to mature, like a benign Burgundy. If you try to uncork your Romanée-Conti 1961 too soon, you will miss the ultimate splendor of its bouquet and body. The Ford beneficiaries had to wait sixteen years before the last round-up. Even the great General Doriot's company hung fire for three years at its start, pottered along on a higher plateau for seven more years, spent another decade on a more elevated plateau still, and only then achieved its summit (with a jump from $93 million of net asset value in

1966 to $349 million the next year).

Backing isn't subject to the same laws as stock exchange investment: on the market, one share is never unique: there is always an alternative. The backer, in contrast, is on the hunt for a Unique Buying Proposition, and if a return of Digital Equipment proportions (360,000%, no less) is the object of the chase, the hunter can afford time. What he can seldom afford is to raise his stake continually when the hopeful provider returns for more. All development projects cost more than their developers estimate. But the Unique Buying Proposition must not run up so steep a bill as to remove its own ripest attraction: the modest size of stake in relation to potential.

The well and truly chosen human receptacle of your cash will detest overspending no less than you. The spendthrift, whose initial request is in the millions and who spends all seven figures in the first few months, is like the locust of Africa: let him thrive, and he will strip you bare.

So the backer is in two hazardous activities simultaneously: deciding on the merits and staying power of a business which he doesn't understand, and judging the ability of a particular individual, usually one with no previous achievement, to develop that business.

The backer needs the genius of a brilliant investment banker and the trenchant insight of a selection consultant. There are men with a Midas touch who instinctively back only winners, but in most cases, the ratio of failure to success is as high as must be expected when playing against the odds. The correct response is to spread the risk, even though this dilutes the profit, and to apply rigorous rules to both the backer's functions.

Most so-called "venture capitalists" do not. The only estimate ever made, by *Time* magazine, is that some six hundred firms exist solely to pump money into other people's ventures. They deploy around $3 billion of assets, according to *Time,* and have pumped in annually as much as $700 million, which would exhaust the kitty in little over four years if nothing came up trumps—and often it doesn't. Some four hundred of the US government-backed Small Business Investment Corporations have died since 1964.

Some of the backers have little faith in their essential judgment of the venturer. Take a scion of the Phipps steel line, Paul Bancroft III, who says, "I do not want the president to have control. If his management is not going to make it, you have to be prepared to remove him." But if his management isn't going to make it, very probably neither is the business, no matter who runs the shop. And the kind of man who for the sake of your wealth accepts your whip is not promising material. Still, at least Bancroft has a rule to go by—even if it's a bad one. For the best overriding guide is to stick to your own rules.

The correct lodestar is what, in the past, has worked well for you. If you invariably select men with deep anatomical snuffboxes (there are truly people who believe this wrist formation has some psychological significance), or shun those whose gaze is shifty, or insist on getting a graphologist to give your selection's fine Italian handwriting a going-over, don't break the habit—not because your method means a thing (it doesn't), but because it means something to you, and you are the man whose money is going to have to live with the fellow and his faith.

Unless you, as backer, share this faith, you shouldn't be backing. Half-hearts lead to full ulcers. But faith must have foundations in fact, not fantasy—and if you can't get the facts you need (and intelligent backing needs plenty), you have the wrong fellow. Not that the business protégé can ever be expected to conform, either to his backer's demands or to convention. But even an eccentric must comply, within reason, with the necessities of economics.

It takes, as we have seen, a certain eccentricity to slave for years to enrich somebody else. Great backing demands eccentricity. But taking your eye off the balance sheet, the market reports, the cash flow, the budgets, and all other information, which should be gratefully received—that isn't eccentricity, it's financial kamikaze.

ENTR'ACTE

The Collapse of Uncontrol
or
Look Ma, No Hands

"Minginess" is an occupational disease of the millionaire. Money in the global sense has long ceased to have any meaning. Figures are simple statistics, with the noughts left off the big sums in conversation; thus does familiarity breed respect. But the man to whom "two-fifty" means a quarter of a million dollars is likely to be obsessional about $2.50 or even a quarter.

Psychoanalysts have speculated about the infantile origins of this miserliness. If some of the theorists are to be believed, the best course for any poor mother who wants to have a rich old age is to give her little boy hell on the potty. Unfortunately, cause and effect don't work out so obligingly. Even if all or most millionaires did acquire their retentive habits at stool, it by no means follows that all men with anal problems are worth a million.

A more confident assertion, however, is that the more retentive the Midas is, the more canny, suspicious, supercautious, and self-centered, the more likely he is to last out the long run and to bequeath an intact and inviolate fortune. The historian of wealth must be impressed by the similarities between Gulbenkian, Rockefeller, Getty, Ford, and Hughes: secretive, taciturn men whose grip on their businesses was or is only matched by a firm hold on their privy purses.

The tight way of the wealthy with their own young is a strange expression of this psychological compulsion. The eldest Rockefeller's heir needed just over a million to buy J. Pierpont Morgan's Chinese porcelains from Frick and Widener. The younger Rockefeller didn't happen to have a million in cash, applied to his father for a loan, and was turned down. Rather than lose the beautiful objects, Rockefeller, a man of forty-one, wrote a begging letter to his father that, even after the passage of half a century, has a pathetic ring.

He told his father that "I have never squandered money on horses, yachts, automobiles or other foolish extravagances." Collecting porcelains ("the only thing on which I care to spend money") was a costly hobby but "quiet and unostentatious and not sensational." Then John D. II delivered the knockout. "The money put into these porcelains . . . is all there, and while not income-producing, I have every reason to believe that . . . a sale under ordinary circumstances would certainly realize their full cost value, and, as the years go by, more. . . ." He got his million—as a gift, not a loan.

A public relations genius, Ivy Lee, converted this vice of Rockefeller I into a virtue by instituting the giving away of dimes by his narrow-fisted employer. Whatever John D. thought about this prodigality, stories about Getty (with his pay telephone kiosk installed at Sutton Place for the benefit of his visitors) and of Henry Ford I show them adhering to the same sound maxim, "Don't look after the pennies, and the pounds won't look after themselves."

Another art story, told by S. N. Behrman, recounts the rare collaboration of the leading New York art dealers, including Duveen, to offer Henry Ford I, the last untapped billionaire in the world (it was during the Depression, and they were desperate), the choicest items from their combined stock. They produced a sumptuous catalogue, which he received with much gratitude. They then tentatively suggested that Ford might like to purchase the items he was admiring. "But, gentlemen," asked Ford, "what would I want with the original pictures when the ones right here in these books are so beautiful?"

Men with deep collective experience of the excessively rich should perhaps have known better. Their success, especially Duveen's, in persuading equally close men, like Frick and Andrew Mellon, to pay astronomical sums for the priceless and for its housing (Frick's palazzo on Fifth Avenue and Mellon's marble National Gallery in Washington, thanks to Duveen, are the costliest monuments of the epoch) blinded them to the equal tendency of the rich to grasp free handouts.

One transatlantic emigrant to Britain, although rich enough to eat a hundred dinners a day at the Mirabelle or Savoy Grill, was constitutionally incapable of refusing an invitation to a free meal. Nubar Gulbenkian, the free-spending, chatty son of the tight-fisted, close-mouthed Calouste, was another who found free food all but irresistible —even though he could and did afford to have Lucullan repasts delivered from his favorite Caprice during a particularly enjoyable legal action in London. Nubar was the author of the perceptive remark that "not knowing how to spend a lot of money is the least of life's problems"; although, since his father Calouste kept Nubar on a tight financial rein, getting a lot of money to spend was Nubar's own major anxiety.

Possibly the rich feel easier about accepting gifts because there is no prospect of their being bribed. But whatever the cause, they can never resist the lure of something for nothing, any more than, when offered a deal, they can spurn a profit of several hundred percent. The liking for free samples and free dinners is part and parcel of the acquisitive urge, a lust which they conceal behind standard non sequiturs, such as the immortal line that millions mean nothing to them, because they can only eat three meals a day. Or, as one Francis Leo Cappaert put it, "I don't care how big you are. You can only drive a Cadillac, you can only drink champagne."

To that, the retort discourteous is that, if nature would allow, many millionaires would eat many times more, drive many Cadillacs, and corner the entire supply of Bollinger '69. As it is, they indulge other appetites where satiation point is further removed. Even the Rockefeller-type recluse always has some diversion on which he spends inordinately.

The I-dotting, T-crossing, punctilious, meticulous, introverted recluse even spends in an organized, controlled manner. In business, if not in enjoyment in life, he has a clear edge over the extravagant extrovert who uses his money and the company's with merry abandon. One giveaway of the con company, in fact, is the giveaway itself. The firm which lavishes free liquor, free flights to faraway places, and free entertainment on journalists and other contacts, or the firm whose executive living standards are lush beyond reason, is rightly suspect on those counts alone. There was no greater cornucopia of goodies for all than Bernie Cornfeld's IOS: just as Mr. Nixon's CREEP election committee had many a lavish creep on its secret books.

By the opposite token, stinginess with company money is an encouraging sign, and for good reason. The excellent manager knows in his finger bones that a pound, dollar, mark, franc, lire, or yen spent represents not only an outflow of currency, but the disbursement of the yield, profit, or return from *several* pounds, dollars, marks, francs, lire, or yen of hard-won business. To the professional miser the ideal situation is one in which he spends nothing at all. That being impossible, he concentrates on spending only when inevitability strikes—which to him means when there is some measurable return from the expenditure.

Among the West's richest private accumulators is an eccentric whose septuagenarian hand will not allow executives to travel abroad unless they can prove that their journey is of direct financial value to the company. Such nitpicking is silly, and possibly self-defeating: executives quickly become adept at shifting spending from a banned area to an allowable zone, for one thing: and, for another, nobody ever measures the loss a company may have suffered from hoarding its money unwisely.

But certain benefits flow from the nit-picking mentality. He who stamps on all unnecessary spending must have some system of identifying and measuring what is necessary. He who forbids spending on this, that, or the other frivolity must have some system of checking what is actually spent, by whom, and on what. In other words, he must have control; and effective control, especially of the purse, is the heartbeat of all sustained business successes.

A would-be Last of the Big Spenders, in contrast, has very little idea of who is spending what, when, and why— sometimes even how. This lack of control is a concomitant of the big spending. If somebody is actually counting the outflow of cash, somebody else is liable to break out in a nervous rash at the sums. If nobody is counting, nobody cares.

In the palmy days of Investors Overseas Services, when Cornfeld could still pose as a kind of messiah of people's capitalism, his acolytes were wont to hymn the praises of the unique IOS management system. The uniqueness lay solely in the fact that nobody at headquarters had the feeblest notion of the company's financial condition—even when it was sick unto death. The $52 million raised by the IOS public offering disappeared in five months; in fact, the kitty was down to $1 million on the day this check arrived.

By the time anybody had diagnosed that the worldwide cash flow, instead of running at $100 million a month, as Cornfeld claimed, was strikingly negative, the hemorrhage of money had reached fatal proportions; a $30 million projected profit was heading down first to $25 million, then to $17.9 million, then to $10.3 million, at which point it meant no profit on normal business at all. The company had spent, in six months, $25 million in buying its own stock, $6.3 million to shore up IOS banks, $15 million on loans to outside companies, and $28.7 million on loans to assorted insiders, including $4.9 million for Cornfeld's very own BAC-111 jet.

A moving passage in Andrew Tobias' account of National Student Marketing Corp., another star example of the get-rich-quick-get-poor-even-quicker company, spells out the meaning of lack of control. NSMC laid out $750,-000 a year on renting its Park Avenue offices, in which it stayed one year, but on which it spent $400,000 for furnishings. It maintained offices to a similar standard in five other metropolitan centers; and ran up $1 million a year on a loss-making force of campus representatives.

The annual report, Tobias says, cost $150,000, or roughly $10 a shareholder. A good rule of thumb is that the glossier the annual report, in appearance and literary flavor, the more suspect the company. When Litton Industries started venturing into the higher realms of Western philosophy in its report to shareholders, MENE MENE TEKEL UPHARSIN was written on its walls, as surely as it had been on Nebuchadnezzar's. Nobody who cares about money hires PR boys (known as flacks in the trade) to waffle about Aristotle and Spinoza.

Other items on the wrong side of NSMC's ledger included $100,000 fees for company-wide audits, an effort at producing a company organization chart, and a 278-page proxy statement. On the latter issue, it's another not so incidental point that the takeover game, to which growth companies are incurably addicted, is an appalling expense. When Imperial Chemical Industries made an abortive stab at the Courtaulds textile giant, the futile cost in stamp duty on the shares acquired came to a million—and that takes no account of the fees paid to merchant banks, to newspapers for advertising space, to the PR geniuses, and so on.

When Maxwell Joseph won the Watney brewing business for Grand Metropolitan Hotels, he inherited a vast bankers' bill, rung up by Watneys in its own defense, to add to the fortune that Grand Met had spent on its own account. Even if the Big Spending wheeler-dealer doesn't overspend for his acquisitions, as most do, the bill for the technical consummation of the deals amounts to a generous slice of corporate overhead.

Tobias concludes that NSMC's overhead was actually rising faster than its earnings as the company moved toward nemesis (little items like a $720,000 Lear executive jet helped fly it along the way). It thus followed that, unless the company made acquisitions, its earnings would decline. But it also followed that if it made more buys, the overhead would rise faster still. Nor is it only buys that cripple the Big Spender's accounts: it's also New Ventures.

Because the business which is out of control never counts its costs, new ventures aren't counted, either; whatever is spent, after all, is bound to come back a thousand-fold. Cortes Wesley Randell, who, at the height of NSMC's fortunes, had some $60 million of its stock, a $600,000 castle in Virginia, a hydrofoil, a New York hotel suite, and a fifty-five-foot yacht, was an ace at new ventures as well as new companies. The cost of his forays was allowed to swan out of sight; hence items like $533,000 in "deferred new product development and start-up costs" in the 1969 accounts.

The theory behind such entries is that tomorrow this expenditure will be covered by the profits it has generated; so today you boost the accounts by $533,000 which haven't actually been earned. This, too, bespeaks lack of control: the venturer is running up costs he can't afford, so he pretends that they haven't really been incurred.

Less assiduous overspenders than Randell have one good excuse. Few businesses, even few small firms, have perfect systems of control; they have systems which are adequate (or inadequate) for their present purposes and present manipulators. While a business pours forth cash, whatever system its creator uses is safely hidden under the Niagara

Falls of wealth. But if a dry period comes, and the creator is as slapdash as most Big Spenders, an awful sequence of events automatically follows.

First, he (like the world) finds out about the horror too late. Second, because of the lack of system, he doesn't find out its full extent. Third, the lack of control that allowed the catastrophe to start also means that there's no mechanism to stop the disaster from developing: the vehicle lacks brakes as well as steering.

The Du Pont family, which should have picked up a thing or two about business methods over the years, provides a case in sharp point: an unusual diversification, started in 1931, a brokerage firm called F. I. Du Pont. The second generation nurtured this house into a position of high respect on Wall Street. When Wall Street as a whole stumbled and bumbled into the most appalling débâcle since the Great Crash, a crazy pavement of paperwork and bookkeeping failures, the Du Ponts were in the van. They had to be bailed out, of all indignities, by the Johnny-come-lately Texan computer billionaire H. Ross Perot (who failed no less miserably himself, so great was the shambles).

The initial bail was set at $70 million. It was discovered, among other mind-boggling facts, that this venerable house settled its books not every day, not every week, not even every month—but once a year. Small wonder that staggering sums were missing and couldn't be traced. Before its collapse, Du Pont had hastily merged with Glore Forgan, whose Russell Forgan once observed sagely that "Wall Street firms pay a lot of attention to how companies run their businesses. But we don't pay enough attention to managing our own firms." The catch is that Forgan said this not after the event, but in 1963, long before his firm and then the merged operation with Du Pont went down the mismanagement drain.

The elementary controls on Wall Street, the nerve center of modern capitalism, were so weak that at least $500 million of customers' securities seems to have disappeared by simple theft. One reason for this monumental incompetence was the highly personal nature of Wall Street's organization. The firms are dominated by their partners, who in turn are dominated by the senior members among them, men who have often either inherited their wealth or made it the easy way by moving along some inside track.

John Thackray has calculated that for $300,000, which used to be the price of a seat on the New York Stock Exchange (in 1973 it shrank to $72,000, compared to a high of $515,000 in 1958), a richly structured, none too bright gentleman could in four hours of leisurely work do well enough by selling stock to himself, his rich relatives, and wealthy friends to pick up $200,000 a year, or twice the standard income for a millionaire. With such easy money floating around, its recipients couldn't be bothered with mundane matters of financial and management control.

On top of the thefts, they therefore collectively lost at least another $500 million through rotten bookkeeping; the NYSE alone had to pay out $100 million to pacify the customers of crashed brokers. These crashes, near-crashes, and terrible frights all had a direct effect on family fortunes, because a brokerage business is much nearer than most to the personal affairs of its participants.

In contrast the limited liability company, which has now appeared on Wall Street, can effectively insulate a rich man from what, in all justice, should be the loss of his riches. The company goes bankrupt, the value of the stock thuds down to nil—but if the owner has taken proper precautions, the wolf can be kept far away from his door, or his wife's.

Many a crashed tycoon benefits from the noncoincidental fact that his wife has enough in hand to make substantial contributions to a lavish family budget. "The wife's name" is one of the oldest techniques of financial self-preservation in the book; like many ancient devices, it has been carried to a fine pitch in modern times.

But even if you can avoid, by this or some other device, the extreme penalty of failure, there is a fearful pain in a comedown, a heartache that no amount of millions can wholly ease. For the likes of Jimmy Ling, the fact that his once proud flagship is now under other admirals is liable to hurt even more than the loss of personal status symbols, like $2 million palaces in Texas.

The mechanics of control, in fact, have nothing to do with its effectiveness. Many of the Wall Street firms which bit the dust had computers attempting to do their clerking; some computer software houses, stacked with electronic data-processing aces, fell over their own overambitious plans—like a scheme for automating grocery movements which died, after $15 million had been spent on it, still $5 million short of the amount needed to bring it to realization.

Few no-hands stories are sadder than a tragedy in Toyland, where Ruth and Elliot Handler, parents of the Barbie doll, had to surrender executive control of Mattel, the company which they created—and where they held thirty percent of the stock. When Ruth Handler resigned as president (to share the chair with her husband), the company had just been forced to suspend its quarterly dividends after one loss-making year ($29.9 million of red ink) was followed with another, and its stock had slumped by three-quarters.

The story sprang in part—and ironically—from one of the Handlers' greatest hits, Hot Wheels die-cast toy cars. Hot Wheels appeared to have triumphed over the British competitor, Lesney Products, which had virtually created the market for cheap die-cast cars but had paid the penalty for many sins of omission: lack of technical development (Mattel's thin axles made a vital difference to the speed of the pushed car); lack of merchandising skills; shallow management; excessive factory space; undiversified product lines—and several of the other ills which two ex-servicemen, waxing suddenly rich on a business built on a postwar gratuity, developed as they became older, overstretched, and more careless.

But while Lesney's two proprietors buckled down to repairing their lacks, Mattel grew more careless still: spending disproportionately on advertising and failing to recognize that Lesney had one basic strength: it could produce its little cars far more cheaply. As Lesney fought back, Hot Wheels lost its market dominance: but uncontrolled promotion wasn't the only area where the Handlers' hands were off the handlebars.

A vice president acquired from Litton Industries had been acquiring in the good old Litton manner: playground equipment, magnetic tapes, a circus (Ringling Bros.), metal frames. The latter offshoot, in a typical diversifiers' disaster, failed to spot the trend to frameless home aquariums, and made heavy losses—as did a new venture into electric musicmaking, with a machine called, none too euphoniously, the Optigan. While all this was going on, proper financial control wasn't. Accounts receivable trebled in three years, and Elliot Handler was still able to predict a profit eighteen days before the significant 1972-73 loss had to be unveiled to jaundiced shareholders, some of whom promptly sued Mattel's management, including Ruth Handler, for selling around a million of stock while still making optimistic noises.

The stupidity is that gaining control and keeping it are the basic administrative arts; anybody can buy them. The rich man needs simply to realize that control problems not only may exist, but almost certainly do.

Take a big, famous publicly owned company like Boeing, source of many of the millionaires around Seattle. The Boeing hits with the 707, 727, and 747 had snatched the civil palm from the faltering Douglas kin (and, doubtless, intensified the pressure on the latter to grab something back with the DC-9). The Seattle company was the wonder of the aerospace world; yet, when recession struck, it was revealed by its own internal admissions to be poorly controlled and inadequately managed.

When orders fell sharply, it took the Boeing brass over a year to realize the implications. When the fall inevitably hit the production line, the brass, desperate for economics, found that operations were woefully inefficient, that two separate divisions making the 707 and the 727 were warring pointlessly with each other; that the 727, in one version, had the range but didn't have the economics; while in the other, it made money but couldn't reach its destination.

So the tale of woe unfolded in a company that, after a previous loss of profits, had already undergone far-reaching overhaul of its methods. When the managerial experts can falter so fatally, the surprise is rather that more self-raising millionaires don't slide back into the slough. Probably the fact that the money is all, or mostly, theirs tends to concentrate the mind or at least, to bring them back to reality in time—if not in time to save the ship and the crew, in time to rescue the captain and as much of his gear as the lifeboat will carry. It's not only rats that leave a sinking ship with full bellies.

ACT IV

On the Sense of
Safety First

or

A Bird in the Bush Is
Worth Two in
the Hand

SCENE 1

The Value of Finance

or

Always a Borrower and a Lender Be

Many sound rules of management are hollow counsel for
would-be millionaires. Those words of Polonius to his son
Laertes—"neither a borrower nor a lender be"—are fine
for the innumerable big-, middle-, and small-time managements that have lumbered their companies with dead-
weights of debt. But one of the highest common factors of
millionaires *is* their high level of indebtedness.

If you're as rich as Croesus, how come you need other
people's money? The wealthy use wealth belonging to others (a) because it costs little or nothing to borrow, (b) because the borrowing enables them to achieve a far higher
equity profit, (c) because it enables them to employ their
entire capital in the way they like best, which is gainfully,
and (d) because people are dying to lend them money.

There are odd exceptions, like the booster of Midland,
Texas, who paid for its first hotel with a $1 million check
and financed its extension in the same simple way. Another
Texas oil man, stating that "I worked for Mr. Interest long
enough," displays an ignorance of financial process that is
often no impediment to financial progress. Far more millionaires would subscribe to the sentiments of yet a third
Texan, Clint Murchison, who observed succinctly that
"cash makes a man careless." Henry Ford, notoriously
simple in these matters, thought that you should "get yourself $400 million or $500 million in cash, tuck it away and
forget about it. It will come in handy some time for a rainy
day."

Garfield Weston's Canadian-based food empire, now
ranging from Loblaw's supermarkets to Fortnum & Mason,
enabled him to tuck away so much that he could actually

afford to make the RAF a present of some Spitfire fighters in World War II. Weston nevertheless used to claim in later days that he never had any money in the bank; just debts. And, he might have added, an empire worth $1.3 billion under his personal control.

In constructing these edifices, debt usually plays either a central or a critical ancillary role. The cash-tucker Henry Ford put not a cent into his original company. The most numerous postwar crop of millionaires—the property developers of London—burgeoned from loaned money that ultimately belonged to the mass owners of insurance policies.

The borrowing paradox can be resolved by a truly homely example. In most countries in the postwar world, the shrewdest stratagem open to anybody was to buy his own house in an established and improving area beloved of the middle to upper classes; then to mortgage that house to the hilt of his financial ability.

The mortgage arithmetic is irresistible. Suppose the family bought a £10,000 house and borrowed £8,000 from a home loans company at X percent (the actual rate of interest doesn't matter, for reasons to be explained). Over twenty years, say, the loan must be repaid, but in steadily depreciating banknotes. For example, even if the entire loan is repaid only at the end of the twenty years (which can easily be arranged), a mortgage of £8,000 paid off in 1972 equals a payment of £4,000 in 1952 currency.

All this time, the loan has been safely secured by the house; provided that its value has risen, the borrower can always clear his debt and still come out ahead. The postwar period has staged few exceptions to the inexorable rise in property prices. After twenty years, if the house has managed to rise by seven percent per annum (many have far outstripped this pace), it will be worth £40,000.

Remember that only £2,000 of the borrower's own money went into the house. So in twenty years he has made a profit of £38,000, or sixteen percent per annum at compound interest. That profit is equal to a simple interest on the £8,000 loan of twenty-four percent a year—handsomely higher than any rate of interest conceivably charged; that's one reason why the actual interest rate doesn't much matter. Another is that the interest is deductible against tax: if the top slice of income is taxable at fifty percent, the net cost of £8,000 for twenty years at ten percent is not £16,000, but £8,000; at five percent interest, the net works out at £4,000.

Multiply the key figures by ten, and you get a £380,000 profit on a £100,000 house; a man who would have paid that much in 1952 might well have occupied the ninety percent upper tax reaches. His net cost of borrowing £80,-000 for two decades would have been exactly £12,000 at 7.5%. That's some millstone. The higher the debt, the greater the return on the equity. If every pound or dollar you deploy can be made into ten by borrowing, and you make only one currency unit clear on every *tranche* of cash, you double your money every time.

The trick is either to get the money advanced on the security of the treasure you want to buy—as in house purchase—or to manage matters magically so that the money is loaned on no security at all. Either way, the borrower can take profitable action that would otherwise have been barred by lack of funds.

Borrowing against existing collateral has the same effect—but the disadvantage that you need such collateral in the first place. Many of London's property millionaires were once in no such happy position but knew how to manage. One future financier was markedly short of currency when a beautiful vision, a site behind Fleet Street, swam before his eyes. He hastily purchased a month's option, and rushed around to his bank to procure a short-term loan, secured by the option; he then ran even faster to an insurance company and persuaded the insurers to promise the purchase and construction money if he could find a tenant; he then sped fastest of all to a company looking for new premises and let them the entire future building—the tenant, of course, was impressed by the insurance company's backing. At this point the developer had a guaranteed profit, on an outlay of nothing but his time and shoe leather, which came to a clear million.

In those days, however, British insurance companies were a more innocent bunch. Latterly they have come to demand a piece of the action themselves, which has somewhat reduced the charm of such operations. The reduction was nothing like so great, however, as that accomplished by the property men themselves. Thrilled to pieces by the availability of floods of money under Edward Heath's Conservatives, they put every penny they could borrow into buildings—and were thus caught, hopelessly over-borrowed, when the Heathites meanly smacked property developers between the eyes, fiscally speaking. So much for charm.

The charm, indeed, can be insidious. The ease with which money floats into the developers' hands, plus the rapidity with which rents and thus building values rise, deceives the borrower into forgetting that, if no difference results between the development cost and the resale value of his piece of Throgmorton Street or Wall Street, he earns not a penny.

The craziest force of nature ever to hit the New York property scene, that stout party named Bill Zeckendorf, demonstrated the risks with a spectacular failure. The amounts he could borrow in orthodox ways failed to satisfy his wayward genius. So he sliced up his buildings like so much pastrami, into tiers of convoluted debt; even the debts had debts.

This broke the golden rule of borrowing, which is never to borrow more than you could, by some practicable form of selling, recover in full. Otherwise, the borrower is in the uncomfortable position known as "overextended,"—or, as the victims of the Spanish Inquisition knew it, on the rack. The less you need money, the more easily it can be borrowed; the more urgent your need, the harder it is to borrow—and the higher the interest charges soar.

It isn't merely a question of ensuring that assets cover debts (or, to use the rightly ominous technical word, liabilities). The assets must be reasonably quick: you must be able to realize them in an emergency, such as a sudden voracious demand by the lender for his money back. If you can't deliver, he will devour and you will be dead. In this context, Zeckendorf's words, "I prefer to stay alive at eighteen percent than to be dead at the prime rate," have a ghoulish ring.

Many an overextended entrepreneur has found his fixed interest lender pocketing the entire business. In a bankruptcy, the equity in even a flourishing business suddenly becomes so much dross; the first come, the secured lenders, are the first served—and usually the last, since they swallow the lot. That is why the truly clever borrower aims for the perfect situation: where he borrows at nil interest, where the loan is not secured on any of his assets, and where he doesn't even have to repay it.

Who, you may ask, lends at nil interest? Governments habitually do. Major industrial corporations have been known to, in pursuance of what they fondly imagine to be their real interest: the mighty Imperial Chemical Industries, the leading chemical company in Europe, lent millions for nothing at a time when its own borrowing costs were eight percent. The secret is to offer the giant the one thing for which, above all others, it slavers: guaranteed sales of its products.

Provided that the supplier avoids getting screwed on price, he puts the giant in a tactically impossible fix. To keep the trade, it must keep the supplier's business alive—even if that means largely financing the operation. The executives concerned seldom reflect, even in this sad event, that they might as well have started the operation themselves and kept the whole bundle in company hands—sales, equity profits, and all.

Kaye Metrebian briskly turned himself into a multimillionaire by exploiting the various reaches of trade credit. He had failed to sell America on the somewhat specialized virtues of Cypriot wines, had lost his partner and money simultaneously in a cloth-selling venture on Seventh Avenue, and had suffered an up and down career in Italy; then in 1958 he hit on the idea of selling nylon sheets in Britain on unsecured credit.

He drove to his selected fabric supplier in a large blue Cadillac, parked outside the offices, kept his hand on the horn to pretend it was stuck until everybody in the building, including the managing director, looked out. Metrebian was not asked for bank references; the only question was whether he wanted credit for thirty days or sixty. Metrebian's next borrowing was a more orthodox affair. A bank lent him ninety percent of the £210,000 needed to buy a factory.

But the real take-off lay in Metrebian's deal with British Enkalon, a subsidiary of a Dutch giant desperate to crack a UK market dominated by Imperial Chemical Industries. Metrebian in short order got a cheap price for nylon, ninety days' credit (equal to at least £1 million), and a loan of £1 million, which carried a rate of interest so low that it shamed even the Dutch. The Armenian borrower didn't mind. His 1973 turnover was £27 million and the putative value of the wholly owned Armenian equity was some £50 million; that of British Enkalon at that time was actually £15 million.

In the US, the two promoters who spawned Holiday Inns have made equally constructive use of debt. Kemmons Wilson loves to say that he never wanted to own a million dollars, but to owe it. Significantly enough, both he and his partner, Wallace E. Johnson, started in housebuilding, homes being the easiest security for loans. By 1965 Wilson and Johnson were paying interest on their debts which amounted to $10,000 a day—a comforting situation, if you can meet the interest, but not nearly so comfortable as the formula that founded Holiday Inns.

The first few hotels were built from whatever resources Wilson himself could muster. But once he met Johnson, the pair hit on the marvelous notion of the franchise. They found other men with money or access to money (which comes to the same thing) and generously allowed the latter to build a hotel for the chain, and, what's more, to pay Holiday Inns for the privilege.

The franchisee of a 120-room inn gets a six to ten percent return on investment, and supposedly treble that on equity. But he must find at least $1 million, and will pay, among other tolls, $15,000 a year license fee and a minimum royalty of fifteen cents a night for each room (at 365 nights a year, that comes to $65,700: not a bad return on $1 million of somebody else's money).

Holiday Inns could never have been built to a 400-inn scale, making it the largest hotel chain in the world, without this neat variation of borrowing, at no interest, with no security, and without repayment. The franchisee has to find the borrowed capital, leaving Wilson and Johnson to pursue the delights of borrowing millions on their own accounts, pocketing the equity profits as they come. Those profits came to $65.6 million in 1971; Wilson's and Johnson's creation had a stock market value at the end of 1972 of $1.2 billion.

The obvious question is how, if borrowing is so beautifully beneficial to the borrower, lending can be good for lenders. That depends partly on the lender. Sources of money fall into three groups: the rich, the professional usurers, the involuntary money lenders. The accidental ones are those who had no intention of lending anything to anybody, but ended up that way because they weren't paid.

All trade credit falls roughly into this category. One multimillionaire chain store tycoon used to be visited once a month by the chairman of a food firm; after some pleasant chat about business, the weather, and world affairs, the food boss would raise the subject of the overdue bill for fodder, the store magnate would write a check, and his guest would climb into his Rolls for the ride back home. When somebody suggested to the manufacturer that this was a wild way for the chairman of a major company to behave, he agreed; but, he said, "If I didn't do it, I wouldn't get paid for six months."

The greatest coup in the history of involuntary financing was pulled by history's most inventive engineer, Henry Ford I. He had made the cardinal error of allowing his debts to mount far above his quick assets, and the Wall Street wolves were closing for the kill. At this point, Ford I turned on his dealers; he shipped out every car in the inventory and demanded payment on the nose.

By this inspired device, Henry routed the bankers and tapped a whole new source of free finance: the money-raising problem was passed on to Ford dealers, whose own survival depended on maintaining a flow of Model T's. Up to that point, of course, Ford had been involuntarily banking his dealers; now he merely reversed the position, thus confirming the law that, like water finding its own level, money always eventually flows from the weak to the strong.

This need not mean from the poor to the rich. It is perfectly possible to be both wealthy and weak, especially if the loot is inherited. Many an heir has been a soft touch for the plausible borrower who has no earthly hope of tapping any harder source. Generally speaking, however, the rich are mean—and if they part with their means, they do so at the highest interest that money can fetch and on the most stringent conditions.

One borrower, a millionaire himself, emerged from a borrowing brush with a still richer man, intact but gasping. "The old man does love his rate of interest," he noted— and it is that love that distinguishes the successful lender from the professional sucker; and most professional, corporate lenders sooner or later fit, or get fitted, into the latter category.

American pros have long shown great awareness of the

cardinal truism that, in lending, profit equals the margin between the price you pay for money and the price at which you sell it, less the cost of collection and disbursement. Money can be obtained free by banks accepting ordinary deposits; otherwise its price of purchase is more or less fixed by circumstances outside the lender's control. To a great extent, so is the price of resale; but with one vital difference. Pro lenders pay interest only on the actual sums deposited with them. On borrowings, however, they contrive to charge interest on the entire sum lent, regardless of how much has been repaid.

Installment loans thus enabled financiers to borrow at nine percent and lend at eighteen percent: the double mark-up may look the same as borrowing at three percent and lending at six percent, but don't you believe it. With a million out on loan, the gross profit in the first case is $90,000; in the second only $30,000. The fastest-growing finance houses in the Western world have been those which exploited this simple truth: that the name of the game is the figure on the loan.

Again, by definition, the weakest members of the economic system pay the highest rates: the family buying its car and kitchen equipment on an installment plan, the individual forced into taking a personal loan, the business that is strapped for cash. In 1973 the British government felt obliged to take action against a whole new army of lenders who had battened onto a special group of the middle class: those whose sole security was their already mortgaged home. The lenders offered, say, "£1,000 for only £2.30 a week." In an actual case, those weeks stretched out for fifteen years. By the time the borrower had finished, his repayments would have totaled £3,000—true interest rate of twenty-five percent. That pays back the lender's money in roughly three years, after which the money just rolls in free. In one case, the rate actually reached 280% in a year.

Every now and again one of the new lending operations gets caught in its own web: Billy Sol Estes trapped Walter E. Heller, the shrewdest finance house in the Midwest, into lending money on his nonexistent grain silos. But more often than not it's the big, respectable pro lender like American Express (the principal victim of the salad oil swindling of Tino de Angelis) that falls for the pro fraud.

Not that Amex had any great need to maximize its loan rates: like insurance companies, deposit banks, and other money engines, Amex contrives to get the use of other people's money for nothing—because of the time lag between selling travelers' checks to the customers and the point when the checks are cashed and Amex must turn over the dough. The size of this "float" in 1972 was a cool billion dollars. That's some flotation—an essential part of the skillful use of borrowing and lending. The idea is to ensure that time is always on your side, that you have the maximum use of the money for the maximum time at the minimum cost.

For most borrowers, however, the main problem is to find the money at all. They advance on the sources of cash diffidently, expecting to be refused, and they pitch their demands at a modest level. This is not only bad finance, it's poor psychology. In the first place, borrowers should always have access to more than they need—partly because they are likely to need more, anyway. In the second place, psychology counts: big men are always impressed by big numbers; nobody gets much charge from lending £5,000. But £5 million is another matter—and anybody who wants to borrow that big must (so the idiot reasoning runs) have big ideas and big capacities.

In Britain, an eager venturer named Charles Gordon prised the colossal sum of £50 million for his Spey Investments from a group of institutional backers for depositing in companies of Gordon's choice under Gordon's management (although there was some shortage of proof that the management could cope).

Much of this money was secured on loans that were themselves secured on securities in subsidiary private companies; and what those latter securities were worth was a matter of opinion. True, the generous lenders owned part of Spey; but, even more generously, they had left to Gordon voting control and the lion's share of the profits—had there been any. There weren't: the ramshackle edifice ran into losses and had to be hastily broken up to save the red institutional faces.

But pro lenders are in the habit of feeding fortunes to their borrowers without noticing it. The whole miraculous process was encapsulated in the ceremony that surrounded the delivery of the *Globtik Tokyo,* all 480,000 tons of the vessel, on February 20, 1972. The Kashmiri owner, one Ravi Tikkoo, totally unknown a few years previously, handed over a check for £17.2 million when accepting the ship from the Japanese builders. As the *Financial Times* observed at the time, this was "largely a paper transaction." Mitsui and Co. of Japan had lent four-fifths of the money, at the staggeringly low cost of 6 percent; British banks had paid the rest. On delivery day, the gap between cost and insurance value was £4.9 million, every penny of which belonged to Tikkoo's very own Globtik Tankers, a £100 company. That's nice work—and you can really get it, if you try.

SCENE 2

The Cushion of Corporations
or
The Company Way Is by Me Okay

The balance of economic power has shifted overwhelmingly to the side of the big corporations, which might, for lovers of the free and rugged entrepreneur, spell a sad reduction in the individual's ability to wax exceedingly rich. Not to worry: the coming of the corporation has spawned a host of new, easy methods of making millions—and several of these lush avenues are within the corporation itself.

For those who lack a rich daddy, the safest method is to join a rich company. After all, with sales of $1 billion, profits of $100 million, and a stock market value of $2 billion, you need only 0.1% of the first, 1% of the second, and 0.05% of the last to pass the million mark and head off toward the upper reaches. And if the gambits fail, for reasons of incompetence or accident, the player can still fall back on the soft cushion of a plump salary and a fat pension.

Minneapolis-St. Paul is said to be littered with the millionaires made by 3M, for this salesmen's conglomerate carries the typical characteristics of the big corporation to extremes. Its whole system of rewards, from the commissions paid to salesmen, to the dummy stock by which managers get their profit-linked bonuses, to the stock options that grace the top echelon's safe deposit boxes, is geared to the creation of individual riches.

It is excruciatingly hard, in any country where the taxman knows what he is doing and can't be bribed to do otherwise, to assemble $1 million out of income—let alone £1 million. It's not impossible, though. At $200,000 a year, by no means an uncommon American reward, an executive can pile together $4 million in twenty years at the top. If the statistics are right, and no American pays as much as half his income in taxes, that leaves at least $2 million; if he banks half, that gives him $50,000 a year on which to live—plus, presumably, some income and capital gain from the accumulated savings.

As with companies, moreover, a heavy cash flow has uses and charms of its own—which, no doubt, is why inordinately wealthy men like Henry Ford II (who resides in his company's salary grade twenty-eight) insist on paying themselves inordinate salaries and bonuses (for Ford, $878,746 in 1973).

The wealthy are by no means shy when it comes to using devices originally invented to enrich the underprivileged executive. The Watson family of IBM is among the best-heeled in the world, worth an estimated $400 million in IBM stock alone; not counting what is left from the founding Watson's salary, which was running at $1,000 a day back in 1934. Yet Tom Watson Jr., though by no means the most avaricious or self-assertive of tycoons, didn't count himself out when the stock options were being offered. No: he exercised the option and came up with a paper profit—to take one year as an example—of $1.9 million.

That incident, which is duplicated in almost every company with an heir in the executive suite, should give the lie to the otherwise engaging theory that stock options are there to motivate, sustain, and finally reward executives for their labors on behalf of the shareholders. On the contrary, the options have one purpose, and one purpose only, which is to make the executives as rich as possible and in the

most painless possible way, without risk and at the shareholders' expense.

The beneficiary of the shareholders' involuntary largesse
usually doesn't have to pay a red cent until he chooses to
take up the option—and he makes that choice only if the
shares have risen sharply enough to offer him a pretty
piece of immediate profit. In that blessed event, he can finance the payment by borrowing on the collateral—and if
the price holds up, can eventually convert his paper profit
into the real stuff without having run any risk or spent any
money. If there's no paper profit, being no idiot, he shuns
the option.

The cost to the shareholder is wrapped up in mythology
and mechanics. The myth is that, without these inducements, the cosseted executives either wouldn't work for the
company at all, or wouldn't work as well. There is no
proof that executives garlanded with options are any more
effective than those who simply work for their livings; and
Western Germany, whose economy and companies have
vastly outperformed the US, knows these devices not at all.

If options are so effective, anyway, why would a company also need profit-linked bonus schemes? There is no
sensible answer; yet most big American corporate nests are
feathered in both ways. The object, again, is to maximize,
optimize, and generally elevate the executives' wealth; it
presumably never occurs to the beneficiaries that every extra $2 million paid to the management cadre is $2 million
off the pretax profit—thus to some extent negating the executives' good work on behalf of themselves as option
holders.

The shareholder-robbing mechanics of options are less
blatant but still apparent to the discerning eye. Take the
Tom Watson Jr. case again. He paid $357,000 for his IBM
option; where did the $1.9 million difference between that
figure and the available selling price arise? At first sight,
the money seems to have been created out of thin air; at
the most, surely, you could say that it came from the pockets of unknown, mythical investors who might have bought
IBM shares at the lower price at the same time and instead
are buying them from Watson now (if he sells) at a much
inflated figure.

There is, however, a harder, clearer reality. The effect is
exactly the same as if, at the latter date, IBM had sold the

same number of shares to the public in a money-raising operation, but had turned over $1.9 million of the proceeds to the chairman and chief executive of the day. It is a straight gift of cash from the shareholders' equity to the executive. The only difference between the option and straight pay is that circumspection demands that the latter be kept within reasonable bounds, while the sky is the limit for the option: and the gift, if cashed in, pays lower tax (twenty-five percent in the US, thirty percent in the UK when options were legally privileged) than the salary.

The shares, of course, have to appreciate handsomely to make the beneficiaries into instant millionaires. It used to be said of Litton Industries, a company so red-hot for capital gains that it paid out stock instead of dividends, that Charles B. Thornton and Roy Ash, Litton's inventors, had in a mere decade made themselves millionaires thirty or forty times over and made a score of other executives millionaires along the way. But unless they sold out along the road, none of that happy score are Litton millionaires today—from 1971 onward, as Litton sunk from decline into fall, piling up horrendous losses, mostly under the impact of its shipbuilding fiascos, the share price slumped to a tenth of its former glory. Options can thus backfire for the executive as well as the shareholder; although that will never stop companies from offering instant millions, so long as the law allows.

There is rough justice in options, in one sense. Running a big corporation is no idle game; it may even be excruciatingly hard work, executed under a mighty weight of responsibility. General Motors does, after all, employ some 700,000 people around the world, a force which is larger than most armies. Surely, the argument runs, the men with this awesome burden on their shoulders deserve better recompense than the dealer who merely sells and services GM cars. Yet, without financial schemes, a $200,000 straight-pay executive in Detroit would have no capital value outside his pension rights, while a dealer generating $200,000 net profits (and there are plenty of those) is worth anything from $1 million upward; one fairly typical Ford dealer in the US, for instance, had $2 million net wealth, including thirty-three oil wells and real estate in Cleveland.

The share option thus appears merely a rough attempt to

redress the balance, before all the guys running GM go off to open dealerships. But there is, of course, no guarantee that the management magnates either could or would build up a business of their own from scratch. By and large, the man who does possess that drive and talent proves the point in practice. The man who heads for a big corporation has other drives and satisfactions, and it's stretching the argument to suggest that he alone among all classes of salaried individual deserves to share or surpass the rewards of the true entrepreneur.

The catch with options is that the executive actually has to find some capital from somewhere, no matter how easily, before he can exercise his lovable rights. The cunningly named "performance share" removes even this necessity. Companies like CBS, PepsiCo, Polaroid, General Telephone, and Sun Oil decided simply to give executives shares, provided that they met certain predetermined targets: predetermined by the executives, that is. The idea is that these large gifts—one company set aside $16 million of them over ten years—should *supplement,* not substitute for, regular stock options. (You can see why an executive like PepsiCo's Donald M. Kendall, good and true friend to Richard M. Nixon, wouldn't want to lose his options. In *Business Week's* 1973 tabulation, Kendall is shown as exercising $3.5 million of options, against $8.1 million the year before. That kind of money beats even campaign contributions, let alone the variety of loot made by most individual entrepreneurs).

Some big-time corporate managers, and even little ones, do go into business for their own account; this can be a surer and richer route than even the stock option. There is the illuminating case of Ernest R. Breech, savior of the Ford Motor Company, the man who rid the company of Henry I's appalling legacy of company goons and corporate mismanagement and also brought Henry II along to supermanager status. Initially Breech was foolish enough to refuse an offer of 30,000 Ford shares at $40 apiece, which could have made him a clear million. But he made up for lost ground with the Dearborn Motors caper. This company was set up solely by active Ford executives to distribute Ford tractors; the most active and the largest stakeholder was Ernie Breech, who got twenty percent of the action. Setting up Dearborn cost these inside investors

$200,000; their employer finally took the encumbrance off their hands for a modest return of $11 million.

The pay-off was invested first in a finance company, then in a securities firm, along which road Breech's original $40,000 was turned into $6 million. By then Breech had recovered from his early false start in other ways: $1.9 million of stock options had been converted into holdings worth $10 million. Nobody can say that Henry Ford, financially speaking, left Breech to the mercies of the poorhouse.

Latter-day Breeches, however, have made sure of avoiding that fate before accepting the job. Take, for example, one Lester Hogan. He is the outstanding managerial beneficiary of the convulsions that struck the semiconductor industry in the late 1960s when the prices of these electronic masterpieces had slumped from $15,000 to $750 a thousand in five frenetic years.

Two scions found themselves eyeball to eyeball: Robert W. Galvin, who had inherited a fifth of Motorola, and Sherman N. Fairchild, who derived heftier financial muscle from a far lighter stake in IBM, but who had Fairchild Camera as his own thing. As the two companies found themselves changing from fortune to misfortune, Fairchild reached out not only for Hogan, but for seven other members of Motorola's semiconductor management (Motorola sued Fairchild, unsuccessfully, for damages).

In agreeing to rescue Fairchild Camera, Hogan accepted in short order (a) a salary rise of a third to $120,000; (b) an instant cash bonus of a quarter of a million; (c) stock options with a paper value of $5.4 million; (d) a loan of $5.4 million, enabling Hogan to purchase the aforesaid options, advanced by the good Sherman free of interest. When the path to the executive suite is carpeted with such goodies, who needs to go into the risky business of business on his own account?

Not content with this largesse, Hogan also got the head office moved from New York to California, where he preferred to live (in a house, what's more, provided by Fairchild).

The final sad word, the final proof that the managerial magic of stock options is strictly in the eyes of the recipient, lies in the Fairchild record after Hogan's arrival: in 1970 it lost $19.3 million, and in 1971 followed that triumph of management with a loss of $7.8 million, although the company did get back into big profits as semiconductors got their second wind from 1972 on.

The big Hogan deal didn't harm pay-off levels throughout the electronics industry. In 1972 Mark Shepherd Jr., president of the other major semiconductor force, Texas Instruments, pocketed $2.7 million of options, adding the chips to the pile of $5.9 million set aside the year before. He also gleaned $15,015 and 81 shares in incentive compensation, plus $59,875 and 325 shares in deferred incentive compensation: leading the uninitiated to wonder just how much incentive, deferred or otherwise, a manager needs.

Richard C. Gerstenberg, who at the age of sixty-three became elevated to the top spot at General Motors, pulled in $551,575 in salary and other payments. With his basic needs thus cared for, the veteran was given $251,550 in bonus payable in stock, making a cool half million in a couple of years. Lest this, too, fail to suffice, he took home $15,000 in company contributions to a stock purchase plan: 921 "stock contingent credits" at $78 a throw; and exercised $297,587 of options, on top of more than half a million the previous year, as a further support for his old age.

Only in America are there such fantastic inducements. In Britain, such lavishness would be unthinkable: very few organization men would have much of a stake in their companies, partly because the stock option route has only recently become popular; and shareholders—especially in insurance companies and similar investing institutions—would balk at a package that (like Hogan's) stood to cost the company £4 million or so.

British directors in 1973 would hesitate to offer executives (even themselves) options equal to more than a year's salary—against the level of three to five times annual pay available in US firms. The big fortunes have generally been made the company way outside the major British corporations; but, even by American standards, they are not to be sneezed at.

The example of Rentokil can stand for many. An obscure little company, known as British Ratin, but under Danish ownership, it was given two new leases on life. The first was provided by an Anglo-Dane who developed its business of repelling woodworm, dry rot, deathwatch beetle, and other afflictions of the unhappy home; the second life-lease was provided by a couple of energetic salesmen who greatly widened the company's attack on its insect foes.

Between 1968 and 1971 the profits doubled to over £3 million. At the beginning of 1971, the estate of the Anglo-Dane owned shares worth more than £15 million at the 1970 peak, while his two successors respectively deployed paper fortunes of not quite £3 million between them. (As for the private Danes who still control half the company, they sat on a pile worth £50 million odd, gathered together from an initial outlay of £5,000 between 1927 and 1930.)

Nor are Britons strange to the technique of owning companies that trade with their employer. In one public company takeover, the bidder found that all the patents on which the business depended were owned by a little private concern that was the sole property of the chairman and founder—so that, too, had to be purchased, and for a pretty penny.

The weirdest case of a chairman trading with himself was that of Robert Maxwell, MP, whose Pergamon Press profits evaporated first under the scrutiny of America's Leasco, which had bid for the company, and then of some acerbic accountants; the evaporation was partly explained by Pergamon's transactions with Maxwell Scientific International. The normal fear with executive-owned companies is that the bosses will feed their own sheep at the expense of the stockholder flock; but under Maxwell's magic touch the reverse happened: the company's profits and hence its share price waxed under the benefaction of timely orders from MSI.

Since Maxwell was the biggest Pergamon shareholder, Leasco's Saul Steinberg can be forgiven for wondering if MSI would have been quite so helpful to a Pergamon under Leasco control. The whole episode caused much indignation in the City of London—although nobody in the wide world is more adept at feathering nests from the inside than your fully-fledged City gentleman.

Behind that immaculate suiting and off-hand manner lies a sharp eye for a passing bank note; and not many pass. The bankers and brokers feed their young, and their old, from pieces not only of their own action, but of other people's, and in a perfectly legal manner. For instance, suppose that a promising youthful growth business comes a bank's way. In exchange for what is wittily called its financial expertise and for loans of hard cash, the bank picks up for a song perhaps a quarter of the equity that will, with growth, be sold to a fond public at a far higher multiple.

At various points along this route, the bank may choose to cut its executives in on the profits—and may even lend them the cash (à la Sherman Fairchild) to finance the cut. The technique has certain virtues compared to the stock option. First, there is no nasty area of doubt: the capital gain is dead certain. Second, the banks' shareholders never know a thing. Third, the process can be endlessly repeated. The snag is that the game shades over all too easily into the dubious area of insider trading: buying shares on the basis of knowledge fed to the bank in its professional capacity or on the back of deals that the bank can promote or control.

A recent American list of inside enrichment includes kickbacks to a couple of American Airlines executives in connection with printing the in-flight magazine (it's called, appropriately enough, the *American Way);* profits made by Kaiser Industries executives from inside dope on a Canadian subsidiary; and some fast moves by Ling-Temco-Vought in the days of Jimmy Ling—like paying Ling and three others $1 million for a ranch, later sold for $1.4 million to another LTV interest, or selling warrants in a stock to LTV insiders that enabled them to treble their money.

Even if stock options have not made the executive a millionaire, fringe benefits can enable him to live like one, which is the next best thing, or to die like one (not quite so satisfactory). Retirement benefits are not peanuts. If an Englishman goes out to grass at £100,000 a year, his pension entitlement could be £66,000, and a benevolent law allows him to "commute" a quarter of this sum for lovely, tax-free cash. A standard multiple would be thirteen times £16,500, or halfway to becoming a dollar millionaire, simply for still being alive at the age of retirement.

It's not only corporate executives that share the fruits. A well-directed labor leader in the US can garner a decent harvest: former convict Jimmy Hoffa is said to have a million dollar pension entitlement, while his successor, Frank

E. Fitzsimmons, a confidant of President Nixon, not only shared the use of the Teamsters' family jet, Lincolns, and Cadillacs, but enjoyed $125,000 of salary, a free house, and a freely disbursed expense account, one almost worthy of the champions of expensive expense-account living, the Japanese.

Those industrious Easterners are supposed to churn through $5 billion of expending every year, plunging 1.5% of the gross national product into gross bills for booze and beauty. Activities that in the West are concealed for fear of dismissal, like recording fictitious entertainment of a client, are a frank part of the Japanese game. Their ingenuity beats even that of W. C. Fields, who once padded his expense account with $25,000, allegedly disbursed on milk for entertainment of newsmen. According to *Time*, there is even a Japanese phrase for it—*shayo tengoku*, or "paradise for the corporate set."

British ex-accountant Wilfred Harvey had built up both a printing company and his salary to considerable heights. In his last year, thanks to a merger that vastly boosted his commission entitlement, Harvey could have taken over a quarter of a million pounds for his paycheck. Of that, however, tax would have taken a lion's bite; and it transpired that Harvey, in addition to Rolls-Royces and houses on the good old firm, had conducted some highly peculiar business deals therewith.

He found, according to the company, an attractive business that could be had for £36,900, bought it, and passed it on to the company (whose board was not in the habit of questioning its master) for £168,819. All this type of activity was the result of the emergence of professional managers before the era of options.

The corporate bureaucrats of today know about options. Their cash flow is guaranteed by salaries and bonuses of enormous size; in a recession year like 1970, Robert B. Walker of American Brands, for instance, pocketed $301,-047 in wages and $173,097 in other payments. These extras alone were more than the president of Monsanto got that year for running a company of much the same size, or than Charles B. Thornton of Litton received for managing an even bigger colossus.

For the sake of nostalgic comparison, however, Sir Henri Deterding, the omnipotent between-the-wars boss of

Royal Dutch-Shell, pulled down a quarter of a million in the solid sterling currency of those bygone days. The great earners of today—even $800,000-plus men like Gerstenberg, Ford, Geneen of ITT, and Philip B. Hofman of Johnson & Johnson—are not truly in the same league as the prewar emperors, or the postwar Japanese. As far back as 1961, the founding Matsushita pulled in the small matter of £356,000. Even at the old, undepleted exchange rate, Thornton of Litton (still on $200,000 after a sorry run of results) would need to labor for five years to match Matsushita's 1961 take.

But the company man, in any country, manages to win both ways. With the left hand he dips into the corporate cash flow for the comforts and luxuries of bureaucratic life, all neatly docketed and documented. With his right hand, he dips into the shareholders' pocket for the pleasures, without the pain, of the individual, infallibly successful capitalist.

SCENE 3

The Beauty of Bargaining

or

It's a Deal, It's a Steal

"A year later I was offered the Cleaver Lease in Alamitos Heights by a man who had bought it less than a week earlier. I knew the property, and felt certain that there was oil on it." J. P. Getty is describing an incident from his early days as one of his lessons in *How To Be a Successful Executive.* " 'How much do you want for the lease?' I asked. 'I paid four thousand dollars—and I'm satisfied to double my money,' came the reply.

"I didn't argue—not for a single moment. 'You've just made a sale,' I grinned, taking out my personal checkbook and writing a check for $8,000." Then comes the punch line. "The four wells I drilled on the Cleaver Lease property brought in almost $800,000 in clear profit during the next twelve years." This little anecdote tells more about the road to business success than all the rest of Getty's writings put together.

The text reveals, first, knowledge: Getty was aware not only of the property, but of its oil possibilities. Second is absence of risk, or at least insecurity—he "felt certain." Third is an absence of any awareness of a higher, or different, morality than commercial ethics, even if both Getty's account and his memory are accurate; his attitude would presumably have been just the same if the offer had come from his side. *Caveat vendor* is the principle; and if the seller doesn't look out, that's his lookout. Here Getty was showing, as his vendor was not, the single most important quality in getting rich: the ability to sense the difference between a buying price and a selling price.

The vendor had clearly recognized that the lease was cheap at $4,000. His error was to suppose that, because a hundred percent is a large and satisfying profit, it must be large enough. The correct price—say, $100,000—would still have left Getty with the lion's share. In this way do the successful feed off the mistakes of weaker brethren. Getty could have grinned less and paid more; he could even have offered the vendor a share in the eventual proceeds, although to be truthful, he probably couldn't: the chief characteristic of Getty's career has been a passionate drive for total control.

Tidewater Oil, too, was a steal of a deal. The first *tranche* of shares in it was picked up in the Depression for peanuts. What cost Getty less than a million dollars must now be worth a billion—which puts the profit on the Cleaver Lease, a mere hundredfold, in its proper perspective.

He who deals with a master of the difference between selling and buying prices usually ends by giving him a present, sometimes of the whole business. That is one interpretation of the deal by which the visionary Canadian Roy Thomson gained control of Kemsley Newspapers and thus embarked on a road that led to gaining a peerage, hobnobbing with monarchs and presidents of the Presidium, and acquiring ownership of the loss-making *Times* (the kind of expensive hobby to which a formerly shrewd millionaire is entitled in his seventies). Starting unusually late in life,

Thomson began in Timmins, Ontario, with one radio station, bought to stimulate sales of the radios in which he dealt, and didn't stop buying until he had over one hundred newspapers of various political and intellectual hues, but mostly only one economic color: green.

The Kemsley family commanded the *Sunday Times* and a powerful chain of provincial papers, and it was ready to sell. The price, after Kemsley himself came down from £6 to £5 apiece for his own controlling stake, was plainly right. The difficulty was that Thomson couldn't lay his hands on that right price. At that time his richest asset in Britain was Scottish Television, the original "licence to print money," in Thomson's own phrase. While the return on capital from the Scottish TV franchise was over a hundred percent it still wasn't printing enough money to swing the Kemsley deal.

Actually, Kemsley would have faced no problem in buying Thomson. And this paradox became the basis of a most ingenious settlement worked out by Thomson's merchant bankers. Kemsley bought for shares Thomson's controlling shares in Scottish TV; Thomson was then in a position to buy up all the Kemsley interests, thus regaining the Scottish golden goose, by exploiting his now dominant position in Kemsley itself. The Kemsleys went comfortably off to green pastures having, in effect, facilitated their own takeover.

That is the essence of a good dealer's perfect deal. It should be self-liquidating: in other words, having paid for the property, you should still be richer by its full value. One of the earliest practitioners to strike the public eye in Britain was Sir Charles Clore, who long before the days of the hotel and property ventures chronicled earlier, made his first six-figure fortune with the purchase of the South African rights to the film of the first Tunney-Dempsey fight.

Then a clever London estate agent told him that the Freeman, Hardy and Willis shoe chain owned freehold properties in virtually every High Street. They were in the balance sheet for little or nothing, but in shrewder hands, their capital value could be realized by selling the properties to an insurance company and leasing them back again, thus stripping the wealth without stopping the trade.

Clore is said to have cleared £6 million by this elegant

footstep. But sale and lease-back proved to have disadvantages for the continuing businesses, since it substituted a commercial rent for a free freehold, doing no good to cash flow and reported profitability. So Clore developed a taste for undervalued money: a Scottish motor company, for instance, had millions sitting idly in the bank; that nest egg, too, became another contribution gratefully received. Clore's onslaughts had a catalytic impact on other companies which had grown accustomed to sitting like so many Lord Chancellors on great woolsacks stuffed full of assets.

The millions prised loose (or liberated, in the word of a later generation of strippers) not only paid for the purchase itself; they provided the wherewithal to finance a fresh upsurge of assets.

All such deals are founded on the ancient tradition exemplified by Getty's $8,000 transaction. Money measures the difference in knowledge between the weak and the strong. A large part of the billion dollar fortune amassed by the far-right Texas oilman H. L. Hunt measures the distance between his mind and that of C. M. "Dad" Joiner, discoverer of the East Texas oil field that Hunt exploited, who died broke. Alfred Irénée Du Pont's fortune measures his ability to see (a) that in 1902 the company was worth far more than the $15.36 million for which his relatives were willing to sell, (b) that they wouldn't be so disobliging as to demand cash: he paid them with $12 million of notes plus shares in the new company.

In the US, the conglomerate movement finally foundered in the flood of different kinds of security dreamed up to conceal from the vendors the fact that they weren't actually being paid for their assets. Whoever invented the convertible stock, in fact, deserves some special niche in the Hall of Fame for Creators of Imaginary Wealth.

A convertible is simply a dollar bill or pound note printed by the issuing company itself. Normally, this might be taken as worth less than legal tender; but the recipients commonly believe the engraving is worth more, because it carries with it the right to convert into shares at a later date—sometimes much later. This basic art form, with all its so-called Chinese-money mutations, turned any number of slick young men into solid financiers on both sides of the Atlantic.

If you can't buy pound notes for nothing, which is the purest form of good deal, in other words, you can buy them for imaginary pound notes. In Britain, by the time Charles Clore's crop of successors had cottoned on to both funny money and the Clore technique, the truly rich prizes of his prime had become harder to find. But there were plenty of middling ones around to create more than middling fortunes. One practitioner bought nine drug wholesalers for $4 million, wrapped them up in a nice new package, and resold them for $8.2 million in cash and a parcel of shares also salable for hard currency. Unfortunately, he also bought a mess of pottage when purchasing the remnants of a failed toy business and was lucky to emerge with his hide. Bankrupt stock has always been a dangerous temptation to the greedy. True, it's invariably cheap. But in a deal all that matters is *relative* cheapness: how the purchase price relates to the business possibilities. If a business goes bankrupt, there's usually a good reason; and the explanation may lie within that discarded pile of old assets in the bargain basement.

Given that the difference between buying and selling levels is critical, how does the dealer work out, for a start, that the price is right? In many cases, perhaps most, he doesn't. The natural man has a feeling in his bones—the Germans locate it in the tips of the fingers, and call it *Fingerspitzengefühl*. Just as a knowledgeable musician can recognize an entire symphony from a few stray chords, or a textile expert can identify a cloth by rubbing it between those *Fingerspitzen*, so can a true dealer judge value instinctively from the smell of a proposition.

The dealing instinct was about the only common factor deployed by the property millionaires (108 men and two women, according to a careful business historian) created in Britain between 1945 and 1965. By all odds the shrewdest deal in which they collectively engaged was to off-load shares in their companies on the public. Starting at a value of £103 million in 1958, property shares on the London stock market had blossomed into £800 million by four years later as the dealers took their top slices out of the action.

The company with which Jack Cotton, coauthor of the Pan Am Building, started on his way was called Mansion House Chambers. An investment of £1,000 in this recepta-

cle, renamed City Centre Properties, was worth £200,000
by 1964. As Cotton's business methods grew as flamboyant
as his manners, his dealing expertise flagged. He made
questionable deals for questionable reasons, including the
Pan Am venture and the purchase of Charles Clore's
property company. The delicate question of title was
worrying Cotton and delaying the deal. According to Oliver Marriott, Clore remarked to the associate who bore
these tidings, "Douglas, for seventy shillings a share, I'll be
the office boy."

But the fights in the City Centre boardroom, mostly over
Cotton's erratic procedures, grew so severe that a solution
had to be sought. Cotton's interests were sold to three parties: Sir Isaac Wolfson, Charles Clore, and merchant bankers Hill Samuel. The shares, after Cotton's death, promptly
went into a swoon from which they took six years to
recover.

When the Hotel Corporation of America was a willing
seller of the Carlton Tower in Knightsbridge, Sir Charles
Forte was willing to buy, but he found his colleagues reluctant. Forte, who had progressed from milk bars to the
George V in Paris by watertight deals, simply reckoned
that £4 million had to be cheap for an established hotel in
a prime site. The managers who opposed the deal were
trained in economic and financial analysis. To them, the
Americans' price worked out at too much per room, the industry's standard measure; on that irrelevance, the deal
was lost to a sharper bunch of traders.

It often doesn't pay to concentrate on the narrower as-
pects of a deal. When J. B. Fuqua went into television in
Augusta, Georgia, his minority partners were the far richer
Martin family. The Martins didn't like the lack of cash
dividends, even though they loved the profits; so in 1957
they agreed to take $350,000 for their $130,00 investment of a few years back. Had they not sold, the Martin
stake would have had a $10 million paper value in the
early 1970s. They had misjudged their partner's potential—an easier trick than it sounds.

The tips of the fingers, or pure hunches, are invaluable.
But they need to be supplemented by sound factual assessment—and that can have only one basis: perusal and pay-
back. The perusal is needed to ensure that what you think
you are buying is actually there. You can't afford, like an-

other young British financier, to buy four American furniture plants without visiting a single one. The accounts, the stocks, the snags, all need perusing with a suspicious mind. Remember that whenever you buy, someone else is selling.

The pay-back, the simplest financial measure of them all, is your golden guideline. Joseph P. Kennedy, one of the most assiduous dealers ever self-made, was reputed never to enter any transaction if he couldn't see his money coming back home in eighteen months. That represents a fifty percent annual return on capital, the kind of yield big company managers don't dream of. In a deal, however, it's a perfectly realistic objective; after all, you are never, as purchaser, compelled to complete a deal—the process is entirely optional, and it's nobody's fault but yours if you settle at an unremunerative price.

A high yield in a continuing business means that, once your money has come back, you have a valuable stream of free and clear income remaining—and also means that the capital can be turned over at a brisk pace. The faster capital moves, the better; it enables the dealer to make more deals, which (barring accidents) means more profit, which means more deals still.

The good dealer would never emulate the mistake of the large British food firm that bought its way into a new sector at the cost of £7 million in cash, every penny of it paid to the owning family. The purchasers had underestimated the extent to which the business depended on the family management. When the latter, bored with being offered marketing advice by headquarters, abruptly followed their millions out of the company, the purchasers found themselves facing fallen profits and a fifty-six-year pay-back.

The right buying price has nothing to do with the going quotation. If the whole market is grossly overpriced, picking up a deal at ten percent below the market carries no compensations. Had a bright real estate speculator picked up a Manhattan cooperative at ten percent below going prices at the creamy top of the market, he would still have been weeping his heart out in 1972, when going prices had dropped by fifty percent. Nor is the right price necessarily the lowest level you can squeeze out by bargaining. Getty, when offered an $800,000 potential for $8,000, didn't, according to his account, try to press the vendor down to $7,000, even though $1,000 means more to Getty than to most.

A British wheeler-dealer still has cause to rue the day when, with terms agreed, he sat down at the conference table to sign the contract for delivery of a whole, beautiful chain of shops. As he raised his pen to sign, he suggested that, as a gesture of goodwill, the price should be reduced by £10,000. His aristocratic counterpart screwed up his gold fountain pen, gathered his colleagues, and departed for the nearest competitor.

Love of bargaining should never be subordinated to the object of the exercise, which is to make a rich deal. S. N. Behrman told a cautionary tale about one of Duveen's customers, an American multimillionaire, who grew fascinated by the permutations and combinations possible on a collection of rugs carried by one of the itinerant Arab peddlers who adorn Mediterranean spas. After a glorious passage of how much for these two? how much if I also take this? what if I don't have the first one? the disgusted peddler thrust the whole pile in his customer's lap. Buying cheaply something you don't want is almost as bad as buying too expensively something you want.

There's another problem concerning objects for which the would-be purchaser lusts: their availability. If the owner won't sell, it is axiomatic that nobody else can buy. Lord Thomson, after his Kemsley triumph, was once asked by another company chairman how one went about the delicate business of finding out if a property is for sale. The Canadian replied simply, "I ask." It's like the old legend of the direct approach to women: you get a lot of refusals, but a surprising amount of sex. By him that seeks, much will often be found.

The great financier William C. Durant, creator of General Motors, once got Henry Ford I to the point of parting with his company for $8 million; but the prospect literally gave Ford so bad a stomachache that he writhed on the floor and the deal died. But Henry I, of course, was no dealer. He belonged to that class of builders who, if not protected by native caution or good advisers, fall into the hands of men with a better eye for the main chance.

There are two classes of dealer, however: those who believe that the other man should always be equally happy when the chips are safely gathered in; and those who argue that if the other man allows you to take his business, house, wife, and Mustang Mach I for a bag of old peanuts, that's his problem. The first school always leaves something for the other man; the second school is interested only in maximizing the something that the dealer gets for nothing.

If the Metropolitan Museum is willing to de-access a Rousseau and a Van Gogh which the Marlborough Gallery can promptly sell for a quick double million profit, one to an art-struck Japanese, the other to a European collection, is it up to the gallery to point out this fact? Those who worry about such problems, those who agonize on spotting an equestrian Staffordshire figure of Sir Robert Peel in a junk shop for £5 as to whether to tell the proprietor that it is worth £1,565—those, alas, may be numbered among the angels in heaven, but they are most unlikely to join the millionaires in the Cloud Club.

This establishment atop the Chrysler Building was where the president of Vick's Vaporub gave a class that included William S. Whyte a lesson in the difference between commerce and ethics. As Whyte described it in *The Organization Man*, the Vick's king asked what the class would do if a long-time supplier, entirely dependent on the company's business, had his price undercut by a new competitor. Should he be given a chance to meet the new price, or what?

The president, in fact, swept aside all such discussions. Either you were a businessman or you weren't, and if you were, there was only one possible course of action: you axed the old supplier and took on the new. Much the same considerations apply to a deal. If the businessman takes his eye off the deal to consider higher things like corporate strategy or the effects on the other guy, he won't do as well as the ruthless opportunist to whom weakness equates with loss of money, and who can abide neither.

It's this which gives the Lone Eagle his advantage over the assembled mass of corporate man. His motivation also gains from the fact that they can hide their mistakes inside billions or millions of other people's assets, while he must personally and painfully feel the pinch. The Lonest Eagle in legend or fact, Howard Hughes, demonstrated this skill in May 1966, when he off-loaded all his stock in Trans World Airlines, representing three-quarters of the equity, for $546 million, the largest check ever made out for an individual's sole benefit. The stock sold then at $82. By December 1972 when Hughes sold his oil-drilling bit company for $150 million, the TWA stock stood at $47.

Whether Hughes foresaw the collapse of the bull market, or of the transatlantic airfare structure, or sensed that the new broom management put into TWA by the banks had run out of dust, nobody will ever know. Probably it was a case of *Fingerspitzengefühl*—and even Hughes' fingertips have run out of feel at times. He even managed, in one deal, to outsmart himself. This was when Hughes, in what looked like a clever tax dodge, put the stock of Hughes Aircraft, then a small company whose title exactly described it, into his own medical foundation. It turned into one of the hotter electronics properties on the West Coast.

But the beauty of deals is the way they change their complexion and their truth. The story goes that long after Andrew Carnegie sold J. P. Morgan his steel interests for $300 million, enough to make all his partners millionaires as well, the two titans met, walking in opposite directions on the promenade deck of an Atlantic liner. "I have been thinking," said Carnegie, "that I should have asked you for $500 million." "I would have paid it," replied Morgan—and passed on down the deck.

SCENE 4

The Building of Businesses
———————————— or ————————————
Great Woods from Little Acorns Grow

Short of inheriting, stealing, printing, or finding the stuff, the millionaire has to work for his apotheosis. And for self-made millionaires, there is only one method: commercial arboriculture. He has to start from the earth, planting one seed, nursing it to sapling and tree size, and then encouraging the good work until he has either a forest or one towering California redwood.

Any old seed will do: a milk bar in Piccadilly Circus; a recipe for a bread substitute; a garage in Tokyo; a barrow in South London. The list can roll on through every avenue of wealth. These particular fortunes (the Forte hotels and restaurants, Kellogg's cereals, Honda motorbikes and cars, Tesco supermarkets) have only one thing in common: they began with one thing.

From that point the laws of geometric progression took over. The little man who runs one shop or garage well can probably (but not certainly, so watch it) run two. If he can operate two successfully, he can with equal likelihood cope with four—and thus his progress continues until he comes up against the sound barrier, created either by his own competence (or incompetence), by competitive conditions, by the nature of his market.

For most little men the exact speed at which they pass through the barrier or stay permanently subsonic is academic. The overwhelming mass of small business ventures remain single, small, and unadventurous. On one estimate, 10,000 enterprises fail for every one that climbs or multiplies out of sight. Although in the golden glow of hindsight, the tycoon's advance from doing his one thing seems inexorable, almost preordained, that transformation is a rare event, something like spotting a four-leaf clover in a cabbage patch.

To start with, running one small business efficiently is less easy than it sounds. The ability to analyze the shop or the sweatshop, to work out the key ratios on which it depends, to understand instinctively what is good business and what isn't—these are uncommon gifts. Without them, the would-be entrepreneur not only can't exact the maximum toll from his little enterprise, but can't hope to control much more as he sets out on his geometric route.

On his way to becoming Sir Charles, Forte worked out in his little milk bar the set of ratios that was still serving him well in a £250 million empire twenty-five years later. Britain's seaside is festooned by catering emporia operated and owned by various members of the prolific Forte family. But only Uncle Charlie made the big time; and his ratios, together with the quality of business mind that saw their magical relevance, had much to do with his dynastic progression.

The proprietor has to be brilliant at tending his seeds and saplings to have any chance among the great oaks. There are, no doubt, exceptions where astounding fortune, or the advent of a fairy godfather, made the vital difference; and even the brilliant single proprietor needs further propulsion than simple efficiency. He must want, truly and deeply, to aggrandize his business—and this quality is almost as rare as competence.

The fact that he runs one appetizing and successful butchery, owns one monopoly local newspaper, feeds the multitude in one lucrative restaurant, or makes loose garments for a few fat ladies in one lean factory imposes no obligation on him to open more outlets or eateries, or to let out more gussets. Growth is an optional extra. For every butcher like one Raymond Bloye, who now runs a £39 million business called Matthews Holdings and enjoys a personal worth of some millions, there are hundreds of thousands chopping and carving away who can't, won't, and don't want to see beyond a single marble slab.

The world is full of small builders who made it big—construction being one of those delectable industries where, since the main item of expense is labor, you can start with nothing. But for every Sir Godfrey Mitchell, who bought the George Wimpey business in 1919 for £3,883 and retired at eighty-one with fifty-seven percent of a property and construction empire worth £180 million, there are hundreds of thousands who have accumulated nothing more than a financial nubbin. (And plenty of others who have ended with nothing: building being the West's fastest route to bankruptcy.)

The bitter truth is that most proprietors who stick with a restricted lot are capable only of a limited amount of success. There is a small shop selling riding gear in London that perfectly epitomizes the true situation. For several years it has sported a notice saying, "Owing to pressure of business this shop will stay closed on Mondays." The small businessman grown big never has that lack of energy.

Those whose little acorns grow are often astonishingly fast at performing calculations in their head. One statistically trained boss is supposed to go through complex operational research routines in his head while cruising along in his Rolls; another had total recall of the latest figures, or the old ones for that matter, of every one of over a hundred divisions.

This encyclopedic knowledge of the firm is a good sign, evidence of both flair and thoroughness. But a specialized computer facility in the head is no substitute for paper-work. The head man is also capable of placing his figures where they belong, which is on paper: a location that has the advantage that others can also get at those precious digits. And the fundamental difference between the acorn and the oak is that with greater scale the proprietor needs to deal with greater numbers of people.

The self-propelled proprietor's methods of managing men often include arrogant repression, or heavy selection from his own ethnic group—and the small source business often does have an ethnic flavor. A high proportion of little acorn to great oak cases are of immigrant stock. There's even a plausible case for arguing that the super-billionaires of America are the supreme exponents of the immigrant drive: after all, a century ago much of the United States was made up of first- or second-generation immigrants.

This factor almost certainly explains a great deal about the fervent thrust of the business empires created by men like Andrew Carnegie (whose father was a desperately poor Scot) or the Du Ponts (refugees from France) or the seemingly endless list of German-Jewish merchants and financiers (Belmont, Kress, Guggenheim, Schiff, Altman, *und so weiter, und so weiter*).

The same phenomenon occurred in Britain before the war with the creation of Shell (Samuel) and Imperial Chemical Industries (three gentlemen named Brunner, Mond, and Nobel). The biggest single benefactor of British business, you could assert, was an Austrian whose immigrant thrust destroyed the whole of Germany: Adolf Hitler. The Führer completed the work of Polish and Russian pogrom specialists by exporting to Britain, as well as the US, families that, having nothing to call their own, proceeded to create prosperity from that nothing.

But the impetus isn't confined to any specific nationality or ethnic set. In addition to incoming Jewish emperors from every hot landmark in Middle and Eastern Europe like Cohen (Tesco), Warburg (founder of the merchant bank that once set the City of London by its ears), and Thorn, the immigrant wave included Armenians, Hungarians, Italians, Germans, Persians, Australians, a clutch of Canadians (Thomson, Weston, Beaverbrook), and even Americans (Forrest Mars). It's the transplant, not the root, that is the turning point.

Most immigrants, being broke, have a driving and burning need to achieve economic security. That need strongly reinforces the true businessman's innate expansionary urge, but it isn't the only essential carried to Ellis Island or the East End of London. The newcomer has the golden asset of entering the new culture and its markets free from the latter's values, preconceptions, prejudices, received ideas, and general stupidities. This capacity for what a British theorist named Edward de Bono has called "lateral thinking," or not looking at a problem in the obvious way, is the common ground from which most uncommon businesses have grown.

The successful grower usually does the obvious thing—there is nothing, after all, very original in activities like selling people food—but he seldom does it in the obvious way. The outsider (and all immigrants are outsiders) is not blinded by the knowledge that things simply aren't, or can't be, done in the way they want; so that, consequently, is the way in which outsiders win.

Although the combative, competitive urge is invariably part of the do-it-yourself millionaire's kit, the immigrant must win not only for winning's sake but to survive. This double urge gives him a thick edge over the Establishment firms, which have often forgotten quite why they are rolling along.

Rarely does the small man grow in a field where the Establishment hasn't been tilling for generations. Like the two exservicemen who seemingly invented, but only improved, the diecast model car, the new boy bursts into a field in which some somnolent giant has been thoughtlessly earning an easy income. In Britain, not one of the large existing food chains caught on to the significance of the supermarket—plain enough to anybody who could afford a plane ticket to America, or even a seat in the movies—until their minds and profits had been jogged by a crop of eager newcomers.

Economic motivation, the desire to profit personally from geometric progression up the business scale, is vital; and this, too, has an especially awful and useful clarity for the outsider. To him, managerial success is directly associated with individual wealth. The business empire, the family fortune, the public prestige are all tied together in a bundle of total personal involvement.

This was the key to the extraordinary battle in which the

pro management of Trust Houses sought to oust what they regarded as the amateur management of Forte, a company with which an ostensibly amicable merger had just been concluded. The pros, who had won over the Carlton tower nondeal described earlier, failed to note that the seat of the pants and the rule of the thumb were only part of Sir Charles Forte's managerial armory. The critical difference, however, was that Forte owned a large chunk of the merged business—it was his money, his thing, his maximized milk bar, in a sense that it could never belong to his opponents.

In short order, Forte plunged most of the many millions on which he could lay his hands into buying more and more shares. He bided his time, let the opposition make all the statements, then struck when the iron was hot by forcing a timely boardroom vote. He repelled not only the internal attackers but a boarding party from a mighty brewing combine.

It was a classic display of the true entrepreneurial drive, abetted by many of those tricks of trade that are learned best the hard way. The margin between a good and a bad decision is personal failure, and a good one demands a mind that is capable of concentration. Dragging a shoe business up by its bootstraps, so to speak, takes long years and a deep devotion to footwear; any lag in concentration, any sign of boredom, is an awful omen—one that appears fatally in the big insider firm that has outgrown its outside origins.

The insiders, however, have always done the outsiders one gigantic favor: they exclude outsiders from the large-scale, capital-intensive, respectable, established industries.

Thus do the insiders generously force the immigrants into nonestablished areas that, by definition, include those (like movies in the first half of the century or electronics postwar) with the most explosive potential. It's reported that the father of Max Pavlevsky, who founded Scientific Data Systems and later sold his computer firm to Xerox, came to America from Russia in the erroneous belief that the streets were paved with gold. Once he saw the wonders of SDS's price-earning ratio, Father Pavlevsky changed his mind. "Max," he said, "the streets *are* paved with gold."

Disestablishment isn't all. The small man, the immigrant

above all, tends to be impoverished. It is therefore incumbent on him to find some racket that needs hardly any capital, or in which others obligingly provide the ready. This delicious category still includes movies and property—even though outsiders now mourn the passing of the glorious heyday when some Establishment muttonhead would put up all the film or property cash, take all the risk, and pocket none of the profit—and it embraces retailing at all times.

This, quite as much as any innate shopkeeping or peddling ability, explains why so high a proportion of the great retailing names have nothing of an Anglo-Saxon ring about them. Gimbel, Saks, Marks, Strauss, Ohrbach, Wolfson—they all demonstrate that if you can peddle from one tray, barrow, or stall, you can peddle from the next step up; and that, if you have no money, peddling is the quickest way to get some.

Again, the phenomenon isn't peculiarly ethnic. In the Outer Hebrides in 1972 Pakistani peddlers were following the same route that sixty years earlier took Michael Marks from Russia to Leeds (then a magnet to displaced Jews) and his first stall in his first market. For the outsider, or the beginner seeking commercial lessons, retailing's most obvious pleasure is that of a high profit in relation to capital employed. But there are other joys: suppliers finance you, providing goods on credit while the customers are made to pay up either on the nail or at stupendous rates of interest. And few enterprises teach more business knowledge more rapidly or familiarize an outsider with new markets at greater speed, or respond more satisfactorily to the laws of geometric progression—or give a more thorough grounding in thievery of all descriptions.

Sensitivity to crooks and crookedness is a talent that the man not made by himself finds it curiously hard to develop. The biggest victims of the great cons, from Kreuger to Estes, have mostly been bred behind their desks, which is no place for developing the seventh sense that protects the not so innocent from those who are not innocent at all. Even as Cornfeld's IOS sank slowly in the East, several highly reputable houses actually believed there was great treasure left for honest men to salvage. One even sent a team of bankers over to Geneva to investigate—only to be told by them to tear up the file and forget about it.

The immigrant outsider has an unfair edge, naturally. One Chinese can nearly always spot a Chinese con man. But to Anglo-Saxons (as some of the barely believable lending fiascos on London and Wall Street have proved) all Chinese look alike. It's a hard truth that, just as an unfair proportion of small men grown big carry exotic names and scanty backgrounds, so do most crooks. There are two paths to wealth open to the outsider—the short cut and the long. A few take the crooked path, at the fork; and many stay confused all their lives over which road they are actually on.

The confusion sometimes stems from a powerful psychological force. When you have started with nothing, avarice, the lust to hang on to the something you have grasped, can achieve truly terrible power. To Rockefeller I, a man of upright personal morality, there seemed nothing wrong in offering his victims a choice between takeover and commercial extinction. That wasn't vicious, crude blackmail; it was good business, sensible progress.

This curious ethical distinction crops up in case after case. One self-made entrepreneur sold his chain of shops to a like millionaire in exchange for shares; the purchaser suggested that since the vendor now had several million he hardly wanted horrible, taxable dividends. The vendor agreed to waive his dividend. Later, when the two failed to get on, he agreed to accept the market price for his shares, but was horrified when this turned out to be a million or so less than he expected. The purchaser gently explained that since the stock had never carried a dividend, it had been listed separately on the Stock Exchange and had never risen a penny since the day of its issue.

In this case the victim won (at the door of the courtroom). But the sagas of small businesses growing up are littered with tales of immoral advantages obtained and ruthlessly seized. And the annals of big businesses are scarred by stories of moral gentlemen failing to recognize the fundamental amorality of their once small exploiters.

Even as he outwits and outruns the Establishment, the outsider hankers desperately after its established joys. His biggest risk is the desire to come in from the cold; titles, honorific time-wasting invitations, and the corruptions of respectability are all highly tempting to somebody whose formative years were spent in Saskatchewan, Stepney, Alice Springs, or the Bronx—let alone Lodz. The danger sign isn't only a propensity to bestow money on Tudor manor houses, yachts moored in Florida, Rolls-Royces, and diamonds from Cartiers; if you have wealth, after all, you are liable to spend it. The weakness is rather seduction by daydreams that have nothing to do with business.

The now great, once small companies all share the common factor that the founder is as passionately, obsessively involved with his game at seventy as he was at seventeen. He not only runs the business on the same motivation: he runs it in much the same way, or tries to. The supermarket chain is the barrow writ large. Tenacity, in a real sense, is the essence of his career. Although the process of arboreal growth takes less time in business than in a forest, it is still measured in decades rather than years.

From the day that Michael Marks laid out his first stall to the time when his son reigned over a hundred shops took forty years. Even the elapsed time from Thomas Watson's arrival at the future IBM in 1914 to its emergence as a $100 million corporate giant was thirty years. The protean John D. Rockefeller, true, controlled half a million in assets by the age of thirty—but Rockefeller was one of the earliest and most ruthless amalgamation experts.

In the US and in Britain, in fact, only the merger and takeover route has been quick enough to produce sudden empires which are significant, like Litton Industries and its various imitators. But if the average time span that a small businessman takes to grow organically into a true king of commerce is thirty-five years or so (roughly the span of a generation), it follows that no business started immediately after the war has yet had enough time to make it organically.

The necessary tenacity, however, is built into the true grower's own fiber. You can see it in sagas like that of the Friedland family, which was originally in wallpapers and paints in Minsk. After the Germans took over in 1917, the Friedlands moved on to Berlin, where they sank the family jewels into a small restaurant; it failed. With the family penniless, one Friedland started making wireless sets in the kitchen, from where the family graduated to success in small transformers. The arrival of Hitler moved the Friedlands once more, this time to London, where, after the war, they made sweet financial music with door chimes, building up the multi-million pound, publicly quoted Friedland Doggart company.

Possibly, when they look back, growers romanticize their small beginnings. But there is, after all, a romantic quality in sagas like that of Bernard Sunley, who at the age of fourteen (when "I hadn't a penny") hired a horse and cart to move a load of earth—and ended up a generation later selling GM earthmoving equipment so formidably that he was the Goliath's biggest distributor outside North America. The sense of romance is felt, and forcibly, by the men themselves. Romanticism is part of their dynamic, but heavily interlarded with realism—not so much that of figures, but the realism of whatever trade they have stumbled into.

During the fits and starts of his struggle upward, the man is palpably learning; usually, however, more about doing business than handling men. This is the Achilles' heel, the location of the wound that cuts off many half-fledged empires in midgrowth. Every commercial Napoleon needs his marshals, but few are able to choose their assistants as well as Bonaparte; and nature may not oblige by providing a usable son. Henry Ford I needed Sorensen and Knudsen and suffered when he lost them; his grandson needed Ernest Breech, and, after him, a series of men in the Breech managerial mold.

It's probably true that no self-made millionaires who have grown the hard way, by stages from the bottom up, are surrounded by the brilliant teams of which they like to boast. But the final distinction between those who rise like self-rising flour and those who stop or are cut short lies in the ability of the survivors to keep enough able men around during the three decades of growth. If you can't keep, breed, or inherit good men, you can't in the end build a business, even for your own posterity.

ENTR'ACTE

The Price of Priciness
or
Gluttons for Punishment

The rich man whose lavish employment of his riches brings Nemesis down on his expensively barbered head is an often told cautionary tale. In the 1950s the world knew no more conspicuous spenders than the two Dockers; Sir Bernard was a Midlands industrialist whose family money came from machine tools and motorbikes, but whose tastes ran to a great white yacht (the *Shemara*), a zebra-cushioned, gold-plated Daimler (his company, BSA, made them, too), and a diamond-studded wife.

This overconspicuous consumption made Sir Bernard too conspicuous in the eyes of the gray-suited institutional investors who held more BSA shares than he did. The men from the Prudential voted for Docker's dismissal, or, as Lady Docker put it later, "They denounced us and sacked my husband because we had dared to bring some glamor to selling nuts and bolts."

Not that big spending on personal comforts is inherently wrong or dangerous. Very few of the exceedingly or even moderately millioned are parsimonious when it comes to homes, the contents thereof, transportation, women, the decorations thereof, and so on. In the mid-1960s Elvis Presley sported a gold-trimmed Cadillac spray-painted with forty coats of crushed diamonds: a vehicle that makes the Docker Daimlers resemble corporation dust carts. The Presley management could argue that the Caddy was a business investment of high value, adding to the Elvis aura, building up the adulation and admiration which fed the fortune that financed the car.

Lady Docker claimed the same for her special Daimlers: they were splendid advertising for the cars. "I got a million pounds of free publicity and we always managed to promote the product." Despite this assistance, the *marque,* once to be mentioned in the same sign as Rolls-Royce, slipped out of public regard and ended up as an appendage to Jaguar. Spending, in order words, is no excuse for neglecting more fundamental functions of being wealthy; and, if they are being neglected, spending will prove deadly, to corpocrats as well as plutocrats.

When John I. Snyder, the builder of US Industries, died of a stroke in 1965, "we were just head of the sheriff," said his successor, who had the job of selling off a few of Snyder's purchases: seven aircraft, a 110-foot yacht, a fleet of limousines, and a hunting lodge in England.

The expenditure tends to have a certain repetitive pattern: gracious living, big game, and yachts, for instance, were blamed for the reduction of the third Duke of Sutherland's estates, once handily over a million acres, to a mere 100,000. Gambling has also exacted a heavy toll in its day. Gordon Selfridge, the American who brought the department store to London, went bankrupt at the noble age of eighty-three through a passion for the tables which, in his case, was coupled with a taste for terribly expensive women. While his beloved Dolly sisters were in the process of losing $8 million over a quarter of a century, Selfridge would console them for their losses, paid by him, by sending them diamonds. He thus compounded his own misfortunes.

The reason why the Michelin tire family, as frugal a bunch of multimillionaires as France has to offer, own Citroën cars is partly because of André Citroën's insatiable enthusiasm for, and execrable skill at, the game of baccarat. After Citroën lost a record $500,000 in one session, he also lost control of the car firm—which he had built up by his genius—to the banks. By 1935, after another crash, the business had passed into Michelin ownership. The second time around, Citroën was accused of gambling foolishly on front-wheel drive, the innovation which, as it proved, sustained the company for the next four decades: his gambling errors were committed strictly at the tables.

An addiction to gaming need not be gruesome in its effects. John W. "Bet-a-million" Gates, who could afford to lose $1 million in a single year of poker after starting as a barbed wire salesman in Texas, lived and died a millionaire. Even for gluttons, easy come doesn't easily go unless there is a death wish present, a destructive urge for which the wild gambling, like that of Selfridge and Citroën, is only a means of expression.

Gluttony takes other forms: the gluttony for power, for instance. The power glutton surrounds himself with secretaries, official flunkies like chauffeurs, unofficial flunkies in the form of yes-man managers; and is abominably rude to all of them. His greed does no harm to his fortune until that avarice starts to grow; then, like a gambler feverishly raising the stakes to counteract a losing streak, he starts to exaggerate the unpleasant and noxious characteristics that, up to now, have been tolerated by his victims.

When a tycoon discovered that one of his far-flung subsidiaries had dared to raise a price without his permission, he summoned all the offending executives from afar for a breakfast time meeting. They dutifully arrived—to be kept outside the tycoon's office for an entire day before being ushered into the presence. Not long afterward the tyrant was unceremoniously deposed.

The behavior of William Randolph Hearst became intolerable enough; that of his nearest British equivalent, Lord Northcliffe, passed the point of no return. As increasingly incoherent messages arrived from the demented Nero ("fire all red-headed men," etc.), his staff had to ignore them and rely on the restraining influence of his medical attendants and family. Yet, this power-besotted plutocrat was the self-made genius who invented the popular press and demonstrated an uncanny instinct for the motivation of the masses. The power glutton, more often than not, does possess genius. It's almost as if the extra dimension to his mind, which produces intuitive flashes of which other men are incapable, is acquired at the expense of the more humdrum dimension which keeps other, more ordinary human beings stable.

Absolute monarchs get brought down by the corruption of their absolutism. Tycoons who persuade others that they can do no wrong are corrupted by the absolutism of their wealth.

One sad example involved a clever manager who, by dint of hard work and inspired decisions, built up for his employer one of Europe's biggest and most efficient businesses in its field. The work, unfortunately, took him into close contact with men who had many millions; he began to live like his associates, with a Rolls-Royce on every port of call, racehorses in his stable, large piles of gambling chips on the table at his favorite casino.

Imitation, however sincere and flattering, is dangerous if the means to sustain it are lacking. As this glutton's expenditure mounted above his income, so his autocratic power over the company swelled. The two gluttonies fed each other: he began cheating the firm of money, and his personal and professional positions collapsed simultaneously. Long afterward, however, the villain of this piece of gluttony was still to be seen driving in one of the Rolls-Royces; in modern times, the corrupt and the crooked seldom get stripped completely bare.

Very costly hobbies are a characteristic of all millionaires for the very obvious reason that the costlier the hobby, the richer you have to be to enjoy it. The deep purse is usually attracted to the esoteric sport, where shoulders need only be rubbed with those who are similarly well accoutred. There are certain doomed enterprises which regularly attract wasteful diversion of funds—like forlorn attempts to wrest the Americas Cup from the Americans.

In this game, the prime disadvantage is that the world's best designers of yachts and sails happen to be Americans, on whom any non-American challenger must perforce depend. Sir Thomas Lipton, the tea and grocery tycoon, spent a clear million prewar pounds in five tries at lifting the cup from the US. An Australian newspaper magnate, Sir Frank Packer, had no better luck in modern times. Nor did the Bic ballpoint baron, Marcel Bich: he charged his forlorn try to the publicity account. But in Lipton's day this kind of expenditure was pure pocket money, which meant that if the pocket turned shallow, the player was out of chips.

In times of low taxation, that's how the game was played. But with taxes high, the burden of spending, even on pure sport, has been shifted onto the corporation, à la Bich. The box at Ascot, the subscription to the opera, the shooting box in Scotland, the racehorses, the ski lodge in Aspen; with luck, good management, and an understanding tax inspector, all these can be financed by the revenue.

If the beneficiary is spending only ten percent of his own money on each pound or dollar of pleasure, it's far harder to spend himself into bankruptcy than in the good old days, when every cent was actually his own, instead of money that would otherwise go in tax. In the Age of the Common Millionaire, efforts to soak up the resources of the rich have thus enabled them to finance their gluttony at the public expense. A latter-day Gordon Selfridge would probably have had the Dolly sisters on the books as publicity consultants.

The glutton with truly well-bred financial tastes can have it both ways: tax reliefs and capital gains. If the lavish hobby has a direct financial benefit built in, it can cost less than nothing. Buying fine art, especially in the US, is a notorious example: the purchaser can either choose to reduce his tax liability and build up credit in heaven by giving his art purchases away or hang on to the pictures for his private enjoyment and watch the capital gains build up in an effortless manner.

Stocking a large cellar with fine wines, a game with similar advantages, was among the most lucrative activities which the 1960s had to offer. Collecting of any kind, apart from its aesthetic joys, offers constant prospects for this kind of double pleasure. You can control it by buying your own art gallery (Armand Hammer of Occidental Petroleum finances Knoedlers), but unless your appetite for bad art and high prices is insatiable, spending yourself into bankruptcy via the auction rooms or the dealers is a difficult feat.

The glutton's worst danger is either to indulge his tastes at the expense of the time required to run the business effectively, or to engage in a form of gluttony that, like lust for power, ruins the business entirely. Marion Harper's desire to build the biggest ad agency in the world overwhelmed all other considerations, as a prescient Madison Avenue critic, John Orr Young of Young and Rubicam, predicted. "I think Marion *will* make his agency the biggest in the world," said Young, adding, after a pause, "for about ten minutes." As Young saw, it's the regardless nature of the true glutton that is the danger sign: the reckless spender is the one to be aware of, not necessarily the big one.

If spending has become less reckless than in the times of the Whitneys, or Jay Gould, or Diamond Jim Brady, the reasons are in part obvious. First, the necessity to ensure that the spending is in fact going to meet the taxman's approval; second, the fast fading of royalty, which, in its heyday of spending set lofty standards for the proletarian nobility of wealth; third, the fact that in the days of high taxation on income, the latter must be turned into capital—and all rich men with any sort of instinct for survival are reluctant to dig into capital.

Fourth is the change in tastes generally with democratization. Parties or estates on the Edwardian scale have fallen out of favor: one peer had his footmen clad in gold livery for a visit by Edward VII. Today, even if you want a private railroad coach, you can't have one (in the US there are precious few passenger trains to attach the thing to). The equivalents in the terms of minority transportation are nonstarters: a million dollars will buy forty assorted Rolls-Royce, Ferrari, and Cadillac cars, which is too many for anybody's comfort.

True, the private jet comes much more expensive, at 1973 prices of $3.5 million for a Grumman Gulfstream II, a couple of million for a Lockheed Jetstar, almost as much for a North American Rockwell Sabre 75A. The truly ambitious giant of commerce can take to the air in a DC-9 with walnut paneling (Kirk Kerkorian, proud owner of MGM) or round bed and bunnies (Hugh Hefner). But it will be a company plane, tax-deductible and depreciation-attracting all the way along the air corridor.

As the emphasis in status symbols has swung to the air, yachts have slipped down the scale of desirability. President William Tolbert of Liberia moved into the same $15 million mansion which his predecessor, William Vacanarat Shadrach Tubman, built during a twenty-seven-year demonstration of the political route to riches; but Tolbert sold Tubman's $2 million yacht. Very few of today's oceangoing spenders, including men like Stavros Niarchos, are up to the spending standards of real yacht owners like J. Pierpont Morgan, whose *Corsair* could be rivaled today only by the British royal family's *Britannia:* its £1,882,334 annual cost is paid for by the taxpayer; the ship officially belongs to the Royal Navy, and will presumably come in useful one day if the British Isles are ever attacked by a fleet of sampans.

For all these reasons, sheer gluttony, or eyes bigger than the purse, is unlikely to decimate more than a modest for-

tune these days. Even Huntington Hartford, whose glut-
tonous projects tended to run into seven figures (like £5
million on his Hog Island Bahamian resort), didn't succeed
in exhausting the lode.

It's true that the life-style of the type of self-made
tycoon who spends $14,000 on one bathtub may approach
the idea of living standards entertained by tycoons of the
golden age. Eugene Klein of National General planted his
Beverly Hills mansion, according to John Brooks, with
$1.5 million of modern pictures and antique furniture and
bought his Rolls-Royce secondhand (at some removes, be it
said) from the Queen of England. But all this spending
was still a pale imitation of the devotion of a Henry Clay
Frick to the disbursement of his cash. The Frick palazzo
on Fifth Avenue cost $17 million—and that was without
its indescribably beautiful and precious contents, for which
any museum in the world would give its soul.

For every hot, now passé conglomerator who made a
poor shot at becoming a latter-day Frick (and Frick, although addicted to unpleasant habits like machinegunning
his workers, was a tight-dealing and tight-fisted businessman), there were plenty of others whose life-styles, if not
puritanical, certainly showed no trace of Texan or Califor-
nian flim-flam and flamboyance. Maybe Toots Shor, the
Broadway restaurateur, had the right idea. "I don't want to
be a millionaire," he said. "I just want to live like one"—
and in recent times, that hasn't been too difficult.

But the taste for gracious living has spread inexorably.
Financial writers in New York knowledgeably sip their
Clos Vougeot. Managers from Hamburg cavort in Adriatic
resorts where once only yachts carrying the like of Edward, Prince of Wales, could penetrate. Expense account
executives monopolize the expensive tables of Lasserre.
Some 2,850 people every year take delivery of a new
Rolls-Royce (or rather, their companies do). In such sad
times for the exclusivity of exclusive spending, it may not
only be safer to be like Alte Yebsen, the Norwegian
shipowner (fifty vessels) and industrialist, who drives to
work in a battered station wagon, and the small number of
other truly frugal millionaires: in this age of lesser glut-
tons, such frugality may even come to be the new
smartness.

ACT V

On the
Availability
of Presents

or

Trust the Greeks When
They Bring You Gifts

SCENE 1

The Graft in Government
or
This Mess in Washington

From Teapot Dome to Watergate, from the Marconi scandal to the Poulson affair, society has always been anxiously alert to the danger that politicians will enrich themselves and their cronies by their access to the public power and the public purse. Society has always been right. But in the Age of the Common Millionaire politicians have been making other men rich, and making rich men richer, as never before—and nobody much has noticed, largely because the millions have been made in new, indirect and inadvertent ways, and not by the deliberate corruption which businessmen, among others, have always deplored (unless, that is, they have benefited thereby).

Corruption in government still exists, of course, and still excites almost as much scorn in the ranks of business as does the government's bureaucratic proliferation and constipation. But in truth, big business can teach even the civil service a knot or three when it comes to red tape, protocol, and waste of money: like the German oil firm which kept one quarter of a car park empty because it was behind the summit offices, whose occupants didn't want to have either their slumbers or their deliberations disturbed by the shutting of proletarian car doors.

By the same token, big business also knows no peer when it comes to exploiting for its unique benefit the mess in Washington, London, Paris, Bonn, Caracas—or wherever in the world some unstable mixture of politicians and career officials tries ineptly to manage an economy which is swimming with financial sharks.

Straight corruption, while flourishing like a dirty green bay tree, is not the problem. The bulk of the bezzle (bribery offered and taken is nothing but an indirect embezzlement of the public's hard-earned bread) lies in bribes. An unpleasant odor was exuded, even before Watergate, by US campaign contributions. (The Nixonian acceptance of $200,000 in bills from Robert Vesco, the alleged picker-over of the IOS carcass, was no nastier than the much larger amounts with which the US dairy lobby greased its way to higher price supports.)

In the same category lie the fat jobs offered to former officials; the largesse scattered around useful contacts; the obligatory payment concealed in tenders submitted to Latin American bureaucracies.

In the latter method, at its most methodical, bank notes of ascending denomination are interleaved in the tender, enabling each succeeding official in the hierarchy to take his appropriate cut as the contract wends its way to the top. It's the same principle that governed between-wars tipping in restaurants in Gay Vienna: customers left piles of coins for each rank of waiter spaced round the edge of the table, the principle being that whatever the hand of the head waiter could span was his alone.

But the criminal bezzle is as nothing compared to the legitimate take. Even if you throw in the depredations of Latin dictatorships like the Trujillos or Pérez Jiménez (who is supposed to have taken the Venezuelans for $250 million, or more than Meyer Lansky, father of the modern Mafia, purportedly put in his poke), the grand total is still only a drop in the ocean of legislated transfer of funds from the taxpayer to the pockets of the rich.

The billion dollar burglary of the public purse arises not from mutual back-scratching, but from the ineluctable nature of economic forces. These can be visualized as a mighty torrent, fed by innumerable tributaries. As it surges down the river bed, events threaten—a village swept away here, a cornfield ruined there—which no responsible government can allow.

So the torrent is blocked in one place, diverted in another, by measures which are economic in effect but political in motivation. So long as their interference meets the political requirements (or appears to), the politicos are indifferent to the economic effects. These, however, are gigantic—not only directly, but indirectly. For the force of the torrent is in no way lessened by a blockage or diversion. Narrow the stream in one place, and you must enormously increase the force of the flow somewhere else; someone will be waiting there to drink.

The classic examples include the US farm price supports, with men made rich for agreeing not to farm their land (under Ike they got $100 an acre), and also troubled industries like shipbuilding the whole world over. In Britain at one point the Labour government was innocently offering cash grants to non-British shipowners who were building ships in foreign yards for operation by non-British crews under the non-British flags-of-convenience (the convenience in the case being no tax).

All that the lucky Greeks needed was a plaque on the door of a London office. Some £60 million is supposed to have plopped into Greek and other foreign pockets before the civil servants of Whitehall, as ever slow to correct a ludicrous error (it never occurred to them that London shipping firms weren't necessarily British), were persuaded to block the drain. The Labour Minister, a businessman himself, who spotted and ultimately scotched this boondoggle, was convinced that the drain failed to gurgle more only because most of the Greeks simply didn't believe that Santa Claus had been so miraculously reborn.

"Greeks" is now a misnomer. Mountainous new shipping fortunes have been assembled by a Taipan (Y. K. Pao), a Japanese (Sanko), a pair of Israelis (Brener and Meridor), and a Kashmiri (Tikkoo). The scale of their fleets (Pao's 1975 plans envisage 13.3 million tons; the Israelis owned $450 million of ships in 1973 at cost price) is no more amazing than the tininess of their equity stakes.

At the time when Brener and Meridor offered to order $500 million of ships from local British yards, their shareholders' equity in Maritime Fruit was just $31.4 million. Ravi Tikkoo, the prize orderer of supergiant tankers, shares just £1,000 of ordinary capital in Tokyo Tankers. On his forecast, each mighty vessel will yield Tikkoo a £3 million operating profit during its life—yet the British government gave him a cash present of £4.3 million to have the monster *Globtik Tokyo* built in Kure, Japan.

Over in Belfast, in an even more bizarre situation, the government was busily pouring £50 million more into a shipyard that it didn't even own. Half the benefit of this enormous State expenditure will go to the outside shareholders, of whom by far the largest is Aristotle Onassis.

With legitimate gifts like this floating about, who needs graft?

Nor are shipbuilders and shipowners the only beneficiaries of the insatiable desire of governments to make millionaires, or to make millionaires richer still. Economic development, in much of its operation, represents less a boon to backward masses in the neglected corners of the world than a means of creating instant private fortunes out of public funds. In country after country, the government will lend (cheaply) or give you the capital to build a factory, charge you no tax whatsoever (or very little tax) for several years, and impose no restriction on your right to divert the profits to anywhere you have in mind.

Cement plants in Trinidad, engineering or textile factories in Northern Ireland, electronics plants in Scotland—all will do nicely. As for the Mezzogiorno of Southern Italy, the mind boggles at the possibilities, given the generosity of Italian politicians and tax collectors to businessmen all over the country.

Any entrepreneurs who start their enterprises in a British development area (a euphemism which means that the district suffers from above-average unemployment) can spell out some seductive arithmetic. The capitalist is eligible for extra-large investment grants; the local authorities may provide the site at no rent or rent a previously built factory to the entrepreneur, who can write off all plant and machinery costs against the first year's profit. One local authority in Lanarkshire advertised its charms under the headline "How to Make £378,000"; that was the whopping total value of "Tax Benefits and Grants" on a £1 million investment "in Year One Alone."

Many men of absorbing wealth have been made wholly or partly by the government's desire for their technological hauteur. Georges Dassault is one of the richest men in Europe thanks to the Mirage and Mystere fighters whose development was allegedly sixty percent financed by the French government. In this case, it could be argued that defense capability had to be preserved; its preservation, however, also ensures the safekeeping of the riches of its owners.

If a company like Lockheed heads into bankruptcy as a result of egregious management errors (mainly on a civil project, at that), a politician like Richard Nixon will always bail it out not only because of its vital defense capacities and powerful political pull, but also because of the jobs at stake. The curious, or not so curious, fact, however, is that (with exceptions like James H. McDonnell) the defense fortunes enshrined within big corporations have tended to suffer severely from the effects of monstrous mismanagement.

By and large the financial results of major US defense contractors are awful, which takes some achieving, given that the government (a) provides plant and factories for them gratis, (b) advances working capital, (c) always ends up by paying vastly more than the originally agreed price. Any civilian in the same happy fix—a building contractor, say—would clean up millions in a trice. Yet defense contractors like Lockheed or General Dynamics have the utmost difficulty in keeping their shareholders' bodies and souls together.

What an efficient contractor can manage was shown by two British cases. In that of Bristol-Siddeley, the company was found to have made an excess profit of many millions on merely repairing aircraft engines. In the even more celebrated Ferranti affair, the profits from making the Bloodhound missile came to so much more than the government was prepared to stomach that the political recoil forced a hefty refund by the Ferranti family, which owned all the shares.

Many a pile of similarly shining profit must be concealed beneath defense contractors' bushels. But true lack of profit reflects in part the tendency of main contractors to share the mindless extravagance of government. Take Concorde: as that misbegotten project moved inexorably toward £1 billion of spending, many hands must have plunged into the till, if not for negotiable cash, at least for costly facilities, all wholly paid for by the taxpayer.

The British Aircraft Corporation was reluctant to explain, even to interested Members of Parliament, exactly how it was possible to spend £1 million a day on a single project, even a supersonic one. But the Case of the Pilot's Chair explained how easily the spending materializes. Seats for Concorde's crew were originally ordered at a development cost of £54,000. Dissatisfied with the results, BAC as prime contractor upped the ante first to £216,000, then to

£409,000. At this point even the civil servants in the act grew queasy. After a probe they finally approved £351,-000—still over six times the original estimate. If the defense wizards can achieve such marvels with mere seats, it's no wonder that they can provide bottomless pits for tax money with entire aircraft.

To get rich from public contracts, however, the privateer has to tread a narrow tightrope between being efficient and being too efficient—that is, becoming careless enough to let the profitable results of superefficiency show. The other guideline is the same as for borrowing: aim high, think extravagantly, and press the moneybags on whatever is currently their most sensitive point.

The aluminum companies, when being pressured to erect smelters in Britain to save foreign exchange, played this game to perfection. They got multimillion loans at favorable rates of interest, cheap electricity (a subsidy which had the extra convenience of being incalculable), plus all the normal investment grants (i.e., cash presents) and tax breaks. The beneficiaries of this bounty included such poverty-stricken companies as Alcoa, embodying the aluminum interest of the omnipresent Mellon family.

Politicians, like big company managers themselves, are victims of the Paper Number Game. Harold Macmillan (a publishing millionaire by inheritance) airily observed that alerting the forces early in the Suez crisis cost "only £10 million." Now, the professional millionaire knows to the depths of his being that £10 million, or £1 million, or even £1,000 is never "only." But Paper Number Players simply forget that the game isn't Monopoly: the resources are for real.

Governments deal with such elongated Paper Numbers that smaller sums, like the £25 million which Britain pumped into the Upper Clyde shipbuilding fiasco, seem piddling. In the even more amazing Rolls-Royce affair, the politicians kidded themselves that because the original loans for the RB-211 engine were limited to a mere £50 million, they had in some tough way restricted the risk.

But governments are equally benign in circumstances in which they are not actually called upon to disburse coin. The flood principle of economic affairs also applies to physical controls, such as licenses and quotas; hence the huge fees commanded by the lobbyists who cluster around the regulatory agencies of Washington. That city, in the shape of the oil import quota, produced the perfect pork barrel of its day, which lasted throughout the 1960s—at one and the same time protecting domestic prices and profits, and presenting oilmen with valuable, completely free, marketable assets, salable at $1.25 a barrel. A British government, not to be undone, produced the triumph of television licensing (which generated profits so embarrassing that special levies had to be clamped on).

Often politicians would be best advised to observe laissez faire, and to stop monkeying about with economic tides which neither they nor anybody else truly understands. The praiseworthy idea of redistributing wealth by taxing high incomes to the hilt, for instance, has had the paradoxical effect of making the rich still more wealthy. It has very possibly increased, rather than diminished, the inequalities of wealth.

The main explanations are twofold: first, the high-tax principle has put a premium on converting income into capital at all times and in all possible ways: second, the use of the devices by which capital is created (borrowing and investment) has been made wondrously cheap, and the higher the tax rate rises, the cheaper it becomes. For a man taxed at a marginal rate of ninety percent, an interest charge of ten percent comes down to one percent: where a completely untaxed pauper would over twenty years pay two hundred percent of the capital in interest, the millionaire coughs up only twenty percent.

As for investment, any plunge that is tax-deductible is subject to the same pain-killing effect. It costs the millionaire only £100,000 to make a million pound investment, and that investment will be subject to all the automatic rewards by which governments seek to conjure up the genie of economic expansion. If the million of investment yields a modest ten percent, that profit will be offset for ten years by tax allowances, including depreciation; in a decade, the already rich investor thus makes a further clear million on, effectively, a risk of only £100,000.

If he invests in the special situations which governments adore, the returns become still more astronomical. The British government even gave special assistance, at £1,000 a room, for the benefit of the tourist trade and hence of the country's beloved balance of payments, for the construction of luxury hotels in London. The government's generosity, naturally, resulted in an oversupply not only of hotel rooms, but of excrescences on the London skyline.

The danger which Eisenhower warned America against in his valedictory address was the military-industrial complex. But there is a far more insidious conspiracy of which the Pentagon capers form only a part: the Old Boy Net of rich men, who finance and flatter the would-be statesmen, batten off their economic ignorance, and work their way into political favors by natural means.

Businessmen do their utmost to encourage the politician's natural desire to live well and die (or lose office) in dignified economic circumstances. In the US, because of the spiraling cost of elections and the clear relation of expenditure to electoral chances, the tendency is for politicos to have their moolah before plunging into the fray; in the 1960 election, out of all the candidates for nomination, only Hubert Humphrey and Richard Nixon were not millionaires. Any candidates who are not provided for prior to their election have a strong chance of being well looked after subsequently. Wealthy to start with, George Washington died worth $530,000 in 1799; Dwight Eisenhower benefited from special tax legislation which made him a million. While "resting" (as actors put it), Richard Nixon was converted from a poor boy to a well-heeled ex-corporation lawyer with real estate in choice locations on both sides of the United States.

Similarly, Edward Heath's time in the City, where he was employed as a merchant banker before leading Her Majesty's Government, presumably helped him to enter 10 Downing Street better than empty-handed. Indeed, Heath could by then afford costly racing yachts and private madrigal concerts. Given the limited amount of time which politics can have left for banking, presumably fortune favored the politically brave.

In an earlier generation, Lord Beaverbrook made it his business to see that ill-luck never ran the way of his political friends. He would buy choice investments on their behalf and present them with the profits when he sold. (If, by some savage quirk of fate, the investment fell, there are no prizes for guessing who stood the loss.) But nothing which Beaverbrook contrived for his favorite Prime Minister, Bonar Law, can match the accumulative feats of the poor young Congressman from Texas, Lyndon Baines Johnson, who ended up not only as the most powerful Senator in Washington, and the most arm-twisting President, but as the owner of broadcasting stations, land, securities, and other odds and ends which the *Wall Street Journal*, back in 1964, assessed at $9-14 million.

Yet this is picayune compared to the amounts accrued by LBJ cronies such as oil tycoon Sid Richardson, and it doesn't rank particularly high in relation to the estate of a relatively minor state official, Paul Powell, the former Speaker of the Illinois House of Representatives. He died in 1970 worth $3 million, of which $175,000 was found in notes in a shoebox in his hotel room. The accidental revelation of the Powell hoard, a consequence of sudden death, coincidentally reveals just how much swan's down must have stuck to the nests of politicians at all levels of the American system.

The American habit of blatantly selling embassies in return for campaign contributions, indeed, has long been a source of wonderment to more sophisticated machinists in this shady area where politics and plutocracy overlap. A little embassy like Luxembourg, purchased by Mrs. Ruth L. Farkas in the Watergate election, fetched $300,000. The *New York Times* suggested that the $254,000 Nixon contribution advanced by Walter H. Annenberg (who could afford it, having sold the family newspapers for $55 million) could be regarded as the renewal of the lease on the London embassy.

As Watergate revealed so horrendously, however, the exchange of American plums is private as well as public. Richard Nixon expressed no qualms in reporting, although under intense pressure, that the aerosol king, Robert Abplanalp, had helpfully lent him $625,000 to finance the purchase of San Clemente, and, even more kindly, had relieved the President of his surplus Californian acreage for a nice price. It must help a millionaire to have an indebted friend wearing the crown. But there is more to the courtship of the rich by the powerful than sheer greed for possessions and their enjoyment.

It's no accident that plebeian politicians, Eisenhower, Johnson, Nixon, Wilson, Heath, have chosen favored sidekicks who are among the self-made rich. Those who don't have big money are fascinated by those who do. But there is one ever present danger in rich sidekicks: the threat of rich kickbacks, if not at the top, somewhere down the receiving line.

SCENE 2

The Logic of Luck

or

Someone Up There Loves Me

If the good fairy ever offers an aspiring businessman one wish, there's no question what he should ask for: luck. Good fortune is the essence of all fortunes, but the one prime factor that few of the rich, nouveau or otherwise, are honest enough to acknowledge. Maybe Julius Rosenwald of Sears Roebuck was exaggerating when he attributed as much as ninety-five percent of business success to luck, leaving only a twentieth to aptitude and application. It is still no exaggeration to say that, without luck, all the other virtues are only slightly more useful than a bridge player who consistently draws bad cards.

Fortune presents the opportunity at the time when the opportunist can exploit it: cometh the man, cometh the moment. And fortune has to attend most subsequent actions if the man and the moment are to combine in satisfactory monetary terms. A goodly, if not particularly godly, crop of London's property millionaires owe their wealth to the blind workings of chance. For a start, it was precious fortune to be in, or even near, the property business at the time when building restrictions were removed by the Conservative government of the day. The crop thus blessed included solicitors, estate agents in fair number, surveyors, the odd architect, property developers of the old school—and several businessmen who merely happened to have a piece of London, where the action started.

One such was Max Rayne, now Sir Max, chairman of

the National Theatre; artistic, social, and financial prestige have an engaging habit of marching hand in hand. Rayne first got interested in property when, finding that his father's business didn't need all its modest premises, he arranged a sublet and discovered that renting was far more profitable than making clothes.

Encouraged by this tiny start, Max Rayne moved on to mightier things. The company that owned Selfridges in Oxford Street allowed him to develop the site at the rear of its store. At this point, Rayne owed thanks to fortune twice: for the initial discovery of property and for the folly of the owners of Selfridges. His third stroke of luck must have seemed heaven's brightest gift: Marks & Spencer, the bluest chip chain store in the land, intimated that it would lease Rayne's new building.

Enter calamity: Lord Marks decided on another site to the north, leaving Rayne apparently stranded. Rayne scurried about, obtained additional backing in the property world, and went ahead. By the time of his building's delayed completion, rents and hence its value had soared far beyond the terms abandoned by Marks & Spencer; Rayne was most of the way to his first million—and he had as tenants IBM and 3M.

The story, with variations of time and place, was repeated many times in the property heyday. The men who made the most of these chances had to display acumen, persistence, and initiative; but fortune kept on dealing the right cards.

Charles W. Bluhdorn, the founder of Gulf + Western (the plus sign is his own invention), was once a Wall Street wonder boy. He was then infested by the bubonic plague which hit nearly all conglomerates. Behind Bluhdorn's share slump lay the usual conglomerate hang-up. As sales continued to pile up, operating income first took a sharp tumble and then resolutely refused to grow. But among Bluhdorn's acquisitions was Paramount Studios, picked up, so report had it, as much for its real estate potential as for any money in the allegedly moribund movie game. As it turned out, Hollywood came to the rescue of the front office.

When Bluhdorn's shares plunged to just 9½, compared to 64¼ at their brightest and best, his boys must have been grateful for the $80 million from *Love Story,* one of the hot properties in Paramount's can. This success didn't generate any marked front office fervor at Paramount for another best-seller—who was interested in a gangster movie these days?—but *The Godfather* was allowed to devour a $6 million budget; and the results, an expected gross of $120 million, will gladden Gulf + Western's lucky balance sheet for years to come.

In fact, everybody is lucky in some degree. The luck may not be readily translatable into capital; the lucky one may studiously or stupidly fail to recognize his good fortune; or he may make the elementary error of thinking that luck is the sole ingredient of success, whereas in truth nobody, apart from the winner of a football pool, a lottery, or a surprise inheritance, ever has wealth poured on his head without any need for effort.

Consider the case of Zographas, one of the two Greeks who gave their national name to the five-man Greek syndicate. Nobody can survive in big-time professional gambling without being luckier than average, even with the mathematical advantages of baccarat, the Greek pastime. For all that, one disastrous week in 1926 Zographas lost the equivalent of $672,000 in play at Cannes. On the last night he risked a further million francs and won everything back. The romantic would call this pure chance. The realist, the Greek himself, knew the odds exactly, knew that their failure to work in his favor before was unlikely to be repeated, knew himself, knew the game, and judged his decision accordingly.

The pure gambler, unless the table or cards are impure, loses a great deal of the time. Nicholas Andrea Dandolos, alias Nick the Greek, is said to have seen $500 million pass through his hands (including $6.4 million of winnings at stud poker) as he passed between the opposite poles of wealth and penury seventy-three times. That is because ultimately the run of the cards is something which the gambler cannot influence. This fact, paradoxically, makes it bad luck that gaming should be their profession.

There are those who, with similar varieties of flair and equal application, stumble into fields where the cards are more closely under their own control—and that fluke start, part of the perennial mythology of capitalism, is where luck truly comes into its own. Starts don't come much flukier than in the case of Dr. Osman Khalil Osman, now a

Sudanese of many millions, who originally set up shop in Kuwait as a veterinary surgeon. In this capacity, Osman treated and cured a cow which was the prize milk producer of the then Crown Prince.

In his gratitude Sheikh Saba al Salem, the present ruler of the richest country on earth, helped to set Osman up in a business career that is a combination of textiles and courtship of the appropriate rulers. Being called to that particular cow's bedside was (if the story hasn't been embroidered over the years) pure luck; curing it was skill; gaining the Sheikh's business confidence required visible talent; capitalizing on that confidence, and recognizing that in the underdeveloped world politics is where the pay-off is, demanded less assistance from fortune; but by far the greatest contribution came from the talents of the world's most moneyed cow doctor himself.

Now that the vet is rich, the odds of fortune that favor the well-stacked can come freely into play. But the dividing line between the luck and the hard work of the wealthy is a fine one. For instance, it was a misfortune for the McAlpine family that the clients for whom they were putting up the Dorchester Hotel in Park Lane ran out of ready cash in the Depression. But the McAlpines owed their own financial security, which enabled them to take over the hotel, to their own Scots diligence and prudence. Sir Robert had begun as a Glaswegian bricklayer; there are few starts more basic or less blessed. In 1962, the family was offered £6 million for the hotel, which they very properly refused; its present-day value is between £15 million and £20 million.

The McAlpines can't originally have known much about hotels, except how to stay in them. But knowledge can be bought. The courage to seize a chance opportunity can't be acquired. Like sex appeal, either you have it or you don't.

But if an investment which turns unluckily sour is in a security about which the investor is profoundly ignorant, that isn't unlucky at all: it's incompetent. Take the sad case (or the sad cases, millions of them) of Scotch whisky. A distiller warned in early 1973 that up to 200 million gallons of grain whisky (the stuff that is mixed with malts to produce the blends) might have to be poured down the drain. Most had been bought by oversold, overeager Americans, some of whom in the mid-1960s had paid up to $3 a gallon for this whisky that in 1973 couldn't bring even the nominal price of fifty cents—for the blunt reason that nobody wanted it.

Just as the price of folly can't be described as misfortune, so the reward of shrewdness cannot be perfectly described as luck. Take the case of Colin Forsyth, an Oxford man who was learning the investment trade on Wall Street, when he found Hampton Gold Mining Areas in a London Stock Exchange reference book. The shares, 4 million in all, were selling at 1½ d apiece. But this unconsidered trifle owned freehold land in Australia; dividing the market value by the acreage, Forsyth worked out that land anywhere in the whole wide world, the Sahara and odd tundra excepted, must be worth more. He told his broker to buy any shares that came up at 1½ d to 3d; and, during the period from 1962 to 1964, collected a bundle thereof.

Forsyth went out to Australia for a general look, which confirmed his particular view. He formed a scheme to sell land to Americans as an investment for their grandchildren: the Trans-Australian Highway was due to pass by Hampton's land, and the Hampton board, which Forsyth had now joined, didn't mind. But the land scheme ran into political difficulties, and Hampton was still hanging fire when, around 1966, Western Mining found nickel on adjoining land. Those once unconsidered Hampton shares burst into flame after the Western miners negotiated an excellent deal with the company to allow drilling, and hence discovery, on its land. At the peak this ardent enthusiasm took the Hampton shares to £6: representing, on an investment of 1½ d, a profit of 95,900 precent: and on 3d, a gain of 47,900 percent.

You could, if you wished, attribute this to the purest fortune. But Forsyth was looking for his luck, by studying the form, in the first place; he followed not hunch but judgment in working out that the company must be worth more than its market value, even though he had no idea of how much; he took the trouble to inspect what he had bought; and he was, by his own initiative, in the cockpit when the Hampton jet took off into the blue skies beyond. The luck, a colossal stroke of the stuff, came in the unsuspected presence of nickel. But chance, as Pasteur once said, favors the prepared mind.

Commander Eugene McDonald, the quality fanatic of Zenith, lost the hearing in one ear as the result of a car crash in 1940. Forced to buy a hearing aid, he was so shocked by its price that he ordered his designers to come up with a cheaper model. They succeeded, and Zenith went on to become the biggest force in the market. The bash from fate was converted into a touch from Midas not by luck alone, but by McDonald's habit of acting on observation, by his possession of a competent design team, and of the finance to underwrite both the designer's work and the production.

A somewhat different illustration of the conversion of ill-luck into good cash appeared during the awful moment between the wars when salt water appeared in the oil being extracted from the Mexican Eagles concession originally discovered by the first Lord Cowdray (and exploited by him in partnership with the most forceful man in world oil, Sir Henri Deterding of Royal Dutch, and the wiliest, Calouste Gulbenkian).

The initial find, like so many in oil, had been a matter of fortune. (One of the fattest Texan cats, Sid Richardson, liked to tell the tale of how his take-off depended on a choice between two drilling sites: the one he chose, at random, was a fabulous West Texas pool; the other, when he got around to it later, proved dry.) Cowdray, then plain H. Weetman Pearson, had built his fortune largely by building railways all over Latin America, and had obtained the Mexican oil rights during the course of this work. Many millions of shares had been sold to the public before the fatal traces of salt water appeared and ruined the company for keeps.

As some counterblow from fate, Cowdray's heirs, many decades later, decided to dispose of a little-loved painting which had long hung in their Whitehall offices. It fetched a few thousand and was then identified by the deliriously happy purchaser, a dealer, as *Daniel in the Lion's Den*, by Rubens.

The common truth, that bad luck is often poor judgment, afflicts rich and poor alike—the difference being that the rich can afford it. The various British property men who tangled with "Wild Bill" Zeckendorf all survived the psychological and financial shock.

One who escaped with profit and honor was none other than Sir Max Rayne, who managed to extricate himself from Mr. Zeckendorf's toils and end up with what is now the General Motors Building. Rayne's good fortune was to come late in the series of British suckers. Since forewarned is forearmed, at least to the canny, Rayne covered himself in time. But the directors of Second Covent Garden also had warning: their mistake was to suppose that their forearming was adequate. They pumped in $43.7 million on conditions which Zeckendorf then proceeded not to keep; almost half of that amount was lost without trace.

In fact, none of the British property argosies into America produced a lasting business empire. The Britons, by and large, misread the prevailing conditions in the US and also misunderstood themselves. Their fortunes owed their genesis to the lucky combination of their being alive and well and interested in property at the time when the boom took off back home.

The lasting empire requires more permanent talents. For instance, the Vestey meat-packing empire would be lucrative, but less all-embracing, if it were not for the mishap of its founder in meeting shipping difficulties out of the Argentine. Reacting to misfortune in the born manner of the entrepreneur, he built his own shipping line.

Chance, just as mythology says, does play a critical role in establishing a major business. It was chance that led Lord Rank, as an ardent Methodist, to make his religious film *(The Rising of the Sun)* and, on being unable to secure distribution, to buy into movies, which took him into the optical industry, which led to a tie-up with the US camera firm Bell and Howell, which culminated in the epic saga of Rank Xerox.

It was chance, you could say, that led so many of those escaping from Hitler's Europe into an industrially backward Britain where their talents, especially in modern industries like chemicals and plastics, were at a premium. They virtually created whole galaxies of growth industries as a result. One, Sir Frank Schon, began unpromisingly by making fire-lighters out of sawdust. When he moved on to the indispensable ingredient for the new synthetic wonder detergents, Schon happened to build his factory on top of a thick seam of the essential anhydrite rock. This golden stroke was like building a steelworks and finding that it is sitting on a solid deposit of iron ore.

Schon sold out his £1,000 company for £2 million and stayed aboard to manage it for the purchasing chemical conglomerate. He quit in a considerable huff years later when the chemical colleagues, against his advice, insisted on putting up a giant phosphorus plant in Newfoundland. It proved to be an unmitigated disaster, haunted by what the uninitiated call bad luck, like a leakage which poisoned the local aquatic fauna, but which the cognoscenti recognize as the invariable price of bad decisions.

Much the same line of thought applies to the lucky men who catch a tycoon's eye early in their careers. The cow-curing Osman isn't the only multimillionaire who can thank an encounter with the superlatively rich. Cyrus Eaton was a seventeen-year-old office boy when he came to the attention of John D. Rockefeller I, who set him up in business as a protégé. That Rockefeller background taught him how to tackle the Morgan interests in head-on conflict.

Mutual admiration was not the only characteristic which Eaton and John D. shared. They had the greatest good fortune of all—living to a great age.

Those whom the gods love don't die young: they die old and rich, and the older they are, the richer they get. The magic of compound growth, on which all great accumulations of wealth depend, works under their control. The man who dies at seventy loses two and a half decades of compounding, compared to a John D. Rockefeller I, who died at ninety-four; and Rockefeller II, who lived to eighty-six.

Survival to these heights of antiquity is not altogether chance. The ability to purchase the finest and most concentrated medical attention available has preserved many tycoons beyond what might have been their natural span. One American insurance millionaire kept on working for over fifteen years with an interior constructed mostly of plastic tubes. The exceedingly rich, like all potentates, can take their personal physicians with them on trips (President Nixon even took his osteopath to Russia).

If long life is a business boon, it follows that a long career also helps. Many rich men of the past, like Cyrus Eaton or Rockefeller himself, started at an early hour of life because no other option was available. Fate decreed a start which today might be delayed by school, college, possibly even business school.

This wasn't what John D. I meant when he uttered the sanctimonious judgment, "The poor boy is in a position of impregnable advantage. He is better off than the son of the rich man . . . ," but it is possibly the only sense in which that statement is actually true. What Rockefeller meant is that the poor boy has the sovereign impetus of wishing to escape from his poverty, which is true. But, as we have seen, the exercise of that magic motivation and the unsparing expenditure of abundant talent and effort merely lands the ex-pauper in the same situation which the rich boy achieved painlessly by the mere accident of birth.

Some of the once poor rich have arrived in that category by the main accident of time and place and money. The last-mentioned chance is often crucial: the accidental availability of cash when needed has made many careers. Money does tend, in a mysterious manner, to stick to the fingers of certain men in the same way that certain great ball players need only stick out a hand for a ball to fly into it.

The general reaction to money catchers, to men with a modernized Midas touch, is to attribute their acquisition to luck; in the sense that all natural talent is God-given, they are lucky. The curious fact is that the very rich often do talk of their success in terms of acts of God rather than acts of themselves. Julius Rosenwald's attribution of success to ninety-five percent good fortune is echoed by "Big Al" Abplanalp, Nixon's pal, who believes that genius is "two percent inspiration, eight percent work and ninety percent luck"—and leading luminaries in oil's Hall of Fame seem to think likewise.

H. L. Hunt declared that "you have to be lucky"; Sid Richardson that "luck has helped me every day of my life, and I'd rather be lucky than smart, because a lot of smart people ain't eatin' regular"; R. E. (Bob) Smith that "My West Texas oilfield was solely luck. It has 38 million barrels in reserve and cost me $5 an acre. The lesson you learn as you get older is that it's luck." In oil, no doubt, the good luck story is truer than in most contexts—although the fact that the great discoveries were made by men who died broke demands some explanation. In truth, the emphasis on luck is a variation on the theme of false modesty, the opposite of whistling to keep your spirits up—moaning, so to speak, to keep your guilt down.

Close analysis of a brilliant player of any game, including the oil and money ones, always shows that behind the success lie application, method, and motivation that anybody can imitate—with a difference: for mastering the mechanics of Arnold Palmer's swing won't turn anybody into Arnold Palmer. The distinction is exemplified by the bad, black day of one publisher who turned down Joseph Heller's *Catch-22* in the morning and Joy Adamson's lioness saga, *Born Free*, in the afternoon. Bad luck, you might say, thus unwittingly condoning what was truly poor professional judgment.

Not that making million dollar mistakes is in itself a condemnation of the professional concerned: being wrong, sometimes is a corollary of often being right. The Midas millionaire simply has a surer instinct for when to be right, when to be wrong, and when to get out before a mistake exacts its penalty. Luck has merely an ancillary role in this connection. It's said that George Gershwin, traveling across America in the days of luxury trains, looked down from his upper berth at his wonderful pianist, Oscar Levant, and said, "You know what this represents, Oscar? The difference between talent and genius."

Rightly Gershwin didn't mention luck. The would-be millionaire who blames his failure on bad luck deserves his unlucky fate.

SCENE 3

The Bounty of Bigness

—————————— or ——————————

Inside Every Fat Company

Inside every fat company there is a lean entrepreneur screaming to get out. Some of them make their escape, armed with all the experience, contacts, and other equipment which a fat company can provide, but free of the main impediment to that company's freedom of movement, its lard. The large, unwilling parent may be efficient, like IBM, or merely prolific in hiring, equipping, and losing managers, like Litton Industries when a star conglomerate. Whatever the parent's powers, however, Baby often outdoes Big Daddy when it comes to the main point, which is the creation of personal wealth.

No firm has spawned as many profitable breakaways as

IBM; it is perhaps the only company which has accidentally created so much of its own competition. That is the inevitable price of being a scandalously rich monopoly in a hotly attractive market: anybody who has worked for you literally has a price on his head. At one point the only two computer companies making money, apart from IBM, were both breakaways from fat computer firms—Max Pavlevsky's Scientific Data Systems and Ken Norris' Control Data Corporation. They were joined in the money-spinning game by Kenneth H. Olsen's Digital Equipment.

Combined sales of these three before SDS went back into the fat company matrix by selling out to Xerox were a long way short of the mighty $11 billion of IBM, daddy of them all, but still generated fortunes worthy of the IBM Watson clan. Since IBM's Tom Watson Sr. was himself a breakaway from National Cash (forced out by a megalomaniac master), there may be rough justice here. But all three made their mark by competing in areas where the corporate father of all computer men, for all his big talk, was surprisingly ineffective: in very large, complex computers and in small, specialized ones. (IBM's fat company competitors, like GE and RCA, both now defunct in this line, made the mistake of competing in-between, or just where IBM bulged with muscle.)

Nor was it only making computers that extracted riches from IBM's groaning table. There, fighting equally hard for the meats, were the leanest and hungriest of the salesmen on whom the great company has always depended for its penetration. The most energetic soldiers in these ranks also spotted chinks in IBM's armor: like the fact that it overcharged on rentals, if a less conservative view of depreciation was taken; or that the company's customers, while spending millions on the leasing, care, and maintenance of the computer and its servants, had only the faintest idea how to use either.

The first vision gave birth to the leasing game, which for its brief, butterfly time in the sun, spread fortunes like wings and with no more difficulty. The second vision produced the computer service concept, which, while it needed harder work, proved longer lasting in the hands of clever men.

The cleverness of one ex-salesman, H. Ross Perot, deserves its legend. The computer company thought highly of Perot, as well it might: as the ace of the Texas territory,

Perot chalked up terrific sales for IBM, and terrifying amounts of commission for himself; that is, they terrified the bureaucrats at head office, who couldn't bear the idea of a salesman earning more than the chairman.

Head office, reacting in the way of all fat companies since organizational time began, slammed a ceiling on commissions: nobody could earn more than $250,000 in commissions in a year. So Perot made his maximum in a couple of weeks—and quit. He put a tiny fraction of his quarter of a million (the standard, legendary $1,000) into a company called Electronic Data Services, which would make computers actually work for the people to whom he had sold them. By 1972 EDS was earning $16.5 million, which, since profits the previous year had been $14 million, was valued by the investing public at a growth (or lofty) price-earnings multiple that made Perot's company worth $645 million at the end of 1972—on paper, that is; this paper value crumpled in 1973.

Another Texan, Sam Wyly of Universal Computing Corporation, now renamed after its progenitor, was behind in the paper gold stakes—but his fortune from UCC was still worth several hundred million dollars in 1968; a fine feat of multiplication, given that UCC's profits that year were a mere $8.5 million. Wyly, ex-IBM and ex-Honeywell to boot, had also started with only that magic $1,000.

These crumbs from IBM's cake were once worth even more than the stakes of the pioneers behind CDC, SDS, and DE who actually made computers.

Big corporations, just like big governments, have a penchant for accidentally scattering largesse about them. They share their fat in all manner of ways. They lend money at low interest, sometimes for nothing at all. They go into partnership with lean men on terms which give the latter all the butter (if any). They buy out lean men at gross prices. Above all, they hold up umbrellas which keep off the rain while the leanies dig their gold mines underneath.

This is because the fat company, like any bureaucracy, likes to do things in the way in which it has always done them. It objects to changing its fixed practices or its fixed ideas—and if a lean man spots that the rigidity has provided an opportunity to make a killing, the fatty takes an unconscionably long, bureaucratic time about seeing that it is being taken for a Chicago-style ride.

Saul Steinberg's fat company formula is a textbook

model. He noted that IBM depreciated its computers over a period of four or five years. The boy wonder observed in his undergraduate thesis at the Wharton Business School that this exceedingly conservative approach made it cheaper to buy an IBM computer than to rent one. If the buyer then took a more realistic eight to ten year depreciation, he could undercut IBM's own leasing terms by ten to twenty percent, while relying on the obliging fat company to go on servicing and supporting the machine free of charge.

If, moreover, this shrewd undercutter borrowed the purchase price of the computer, he had the greatest prize of all: instant money. A million dollar computer, financed almost entirely by a bank loan, would rent for $225,000, say, against $251,000 from IBM (of which some $200,000 would have been IBM's depreciation). After paying his lower depreciation and his interest charges, the Steinberg-type wizard ended up with $64,000 net profit. Not only would this return his entire equity investment in a year; but the stock market was then prepared to value leasing companies at up to thirty-five times earnings.

Now, thirty-five times $64,000 equals $2.2 million. Thus, if the formula worked out perfectly, as it sometimes did, the leasing genius made a clear, untrammeled million the minute the lease was signed. Small wonder that Steinberg and family, even after their share price was cut in half in 1969 by an abortive stab at buying the Chemical Bank, a lamentably successful bid for the sorrowful Pergamon Press, and a collapse in the leasing market, was still worth $100 million in Leasco stock.

The whistle was blown on leasing by the fat companies, which finally noticed the fortunes being made on their backs and revised their leasing terms. They screwed the leasers so painfully that in 1969 Leasco gave up the activity which had taken Steinberg most of the distance from a borrowed $25,000 and a loft in Brooklyn. A year before that traumatic event, however, Steinberg had ensured Leasco's and his own financial survival by buying an insurance company. In exchange for some paper, Steinberg bought $550 million of real-life assets in the Reliance Insurance Company, dropped the Leasco name in Reliance's favor, and lived, if not happily, at least ever after.

The money company move, or the Steinberg-Geneen

Defense, has been played in time of trouble not only by Leasco and ITT, but by the biggest of the computer breakaways, Control Data Corporation. The Defense is made possible by the highly developed adipose tissues of money companies that are prone to pile up wealth by unglamorous methods like collecting premiums, breaking even (if lucky) on the insurance, and making profits by investing the cash.

Their time horizons are so distant that, even with the usual inexpert handling of the funds, capital gains accrue. But investors are unlikely to get excited over so humdrum an enterprise as an insurance company—and that makes the insurers easy prey for corporate anglers who offer highly valued paper. The fat company hands over its accumulated cash and cashable investments to the skinny man, who thus rescues himself from the main difficulty of the lean: the lack of ready, fat cash.

CDC bought a finance company, Commercial Credit, three times CDC's size and so desperate to escape from the arms of Loews that the deal, worth $600 million, went through in seven weeks. CDC's Norris had broken out in 1957 from the Univac division of Sperry Rand. A group of Univac conspirators asked Norris, the head of the division, to lead them away like a modern Moses to set up their very own computer factory.

The team quit *en bloc*, and inside two years marketed the first brain child of its big computer design genius, Seymour Cray: his big baby actually made a profit. By 1964 Cray's team at tiny Chippewa Falls, Wisconsin, had given birth to the mammoth CDC 6600, six feet tall, seven tons heavy. In that fiscal year sales all but doubled, and profits rose six times. In the first eleven years of its life, CDC had grown from seven men sitting on a capitalization of $600,-000 into a 2 billion dollar company, making Norris a millionaire fifty times over.

So much for Univac. But Norris and Co. were so successful, in fact, that the fattest competitor of them all, IBM, felt seriously threatened and retaliated savagely—and another fight developed between the fat and the lean. In 1965 IBM announced that its 360/90 would be better than the 6600 ("IBM is out to get us," Norris told the *Wall Street Journal*, "and you can print that,"); the 6600, which let itself down by some poor performance in the field, was stopped cold in its tracks; and Norris wasn't a bit pleased when the 360/90, like other IBM giants before it, disappeared from the market and from sight.

Norris took an unprecedented step against his fat foe: he filed a private anti-trust suit. Four years later CDC had its reward. In an out-of-court settlement, IBM sold Norris its computer service bureaus, worth an estimated $60 million, for $16 million, and paid off CDC's legal bill, which came to $15 million more (no wonder lawyers love litigation).

Computers, because of the rapid growth of the market in all directions and because the market was dominated by one super-large firm, with only other fatties competing, was the ideal postwar set-up for little outsiders, or for insiders moving outside. But the governing factors are identical in less highly charged and high-flown situations.

These dominants are the sheer size and strength of the giant, which encourage it to believe that small intruders or extruders can be ignored; and that, in any event, the latter are highly unlikely to spot or snatch any opportunity that the big managers have missed; and that, in the final sweet analysis, they can always crush the attacker, or buy him (a device that, once the small company is in the fat one's embrace, often has the same effect as crushing).

Conceit, apathy, and ignorance are not the best ingredients of a commercial brew. The United Fruit octopus, for instance, although its banana-like tentacles reached to every corner of the globe, refused, in its lordly and ignorant way, to believe that bananas could be grown in the Windward Islands. Two brothers named Geest, who knew nothing much about bananas but had deep lore about growing, acquired from early days in the Dutch bulb fields, saw no objection to the islands. They duly planted their bananas and reaped a harvest which gave them half the British market, raising the profits of their entirely private operation to £2 million a year—at which level the family business was worth a minimum £50 million.

Even when a marbled company shares a lean vision of a market, the fatty somehow often manages to get what Marilyn Monroe in *Some Like It Hot* called the fuzzy end of the lollipop—as when the British Printing Corporation, paving the way for Saul Steinberg, fell in love with Pergamon's Robert Maxwell. The biggest printer in Europe had originally ventured into encyclopedias for a very common big company reason: a customer, in this case a publisher, owed it money. By sharing Maxwell's vision of a world brimming with encyclopedias, and forming a joint company, the printers cleverly thought they were exchanging a liability (a £300,000 after-tax loss) for a golden future.

One of the oldest precepts in commerce, which is to compare your prospective gains with your prospective risks, was ignored; so was an equally aged maxim, which is what you don't control, you don't dare to trust. In its first eighteen months the grandiosely named International Learning Systems Corporation was first reported to have made a profit of £806,000; after the auditors got to work, they cut the figure to a draft profit of £40,000; when the accountants had completed their labors, they came up with a slightly different answer still—a loss of £2.6 million, which fell like a thunderclap on BPC's unhappy head.

The innocent may argue that, surely, big companies rarely go into an expensive enterprise without careful investigation, without ensuring that they have adequate control, either managerial or financial, and without limiting their liability. But the ILSC case is no isolated example. When the International Publishing Corporation decided to back two software pioneers in that insidious computer game, it not only paid £600,000 for their nascent company, it accepted their dictum that, since publishers knew nothing about computers, they should have no votes on the board—where their ignorance might upset the experts.

At the end of the day, the publishers' losses had come to at least £3 million; ignorance is seldom bliss. Nor were they alone. A little later a City merchant bank led a group of institutions into backing the same entrepreneurial pair with £6 million cash: it wasn't supposed to be that much, but the two went through the original amount so fast that good money began to flow after the bad. Faced with entrepreneurs who use big numbers and make rich forecasts, even financiers, although supposed to be able to do sums, lose their senses. Poor, simple managers, who can't add up at all, are utterly lost.

For instance, one modest entrepreneur had fallen into the majority control of a larger company by a series of accidents: the lean man retained an option to buy his big brother out, which proved, in his hands, to be a marvelous asset. The fatty, strapped for cash, decided to sell; and the lean man exercised his option for $2.5 million, financed by a group of banks in a deal that raised his own stake to sixty percent. A little later, the fat boss inquired after the health of the lean purchaser and was informed that his condition was excellent, as you would expect after receiving a present of nearly $1 million. The fat boss was astonished; it was gently explained to him that, since the deal valued sixty percent at $2.5 million, the extra fifth was worth over $800,000. Within a couple of years, even that assessment was falsified: the profits having risen in the interim, the entrepreneur's stake was worth $15 million, of which $2.5 million represented the large company's putative loss.

The bigger the company, the larger the largesse, because big-time managers, like politicians, like to play the Paper Number Game. If the board rejoices in a turnover of 1.5 billion, a million isn't even petty cash—unless one of the submanagers wants to spend it, when the proposal becomes the subject of earnest board room deliberations. Even £15 million is only one percent of sales; but if you drop twice that much, as the International Chemical Industries board did in its vain attempts to finance the British textile industry into prosperity, it offsets the value of many minute examinations of managerial spending plans.

The most spectacular of ICI's exertions involved Joe Hyman, whom ICI's grayer managers correctly saw as the strongest individual force in the industry. So they backed him with a vengeance: ICI took a quarter of the Viyella textile shares, which Hyman had revitalized, and provided him with £10 million—most of it in the form of an interest-free loan. Within a week Hyman had spent it on buying British Van Heusen. "We like to see things happen fast," said an ICI spokesman lamely. Presumably, the ICI directors could see that they were perfectly capable of buying the shirt company themselves; they probably didn't see that their action made automatic millions for Hyman in person, just as surely as if they had pressed the cash into his hand.

If you have the use of millions free of interest (as Hyman did), any one of them will purchase after-tax earnings of at least £100,000; if that is multiplied by a very average stock exchange multiple of fifteen, the capital value to the equity holders is £1.5 million, half a million of it pure profit.

Hyman, as the largest individual shareholder in Viyella,

reaped the harvest sown with ICI's seed. In 1963 alone his shares shot up two and a half times; at least, in this deal ICI made a profit, which is more than can be said for its other textile forays. Desperate to salvage one wrecked customer, the chemical giant merged it with another, run by an entrepreneurial family whose previous run was of unbroken glory; ICI ended up with the whole profitless caboodle.

With his Viyella and other proceeds, Hyman, ousted by his own board, bought control of a woolen textile company in a brief takeover battle in which he seemed infected by the usually fatal desire to win at any price. Within a year or so of this expensive-seeming deal, wool prices soared upward. The money which Hyman put into Crowther appreciated by leaps and bounds—in a couple of years the shares multiplied almost tenfold. If his directors had not struck Caesar down, the same money left in Viyella would have fared far less well.

The record of the involvement of giants with entrepreneur-built companies the world over makes sorry reading, partly because the two sides don't speak the same language, let alone work in the same way. The entrepreneur instinctively relates a proposition to his individual well-being; the manager thinks of it strictly in terms of corporate strategy. Take the strange example of Sylvania and Sir Jules Thorn. Sylvania, later absorbed into General Telephone and Electric, was the largest shareholder in Thorn Electrical after its founder, who had made extensive use of Sylvania technology.

The obvious assumption was that the Americans were biding their time until Thorn, who was no chicken in years, but not easy to pluck, decided to relinquish control. A plump British affiliate would then fall ready-made into the American lap. While this build-up continued, the US part-owner even increased its shareholding, stirring happy speculation in the City of London. As Thorn grew to a height symbolized by its name in lights high above the West End, the fortune—which Sir Jules held as closely as he controlled the company—grew, too.

Thorn's whole career was founded on the lean outsider principle. Coming to Britain as a refugee from Austria and the Nazis, and deciding to sell lightbulbs, he found the market encircled by a manufacturers' ring. This broke the Law of Fat Company Preservation: every artificial restriction of a market or price level opens up a natural, protected opportunity for any lean man who is not bound by the restriction.

The outsider cracked the ring, and drove his company on to a score, at its best levels of 1967, worth £74 million. He then played his master stroke, by merging just before Britain's color TV boom with another TV rental giant. At this one stroke, the American stake was reduced to non-strategic proportions; it was subsequently off-loaded, while the Thorn equity marched on to a 1972 best level of £732 million, of which the directors' share (meaning mostly Sir Jules) was £48 million.

The fat company's final defense, buying the lean ones out, has the inevitable result of turning the latter's paper wealth into the real McCoy, and the undesirable side effect that the business is often worth less without its lean progenitor—especially as the latter, by instinct or design, tends to get out when the going is good, or, rather, before it gets bad. Xerox paid $900 million for Max Pavlevsky's SDS—of which the founder himself pocketed $50 million in Xerox stock—shortly before the bright lights of the computer market and the SDS profits were abruptly switched off.

Another danger is the old switcheroo. When Gillette paid Pat Frawley and his partner $15 million for the Papermate pen business, the razor men sharply insisted that the lean vendors should not compete in the ballpoint market for five years. Frawley promptly took his millions, bought Eversharp, sold its pen side, and concentrated with all the remaining resources on competing with Gillette—with electric razors and razor blades, only desisting from the latter when the government forced the blade company's sale.

ITT under Geneen has made far more cash millionaires by its purchases even than by its stock options, as in the purchase of the Levitt building company, creators of Levittowns, for a pay-off of $92 million. After ITT had poured millions into making a mess of the business, William J. Levitt bought it back in 1974 for a fraction of what he had gratefully received. In the beauteous cosmetic trade, one entrepreneur bought back his firm, previously sold to a mammoth, with one innocent condition lurking in the large print: the vendor was to take the financial responsibility for the old stock.

The purchaser then cruised around his retail outlets, offered to take back all the stock on hand (which rejoiced the retailers' hearts exceedingly and cemented their affection forevermore), and then passed the goods back, with his compliments, and in return for a large check, to the big company. This effectively reduced the purchase price by a third: there's no fool like a fat fool.

Yet the normal human reaction, when put in a ring with a heavyweight, is to run for the ropes. In making millions, this policy is woefully misguided. The correct course is to search for the weak spot, hit it hard, and go on hitting until the heavy either surrenders or buys you out, which comes to the same thing. If the heavy is theoretically on your side, never make a deal which gives you less than, or only what you want. Aim for the moon: the heavy may give you that body, because it costs those in charge nothing to give it away, but it costs you plenty to miss the chance of your private Apollo money mission. If you can squeeze the fat out of your friend by seemingly modest deals, as Gulbenkian did with his guaranteed five percent of Iraq's oil, do so. (They tried to fob him off with a penny a ton royalty, with no success whatsoever.)

Never repeat the error of Haloid, the little company that became large Xerox. In its youth and innocence, Haloid sold to the Rank Organization, for £600,000, half the rights to xerography in the whole world outside the US. On declared profits alone, that giveaway was worth £89.8 million in a decade. Even skinny companies, at times, can have fat heads.

SCENE 4

The Avoidability of Taxes

--- or ---

The Taxman Cometh Not

The ordinary income earner, the wide world over, is a complaining taxpayer. Small dodges are practiced by most people, such as taking extra jobs which are not revealed to the official predator. This moonlighting may be the largest single category of employment in the Western World. In the more lax, usually Latin areas, undercover, under-the-counter, and even under-the-desk payments play the same role.

But when the taxman can't get at your income, he attacks your spending instead, through the more direct method of what are therefore known as indirect taxes. One way or another, like the Mounties, he always gets his man—except, that is, when the man is really flush with taxable money. It's as if the Mounties, while adept at picking off petty thieves, were totally incapable of catching mass murderers.

This strange situation, that the more tax you are supposed to pay under the law, the less likely you are to pay it, is most clearly seen in the careers not of business moguls, but of movie stars, telegogues, pulp novelists, and the like. An income of $1 million, even after genuine tax, still leaves a sum that is beyond the spending powers of all but the most determined playboy. But the residue, after meeting all expenses, would take many years to add up to a seven-figure fortune, even with the aid of shrewd investment. That factor will probably be offset, anyway, by the poor investments to which stars are prone and by the hugely exorbitant cost of the hangers-on whom show biz personalities accumulate as rocks gather barnacles.

Yet many supertax-bracket stars put together a million in no time at all; and nobody in the taxed rabble seems to wonder how these things can be. The solution is far from complex. The rich pay less tax, sometimes even no tax at all simply because they can afford to employ better accountants, lawyers, and other acolytes, and, equally important, can afford to do as the acolytes advise.

The ordinary hen-pecked taxpayer doesn't even know that the Republic of Ireland, for some inscrutable Irish reason, levies no tax whatsoever on creative artists. The shrewd creator can not only find this out; he can also buy a castle in Eire to take advantage of the benevolent provision.

A swift change of residence is obviously a prerogative of the rich. Best-selling British authors today head for Malta as earlier generations of American actors and writers sped to Switzerland. That trick isn't open to the average or even above-average income earner. Apart from anything else, your average, even your well-above-average, man has to live where his work is; whereas the superbly rich can even buy their own island, like Len Matchan, who is Britain's biggest manufacturer of lipstick cases, or Aristotle Onassis (to go from the financially superior to the sublime). The island proprietor can then, with luck, fix his own tax rate. Nor are the exiles condemned to spend the rest of their lives in Malta or Switzerland.

The overrich Briton, for instance, flees to Malta on April 4, just before the new tax year starts. He stays there until April 5 a year thence, at which point he patriotically returns home. Now, all income from self-employment is taxed one year in arrears. That is, the income of the temporary expatriate for the year of his absence is technically the money earned in the previous year. But since the wandering boy has left UK residence, he has no tax liability for the income in the wandering year—even though he spent every month in which the loot was actually earned living in Esher, Surrey.

That's not all. During his year of absence, the wanderer is not a UK resident for tax purposes. Therefore he can so arrange it that the money he receives during those absent months, be it never so large, is not eligible for UK tax— even though during the months when, in other circumstances, the loot would have been taxable, he is safely ensconced once more in the splendors of Esher.

The result of this strategem is that two years' income can be received free of tax: and it takes little further ingenuity to put three years' income, or sometimes even four, into those twelve months by some judicious deferring here and advancing there. Even so, exiles are liable to find the months of exile trying, and to skip back to London for a brief taste of something livelier than Malta, all muffled up in false beards.

The foreign residence loophole has a different shape and mode of access in every country, but it is a defensive gambit that isn't needed if the player has foreign income. Generally, money earned abroad can be taxed either where it's earned, or where its owner lives—or in some neutral spot the earner selects because its government levies little or no tax. The Cayman Islands came into unwonted prominence in 1973, when it was revealed that former Cabinet Minister Duncan Sandys had money paid him for consultancy services delivered into a Cayman account; and that Sandys' company, Lonrho, habitually rewarded its executives, at least in part, in the same home from home. The saga played no small part in persuading the Labour Government, after Sandys' Conservative friends had been ousted, to slap restrictions on such overseas fiddles—with the unexpected result for expatriate Americans living in London (and in some cases paying no tax at all) of abruptly altering their rosy view of Britain's charms.

Being taxed in several countries rather than one is an advantage for a start, since the combination of rates on ten separate incomes of £100,000 is far less than any government in the industrialized world will settle for on a million—if it can help it.

In countries like Italy tax evasion is almost a second religion. Since no Italian will ever give an honest account of his income, the authorities have been reduced to taxing him on the appearance of wealth. That's why Italians keep private planes at an airfield just inside the Swiss border.

It follows that any foreigner who has income in a land of eager evaders can benefit from the same rules. Being foreign, moreover, he can keep some of his money outside without let or hindrance—and is not reduced, like an Italian who distrusts the lire, the unions, and the government in equal proportions, to passing suitcases full of currency across the frontier which separates Italy from the Swiss paradise.

Most authorities, while tough on domestic money that wants to emigrate, are kind to overseas earnings that decide to come home. A British star can pop his foreign proceeds into a bank account in the Channel Islands or the Isle of Man, where kindly bankers will invest it anywhere in the world. After a few years, the star can bring all the proceeds back the last few miles across the sea without paying any tax of any variety.

That's one of the ways in which the one-year exiles can get more than two years' income saved from tax. During the year they finish another masterpiece which collects foreign royalties. If the filmscript or whatever had been written in Esher, the normal UK tax would have applied. Since it was compiled in sunnier climes, the proceeds can go straight to an off-shore tax haven. Performing artists, of course, never have this problem. Their work takes them legitimately all around the world, and where they choose to be paid (or rather, where their business managers choose for them) is where, if anywhere, their tax is handed over.

Time as well as place is optional. You can defer income over several years, as William Holden deferred his take from *The Bridge over the River Kwai*, or as the original late-night chat hero, Jack Paar, did with his phenomenal contract. The smaller the annual installments, the lower the tax liability in each year. In fact, the deferred trick can confer more benefit on the employer than the employed. In one case, the interest received by the movie producer on the sum set aside for his deferred star substantially exceeded the payments due each year—so he actually got the superstar's services for less than nothing.

Time and place are thus two dimensions on the side of the heavy (or supposedly heavy) taxpayer. Another is space: the wider a man's sources of income, the more room he has to juggle those flows around, to decide in which of the other two dimensions he will receive the gold. He can even decide not to receive it at all—while still retaining almost as much benefit as if he had. This is not only through the dividend waiver, by which a man forgoes the dividend on his controlling shares in a company, thus hopefully enhancing the value of those shares. That is a relatively crude and blunt instrument, not to be compared with the delicate and flexible touch on the trust.

This device, in its family form, allows a papa to "make provision" for his children, which sounds no less innocent than popping coins into their piggy bank. The family trust—the Stranahans of Champion Spark Plugs erected thirty of the things—is probably the most heavily worked device in the whole field of tax avoidance, used even by those families which have graduated to the ultimate in trusts, the charitable foundation.

In the American heyday of 1950, foundations were being created at a hundred a month. The donor could give twenty percent of his income to the foundation without paying tax. If he gave stocks or property, he deducted twenty percent of the value from gross income; yet in seven years the Moody Foundation, set up by a man who owned half of Galveston, gave away a measly $422,000.

Even if the donations are of somewhat nobler proportions, the charitable founder is enabled to spend tax-free money on some of his own desires: supporting the Metropolitan Opera is no less a gratification, even if a worthier one, than owning a yacht.

You can, in fact, get the yacht tax-free, too: by the company way, if not through the trust route. Income earned by a company is different from income earned by an individual—even though it does not possess the sovereign difference of income received in a trust or foundation, which is total exemption from tax (despite the fact that many studies of US foundations have shown that the Moody money deposit is not alone in giving away far less than it receives).

Corporate income can have expenses deducted before the taxable amount is computed—so long as the charge is a legitimate business expense. Enter the yacht. Mrs. Bernard Castro, whose fortune is built on sofa convertibles, has a small liner at Fort Lauderdale; scattered around among the convertibles (a sofa converting into a bar at one end and a stereo at the other, a chair becoming a hair-drier cum ironing board) is Castro sales literature. As Mrs. Castro delicately points out, "After all, we make this boat tax deductible." Another American taxpayer, a manufacturer of footwear, argued that the entire cost of his oceangoing plaything was legitimately deductible, because it afforded the opportunity to study the adhesive performance of various soles on a sloping, slippery surface.

The wealthy taxpayer, indeed, is a sloping and slippery animal. Even three dimensions—place, time, and space—don't exhaust his appetite for evasion. There is also the fourth dimension. As opposed to income received by trusts or foundations, which would attract tax if received in any other than the third dimension, income of the fourth degree is income which is identical to every other form of receipt, except for one thing: that it pays no tax.

This category, almost exclusively reserved for the exceedingly rich, includes blessings like American tax-exempt bonds, issued by local authorities with the benediction of Washington, which loses heavily on the deal; Eurobonds, the new international medium, also tax-free, from which all governments suffer without apparently knowing or caring; the oil depletion allowance in the US, which allows rich men and richer corporations to deduct against tax not only the cost of all holes dry and wet, but also 22.5% of their gross income; depreciation money all round the globe, which allows those with money to build up still larger investments out of untaxed cash.

The classic depreciation cases are not the Texan oil fortunes. No, the strongest depreciation cases, because the industry is not inherently lucrative, are the shipping lines. Ships not only attract depreciation charges, even though they may easily be worth more at the end of the depreciation period than they cost, but in many countries they attract specially generous rates of tax exemption, with subsidies thrown in.

Politicians have a seemingly insatiable desire to foster their merchant marines, lest in some future holocaust their country get cut off from the high seas (the phobia dates back at least to the days of the Spanish Armada). The net result is that one of Britain's most successful companies, European Ferries, engaged in the business of ferrying tourists and their cars to the Continent, earned £20 million, and paid not one penny of tax in four years (then, after a smidgen got paid to the Norwegians, doubtless by accident, the ferrymen paid the gigantic ratios of 0.2, 0.2, 0.3, and 0.2 percent of their profits over the taxman in the next quadriennium).

The extraordinary preponderance of shipping magnates among the world's new rich is partly explained by the remarkable freedom from tax which they enjoy. Thus Y. K. Pao, estimated to be worth $700-800 million, has two main companies, which in 1972 made profits of $26.8 million; neither paid a penny of tax. Ships, like pop singers, travel the world about their business; which makes it that much easier for the owner to locate his personal tax base wherever on the surface of the globe he can best ensure that his private income, like his corporate flow, is tax-free.

There are also tax anomalies and oddities, like the first £5,000 paid, all untaxed, as compensation to a big British executive who loses his job. Once upon a time, the whole "golden handshake" was free of tax, meaning that it paid a highly paid man hand over fist to engineer his dismissal.

There was another lost British beauty which allowed retiring barristers to collect tax-free all fees outstanding at the date of their retirement—no matter how often they retired. One or two made almost as many last appearances as Sarah Bernhardt, taking care that, for a year or so before each retirement, no client was encouraged to pay up. Since a goodly proportion of the House of Commons consisted of lawyers, the chances of this loophole being closed were rated about as high as those of a US Congress in which oil interests were the most powerful paymasters doing anything nasty to the depletion allowance. The tax collectors' victory in both cases demonstrates that the life of all loopholes, no matter how gilt-edged, has a limit. But the ingenuity of moneyed man knows few limits, either, and as soon as one loophole closes, another opens up.

The Middle East of loophole drillers is the differential tax between income and capital. If tax rates rise to ninety-eight percent on income, but fall as low as thirty percent on capital gains (twenty-five percent in the US), there is a profound saving (sixty-eight pence in the pound, flat) in converting the former into the latter. Since capital, in most countries, is not taxed at all until a gain is realized, the advantage of conversion is even greater than immediately appears.

The simplest and unstoppable way is to become a genuine incorporated, publicly owned business. In this event, your wealth is no longer your taxable income; it is your income, taxed at the lower corporation tax rate, and multiplied by the price-earnings ratio: £100,000 a year then becomes, say, £1 million of capital instead of £30,000 post-tax income. Enterprising Britons set up two companies whose stock-in-trade was to get stars like Tom Jones to exchange their future earnings for shares; another company, Booker Brothers McConnell, better known as a West Indian trader, purchased the future earnings of authors like Agatha Christie and Ian Fleming.

This loophole was among those gummed up by the Inland Revenue, but the principle can still apply. One neat method is the Bahamas partnership, in which the partner, a local lawyer, is well paid simply to sleep. After a suitable passage of time, during which the earnings have poured in at the indulgent local rates of taxation, the partnership is liquidated and the profits are paid over as capital increments, and in the previously determined proportions, to the partners.

This is a relatively new wrinkle to an old device, the

Liechtenstein or Luxembourg company, in which, again, a local lawyer comes in as the ostensible part (or even majority) owner. Many a rich income finds its way into these safe harbors—but the catch is that a resident in some country with an efficient tax system, like Britain's, may find it difficult to get his tax-free money back home in the same blissful untaxed condition.

But all is less well than it used to be in the grand old sport of tax havenry. Not the least disturbing aspect to the tax evader of the Howard Hughes affair, or rather the non-Howard Hughes affair, was that a Swiss bank dropped the veil of secrecy, simply to put Mrs. Edith Irving on the spot.

A tenet of the dedicated tax savers who have deposited billions of foreign money in Switzerland ($5 billion is supposed to consist of American tax evasion money alone) was that Swiss banks, no matter if you opened the account in the name of Mickey Mouse, Al "Scarface" Capone, or Nikita S. Khrushchev, would protect your secrecy to the death. In this instance, no doubt, the Swiss banks' dislike of helping to perpetrate a particularly blatant fraud, especially on a man with as much money as Hughes, outweighed the traditional respect for the privacy of the numbered accounts.

But however special the circumstances, the Hughes-Irving incident was another example of the steady erosion of what was once the rich man's inalienable right to keep every red cent he earned. In 1969 the US Congress actually decreed that the wealthy had to pay ten percent of their income in taxes, irrespective of the dodges to which they and their advisers had resorted. A Senator later turned up the information that in 1972 no less than 276 Americans with income over $100,000 paid nothing to the Internal Revenue Service. The minimum tax, it transpired, was to be levied on "adjusted gross income"—and after they had finished adjusting via their favorite deductions, these 276 worthies had an adjusted gross income of nothing.

It transpired further that the man who as President signed the 1969 legislation had led the way in this stampede from the taxman. Not only had Richard M. Nixon taken advantage of every deductible item, large and small; he had by an untimely (in the sense that it was past the official deadline) donation of vice-presidential papers to the nation, at a suitably high valuation, virtually obliterated his liability to tax. The circumstances of Nixon's avoidance, like most of the events in his White House years, are peculiar, but the principle is ordinary enough—the rich man hires rich lawyers to mine riches from the tax laws. The magic word, deductibility, is literally worth millions: in Nixon's case alone (until the press, the IRS, and the Congress caught up with him) it was worth $576,000.

All the same, one by one, stone by stone, the bastions which protected a millionaire's income in his lifetime are, if not coming down, being chipped away; and it follows that his defenses against depredations after his death are also being gradually eroded.

For instance, the Disappearing Estate Trick, a gambit as satisfying and mysterious as the Indian Rope variety, came to the pained attention of the British authorities. It operated on the fact that works of art, instead of being aggregated together, were charged after death separately—at the rate which applied to the rest of a man's estate. Suppose a millionaire was suddenly informed by his doctor that he had only a week to live. His correct fiscal response was to rush to the nearest friendly banker and borrow another million, then race on to Bond Street and the nearest equally friendly art dealer. With the borrowed million, he buys some assorted masterpieces, and then dies as promised.

Then the estate consists of a million of assets, less a million of debts, which equals nil. The art must be assessed at the same rate as the rest of the inheritance, which also equals nil. This loophole, created by the general and laudable feeling that artistic patronage is to be encouraged, has been plugged: the American authorities, too, are getting leery about the tax-avoidance uses of *la belle peinture*.

Time was when a rich man could buy a picture for $100,000, give it after a suitable pause for appreciation to a museum, and deduct the entire appreciated value from his income tax—while still enjoying full possession of the painting during his lifetime. Today he must hand it over to the museum within four years, but the provision, again eminently laudable in intent, still has the prime effect of allowing the wealthy to hang on to more of their income than the taxman has a right to expect.

The politicians are always creating new ways of keeping

fortunes intact—or refusing to repeal old ones. In the US, half of any estate going to the wife is nontaxable. In Britain, matters can be arranged to pass on the entire family insurance proceeds to the wife at a privileged rate. The results are plain to see: in the US in 1958, when estates were supposed to carry duty ranging from sixty-nine to seventy-seven percent, those of $20 million or above actually 15.7%. Incomes over a million, by the same token, paid thirty-eight percent instead of a nominal eighty-seven percent.

In Britain, estate duty has been called an "optional tax": and those who fail to take advantage of such options are often robbed by their own blindness. One was the first Henry Ford. According to an almost certainly accurate estimate, the crisis forced on Ford by his failure to make suitable provision decimated the family fortune; in the emergency, the old man had to give away to his hastily erected foundation the bulk of his interests.

Far lesser men devote their time and ingenuity to the trinity of tax avoidance: (1) achieving the exemption of income from tax, (2) obtaining the conversion of taxable income into capital, (3) accomplishing the preservation of capital for inheritance. One honest scion of a noble house, asked what he proposed to do with himself, now he had come into his fortune, remarked frankly, "Defend it against the Inland Revenue."

The defenders come both low and high. Kathleen Winsor, author of *Forever Amber*, had her income from that work adjudged a capital gain, thus paying a maximum tax of only twenty-five percent. At the other end of the scale, literary and otherwise, Winston Churchill's proceeds from his war memoirs are supposed to have been treated as a sale of his archives (a capital gain, then tax free), not as income from writing a book. Since the great old man got $750,000 from *Life* for the serial rights alone, the scope for savings must have been immense.

The sudden enthusiasm of film stars for forming their own production companies, or getting their fees in cuts from the worldwide take, arose because income derived in this way can be treated as corporate rather than individual. Lucille Ball and Desi Arnaz, by forming Desilu, or Frank Sinatra with Reprise Records, exchange potentially highly taxable income for lower-taxed money; said funds can be retained and invested in a corporation, which then becomes a highly salable capital asset.

In fact, the main wonder, given that so many wonders can be worked by tax advisers, is that anybody should opt for less favored treatment. But it does happen. Edward Boughton was one of an elderly trio whose Automotive Products made three vast fortunes out of Lockheed brake, Borg and Beck clutches, *et al.* On his death in 1973, Boughton left £2.8 million. Of that nearly £2 million went, voluntarily, to the Exchequer, because the ninety-one-year-old Boughton had not availed himself of "ways and means available to reduce death duty," believing that the tax bite was "just and equitable." If Boughton is right, then the rain of tax-avoidance riches has been falling heavily on the unjust and the unfair.

ACT VI

On the Yields of
Achievement

——————————————— or ———————————————

If at First
You Do Succeed,
Try, Try Again

SCENE 1

The Income of Invention
or
The Better Mousetrap Gambit

Invention is as famous and heavily trampled a road to fortune as prospecting—but rockier even than the deserts of Colorado, more hazardous and less hospitable even than the North Slope of Alaska. Great manufacturing companies, with few exceptions, are built on technological advance. It may be scientifically sensational, like the germanium dioxide semiconductor, a mystery to all but the electronic elect, or humdrum, like the moving fly button, alias the zip fastener.

The idea may be revolutionary, like the internal combustion engine in its day, or one that has been kicking around for years, like television. Whatever the circumstances, if the gimmick meets a real demand, works without need for constant ministration by specialists, and can be sold at a profitable price, money is there for the making—and the more astounding the innovation and the greater the technical discontinuity with the past, the richer the prize available to the technological prospector.

Alas, he rarely collects it. Many a brilliant, ineffably creative inventor has seen other men garner his harvest, while he gets a grain or two as total recompense. Take the case of polyester fiber, an innovation which is literally one of the world record money spinners.

Manufacturers of Terylene and Dacron (formerly the ICI and Du Pont near-monopoly), Trevira (Hoechst), and the rest have spun mounting millions of pounds of the stuff in the last decade, which even at the occasional depressed prices, came to a worldwide total of Midas proportions. The two intellects who created this cornucopia, you would think, must have been laden with honors and wealth: you would be wrong.

Their names were J. R. Whinfield and Dr. J. Dickson, and they worked for a company, the Calico Printers Association, which bowed to nobody in its knowledge of printing calico, but was not fit to handle the Whinfield-Dickson discovery made in its labs. In 1947 the bonanza was sold to ICI in return for royalties, which kept CPA shareholders in happy ease for many years.

Whinfield went over to ICI with his discovery (which caused its purchasers no end of problems in its early days; the first all-Terylene trousers practically stood up by themselves). His booty from one of the century's premier achievements was £600 a year. Dickson wasn't even on the ICI bandwagon; he went to work for a company manufacturing linoleum, a product which the Victorians knew well. Linoleum was a long journey away from the product of the finest modern polymer chemistry.

The inventor of the jet engine fared well, relatively speaking, but in absolute terms his money fate was much the same: others made millions out of his discovery. He depended, for his main reward, on a government handout. Sir Frank Whittle's principal misfortune, perhaps, was that his jet made its progress toward realization under the war clouds of the late 1930s. This inevitably made the government intensely interested in his little private company, Power Jets, which had originally been financed by City investment bankers.

In the end the government purchased the entire kit. A few weeks before the historic moment in 1941, when the Gloster/Whittle E28 made an unintentional 200-yard flight during taxiing trials, the total government investment was put at £96,000. Whittle was given £4,000 more than that—or £100,000 tax-free—in 1948: a sum which sinks to its proper proportions before the knowledge that, three years later, the US government alone paid $4 million for the use of the patents.

History is littered with men who similarly made the breakthroughs for others to exploit. The liability of the innocents in these cases is their very innocence. Like the stock character of the absent-minded, muddled professor, they truly are an unworldly bunch. Build a better mousetrap, they fondly believe, and the world will beat so many paths to your door that the problem is merely which road to choose.

In fact, when the improved, Mark II, all-electronic mousetrap does appear, the world says it will never work; if you prove that it does, the world (or rather the worldly) will try to steal the drawings. The skepticism and the thievery are in a sense both justified: every year hundreds of thousands of patent applications are made, many by private individuals whose ingenuity is matched only by their incompetence. Of the small minority with a worthwhile wonder on its hands, an even tinier minority has digits adroit enough to exploit the opportunity which they have created.

The most likely scoffers are, as you have gathered, the giant corporations: partly because it goes against the corporate grain to accept any idea from outside, except on their own initiative; secondly, because the acceptance of the new, the untried, the unknown, must involve the corporation, or somebody within it, in time, trouble, and expense. It's the unknown, more than any other psychological deterrent, which is most effective.

Thus Eastman Kodak listened to the two concert pianists who dreamed up Kodachrome in the bath, because film was its business. It rejected xerography because Chester B. Carlsson's invention had its potential and technology in areas where Kodak didn't, at that time, feel that it belonged.

Kodak's loss was the Haloid Corporation's infinite gain. The executives of that obscure New Jersey operation waxed adequately rich even by the standards of the George Eastman family, and Carlsson, while lagging behind, was financially among the inventing élite: his royalties themselves created a substantial fortune.

That pile, however, was negligible beside that of Charles F. Kettering, inventor of the self-starter and other handy gadgets, who on his death left at least $200 million, the proceeds of his long and lucrative association with General Motors and automotive technology. The closer the inventor nestles to business itself, the better-heeled he must become—even if invention itself is his business.

That is the lucrative occupation of a Dane, Karl Kroyer, who is the proud author of such benefactions to humanity as the nonstick frying pan; he also thought up an ersatz hosiery elastic during World War II, showed how expanded polystyrene granules could be used to salvage ships, and devised a detector for deathwatch beetles. All his inventive activity is masterminded and promoted through a series of companies: a man with a commercially viable mind should have higher hopes of developing a commercially viable product.

But the inventor is more often preoccupied with the problem for its own sake than for its pecuniary worth. Without that preoccupation, he would never have possessed either the stamina or the concentration to solve his conundrum. When Dr. Jonas Salk was working toward the discovery of polio vaccine, or Dr. Selman Waksman toward streptomycin, their thoughts may conceivably have drifted toward the fortunes which attend all pharmacological breakthroughs, but the imagination finds this notion as hard to encompass as the idea that pharmaceutical companies are the devoted benefactors of mankind that they purport to be.

The profits from genuinely new drugs are probably larger than from any enterprise except a successful bank robbery. According to the industry's standard defense, astronomical profits are required to finance research into the new drugs from which greater medical progress will result. But that progress, as the apologists fail to mention, inevitably goes along with still more nourishing profits.

Some idea of this nutritious take emerged in 1973, when the British government decided that the world's biggest drug company had been overcharging it by unholy percentages for two tranquilizers, Librium and Valium, both of which are valuable in treating various psychological disorders. The British offshoot of Hoffman La Roche, a Swiss company so secretive that even elementary financial figures have to be prised loose by detective work, was charged by its parent $925 a kilo for Librium supplies and $2,300 for Valium, which couldn't have cost the parent company more than $22.50 and $50 respectively (the prices at which Italian pirates, who make fat livings out of Italy's lack of patent protection for drugs, were willing to supply the same compounds).

In seven years, according to the investigators, Roche pulled in $55 million, most of it siphoned back to the Swiss parent in the transfer price. Small wonder that Roche was among the pet investments of millionaires. At a mid-1973 cost of 140,000 Swiss francs each, a dozen Roche shares cost a quarter of a million pounds; the stock has become so heavy that trading has long been conducted in "mini-Roches," worth a tenth of a share apiece.

What the millionaires were buying, in addition to a share whose limited supply kept the price perpetually aloft, was an entrance ticket to the inventor's perfect product situation. The sick man is in no position to haggle over price. He isn't the direct customer, anyway: that role is filled by the doctor, who doesn't have to pay a penny. The situation, provided that government can be kept out of the act, is perfect: urgency of demand, total elasticity of price, and floor-level costs of production.

Most inventors design their wonders with no thought for the market's demands, ignore the fundamental importance of price, and don't understand that, since profit is the sum of price less cost, if the relationship between the two gets out of hand, their work will go for nothing. The perversion of that essential basic marriage tends to begin at the beginning, with the cost of development.

Anybody who has financed a noble try in research and development sooner or later stumbles over the fact that inventors always grossly underestimate the cost of getting to even a working prototype. Even then, the final twenty percent of progress seems to cost as much as the first eighty percent put together—plainly, the process is governed by some inexorable geometric law.

Nobody has ever come up with a sane solution to the problem. Sanity is probably ruled out by the tendency of inventors to come up with something for which they weren't looking at all. This was the true of the best businessman who ever made an invention; or, for that matter, the best inventor who ever went into business, Dr. Edwin Land. His original preoccupation with the polarizing of light was founded, wrongly, on the notion that he would create a breakthrough in car headlights, not sunglasses.

But the launch of Land's nonglare glasses in 1937 set Land up in a business that, thirty-five years later, was still selling 25 million pairs a year. This supported him through lean times and fat—the leanest coming after the war, when the loss of military business plunged Polaroid into a $2 million loss. In addition to a good basic business and luck, however, Land was saved by his high degree of the inventor's highest denominator: single-minded persistence.

His original experiments took nine years to pay off. The

first instant camera, appearing in 1948, had been in the works for five years. Its apotheosis, the SX70, was seven years in the making. As time scales go, these were probably unusually short. The inventor has to prepare for a long investment of time, which is money, and of money, which is time: the more you have to invest, the quicker the heavy returns must come to produce the desired pay-back.

In obeying the demands of this iron law, Land by accident or design helped himself mightily by aiming at the top volume end of mass markets. Just as the Land polarized sunglass lens is the dearest, but still sells in millions, so the first Polaroid camera was no toy for the poor at a price of $89.75 (nor was it a plaything for the weak: it weighed in at nearly four pounds).

Another law rules with its rod of iron: prices of innovations always fall after the innovatory honeymoon. To Land's eternal credit (and fortune) he recognized the virtue of this necessity: the virtue lies in the constant widening of the market as prices decline. He simultaneously improved the product, with five major developments between 1960 and 1971, so that it kept the up-market cream while it widened into Kodak's mass-market preserves. Even this process, culminating in the $250 million SX70 development, didn't mark the end of Land's business ingenuity; indeed, that quarter of a billion appeared to be a far from inspired investment—on its own.

But every buyer of a Polaroid camera is a captive customer for Polaroid film, without which he cannot use his captivating purchase; and buyers of consumable accessories are notoriously indifferent to price. By an interesting coincidence, the culmination of work on the SX70 was accompanied by a Polaroid decision to make its own film, instead of buying from Kodak. Looking for ways to build new and recurring turnover and profits on the initial sales is a neglected avenue to making money; the great prizewinners of invention all have this characteristic—like the usage charges on Xerox machines. The ultimate lesson of Land is that the two approaches—the financial and the technological—are equally important; that lesser inventors fail because they are one-dimensional.

Land's dual approach extended its bliss to the stock market. At the peak of the excitement over the SX70, the shares were valued at over one hundred times earnings, making the Land family worth some $250 million. The valuation meant, incidentally, that if Polaroid doubled its earnings every three and a half years, the company's earnings were being purchased well into the twenty-first century. Such are the wonders of technological sex appeal. (They seldom last: within one more year of the twentieth century, the Land fortune was down by half as the SX70 fell behind its schedules.)

Not that high, or even new, technology is needed to achieve financial appeal. The $150 million fortune which Ewing Kauffman, owner of the Kansas City Royals baseball team, boasted in 1972 was started in 1950 with $5,500 and a pharmaceutical product, Os-Cal, confected from crushed oyster shells. His fortune was made by another wonder of medical science, Pavalid, an opium derivative for dilating blood vessels that had been known since 1848. The proceeds from selling these preparations enabled two of Kauffman's executives and one salesman to retire with a million in their money boxes.

In Britain an immigrant of Greek extraction, Demetrius Comino, made his millions with a construction device called slotted angle, which worked on exactly the same principle used in the child's building kit known as Meccano. Robert H. Abplanalp, whose wholly private means are estimated at $100 million, made a basic improvement in a common or garden product, the aerosol spray can valve, which cut down its propensity to leak. That one stroke enabled Abplanalp to grab a patent, sixty percent of the world market, and his notoriety as the financier of San Clemente.

Some better mousetrap makers command neither glamor, headlines, nor much notice even in the industry where they earn their bread, butter, and cream. The car is the dominant, if not overdominant, product of twentieth-century civilization. Yet it has seen relatively few revolutionary inventions since Model T days: possibly the can opener has changed more. Those few innovations which have penetrated the industry's iron curtain have mostly made it big—from Kettering's self-starter to Dr. Felix Wankel's rotary engine, the rights to which cost General Motors every bit of $50 million. Still the name Hub van Doorne, which sounds like something from a German fairy tale, probably means very little to car aficionados, even in

Detroit. Yet van Doorne's mousetrap produced £124 million in sales in 1971, three-quarters of which belonged entirely to the inventor's family.

Like all great inventors, van Doorne did not rest his laurels on one trap. The true inventor tends to germinate a new idea from the solution of an old one. Just as Land moved from lenses to cameras, so van Doorne progressed from the container transporter in 1936 to the infinitely variable V-belt transmission for cars.

This gadget made the impossible a reality: launching a range of small cars in the Netherlands, one of the industrialized world's midget markets, and keeping the company viable at an output rate (100,000 cars a year), which any self-respecting maker would spurn contemptuously in this price bracket. Van Doorne's transmission had its birth pangs before and after birth: the rubber belts of early days tended to snap at uncomfortable moments. But his funny little Daf cars had a cheaper, lighter, and smoother transmission than the combined motor industries of the US and Europe could produce.

On that unique selling proposition the most anomalous and eccentric auto company in the West pursued its singular course—even after Hub and his brother Wim, neither with more than five years of elementary education, had handed over to the next generation. But the technical hopes—in particular that of extending Hub's Variomatic idea to heavier cars—at hand-over time rested on Hub, beavering away in a shed at the bottom of his garden.

For the Daf successors' sake, it was vital for him to find something nice in the woodshed, for genius has one dangerous defect: it is irreplaceable. None of the Edwin Land moves, however well conceived managerially, could have succeeded without his peculiar inventive power—a force that more or less overcame prodigies of uncoordinated mismanagement as the program for developing the SX70 lurched about.

Genius is seldom required to see whether a market exists for an unknown but wholly innovatory product. But you do require perverse genius of a different sort to say (as various worthies did) that the automobile, the electric locomotive, and the instant camera would never sell. Again, those with a vested interest in the technological establishment naturally reject a challenge to their sacred and financially consecrated way of life, like the British motorcycle firms that refused to believe bike engines could rev at the breathtaking speeds which Soichiro Honda developed.

But challenge to established ideas need not mean the pursuit of far-out technology: that chase offends against the well-known rule that the further out you go, the longer it takes to get home. For instance, Honda's "compound vortex controlled combustion" engines for cars sound hideously complex. They are actually much closer to existing engine technology than the contemporary expensive developments for controlling noxious emissions with catalysts, batteries, and so on. Practicality is the trademark of effective inventors. Honda's engine, apparently a foe to carbon monoxide and unburned hydrocarbons, is what the fans would expect from this deskless, workshop-happy multimillionaire. No good engineer likes to waste precious time on chasing an impossible dream.

Honda, like Land or van Doorne, served a long apprenticeship before becoming a master. That, too, is characteristic of inventors. Their tenacity is bred by their experience, and in a world peopled with far richer prowlers, they need to be as tenacious in business as they are at the bench. Witness the doggedness of Harry Ferguson, who let Henry Ford use his revolutionary tractor principle (the engine drove both tractor and tools) on the strength of a handshake. When Ford abused that handshake, Ferguson filed the heaviest breach of patent suit in history and stuck with it until he won (he collected $9.25 million).

This eccentric genius from County Down proved equally hard to pin down when his Canadian partners decided to buy him out. A powerful delegation from Canada found Ferguson willing to talk anything but business; then its leader overheard him telling the butler that the Canadians could be kept cooling their heels. The Canadian threatened to return home at once unless Ferguson signed; he did. One queer feature of the case is that Ferguson was not profoundly interested in money: he once lost $1 million to his Canadian partners on the toss of a half-crown—they generously had the million dollar coin mounted at Asprey's and gave it to Harry as a present.

As it happens, the most inventive artist of the century, Pablo Picasso, exhibited all the traits of the inventing breed: enormous powers of innovation, persistence, instinctive commercial shrewdness (no business manager could have manipulated the market in Picassos more adeptly), and a close-fisted tenacity that made him not just the richest artist in any medium in all history, but possessor of one of the greatest fortunes in Europe.

Would-be Picassos in business need that self-same quality of eccentricity combined with deep understanding of the ordinary. Ultimately, the invention has to find its reward and justification in a marketplace formed by people in the mass; it must find its expression in a business apparatus manned and managed by people who have neither genius nor inspiration. The sad truth is that invention, like most of the admirable qualities in life, is not enough. Salesmanship is essential.

The inventor has to start by selling himself, continue by selling his invention, capitalize by selling the product of his inventiveness, cash in by selling the business that produces the product—and preserve his birthright at all times by refusing to be sold down, up, or across the river. At various stages, he can get off the gravy train; but the earlier the exit, by and large, the smaller the spoonful of gravy. Those who want all the rich juices that invention can provide must, like Land and Kettering, stay on to the end of the line.

SCENE 2

The Secret of Salesmanship
or
Can *He* Sell Salt

A regrettable necessity of commerce, regretted especially by its more respectable exponents, is that it rests ultimately on the disreputable process of selling. Even in the upper realms of high technology or higher art, selling is the Open Sesame. The foot must still get in the door; the pitch must still be delivered; the sale must still be clinched.

The whole embarrassing process is as important to the businessman or professional manager as to the door-to-door huckster. But the god among businessmen pretends otherwise: he calls selling "marketing," or "customer relations"; he tries to sever himself almost completely from the sales operation. Most businesses prefer their customers to buy, thus apparently removing the disagreeable imperative of selling. From this weakness, rooted in the same psychological depths as fear of money, the supreme salesman makes his mint.

An illustrative Jewish fable tells of the grocer whose store and storerooms are heaped high with cartons of salt. "My God," says his visitor, "you must sell a lot of salt." The grocer shakes his head slowly. "I don't," he answers. "But the man who sells me salt, can *he* sell salt." Salt sellers rely on their powers, techniques, and tricks to persuade their marks to buy goods that the marks may not really want or need.

The purchase may be perfectly good value, although the champion salt seller also aims to get the highest price the traffic can bear. But the image of the forlorn housewife standing helplessly on her doorstep holding a set of brushes or encyclopedias that she never intended to buy is what gives salesmanship its bad names—and they even come in Latin. It's the *emptor* who has to beware: all too few say *caveat vendor*. Nevertheless, selling is a two-sided relationship, and the bargain can easily work against a seller—as many who have tried selling a family heirloom to a dealer have found to their cost and the dealer's profit. As Marcus Samuel, the first Lord Bearsted, a seashell merchant who moved on to Shell Oil, once remarked succinctly, "The price of an article is exactly what it will fetch."

The greatest salesman on record was a dealer, Lord Duveen. To a substantial extent, he created his market, the transfer of European art treasures to American millionaires. To a substantially higher degree, he created that market's prices, by paying exorbitant amounts so that he could charge still more extravagant sums. He stalked his prospects with a whole armory of blandishments, from bribing their servants to simple acts of friendship, and he devoted years to the pursuit of an indispensable target, notably Andrew Mellon, the supreme millionaire of his day.

So long as Duveen lived, he went to remarkable lengths to defend the market which made him rich. For instance, Alfred Erickson of the McCann Erickson advertising agency bought Rembrandt's *Aristotle Contemplating the Bust of Homer* from Duveen for $750,000. Hit by the Great Slump, Erickson sold it back for $500,000. Duveen then stored it for his customer until Erickson could afford to repurchase it. (The storage cost Erickson $90,000, but was worth it from his heirs' point of view: the picture fetched $2.3 million at auction in 1961, when it passed to the Metropolitan Museum.)

Duveen made himself the social superior of his customers: spending and living like a prince, acquiring a title (by long, apparently disinterested courtship of Premier Ramsay Macdonald), moving in exalted circles, deploying a considerable scholarship to which the clientele could never aspire. But the whole bravura performance was rooted in the Garden of Eden of all selling: faith. The great art dealer had surpassing faith in himself, bounteous belief in what he sold.

Insecurity is the enemy of selling, and insecurity is the normal condition of man. Cross that psychological barrier, and you are in the Promised Land. The difficulty of making the crossing, however, shouldn't be underestimated. Its hardness and stress explain why so many salesmen, at all levels of the art, hit the bottle with unending percussion. They don't drink to be sociable with their customers; they drink to obliterate the shock to the psyche of overcoming the instinctive urge to hide away in safety.

Selling is no simple activity. It has as many subcultures as the Polynesian islands, each with its own complications. Even the ostensibly simplest form—selling something which is actually better—is complex (and relatively rare). This problem confronted Proctor & Gamble in acute form with Crest, the first fluoride toothpaste. P & G's Cincinnati millionaires had developed to a superfine art the second main division of the sell: hustling a product or service that differs not at all from the competitor's offering.

This is usually the case when the salesman claims that his goodie is superior; just as, if the fellow boasts that the thing is new, you can bet your trading stamps that it is merely an old offering mildly revamped. With such basic techniques did the boys from Cincinnati make P & G world-famous. Crest, discovered in a university, threw them into mental confusion. It truly was a more effective toothpaste—and P & G, having cried wolf in reverse so often, simply didn't know how to advertise the truth, the whole truth, and nothing but the truth.

In the end, Cincinnati was taken off its painful hook by the American Dental Association, which made Crest the first toothpaste it had ever endorsed. Straight ads retailing this fact, with none of the huckster devices which P & G and its agencies had perfected, swiftly turned Crest into the best-selling brand in the US. But selling the genuinely better product, in addition to such subtle problems, has the more obvious heartache of limited lifespan. Sooner or later, somebody is going to match the new marvel, and its superiority will be lost and gone for ever.

The Randolph family had for years been manufacturing superb swords and good, if clumsy, razors. They then suddenly burst forth with a stainless steel blade that left all other forms of wet beard remover far behind. As word of mouth spread like stubble, the Randolphs' only difficulty was to produce blades. After the company went public in 1964, the Randolphs' company was worth, at the peak, £28 million.

When the selling had to start, because Gillette had finally caught up, Wilkinson Sword was no longer in the position of superiority, even if the aura of advantage lingered for a little while. There is only one sure method of maintaining the position known as "company superior"— by eliminating the opposition entirely, by fair means and (inevitably) by very foul.

The father of modern selling, John H. Patterson of National Cash Register, was a devoted adherent of this faith. His techniques, illegal even in their day, included setting up dummy companies to corner the secondhand market and undermine his competitors. The henchman in charge of this department of dirty tricks, Thomas J. Watson Sr., later refined at IBM both Patterson's ways of objecting to competition and his more orthodox approach to organization of the sales force—including the heavy use of evangelistic commercial theology.

The difference between the sales evangelism of Patterson, Watson, W. Clement Stone, ace inspirer of insurance salesmen, or, for that matter, Billy Graham, isn't much in principle. All use the Group, the Cause, the Leader, the Message, the Slogan, the Atmosphere to induce in the subject precisely the reaction which the psychological theory of salesmanship demands: faith, the suspension of insecurity, its replacement by belief in the company and the product.

Patterson and Watson worked their wonders in a field in which the salesman is indispensable, office and shop machinery. Most other selling armies face the logistical difficulty that they cannot penetrate to the ultimate customer. They can use a multitude of methods to get goods on the shelf, but the goods won't move off the shelves unless the mass public buys; and that means advertising.

Clever ads have translated several modest fortunes to imperial heights: for instance, the celebrated Doyle Dane Bernbach campaign for Levy's Jewish rye bread. These one-shot operations are, however, freaks. The big money spent on ads can't be divorced from the intrinsic appeal of the product, the strength of the distribution set-up, the use of other promotional methods. Generally it's an illusion that you can start with nothing and spend yourself via a collection of TV spots into a mini-Rockefeller.

In fact, the more spectacular sellers usually rest heavily on other techniques, even if they also use the media. The appeal of two much favored methods, door-to-door selling and direct mail, lies in eliminating the infuriating gap between buyer and seller. If some worthy citizen will fill in a coupon cut from a publication, or return some junk mail dropped in his letterbox, you have a ready-made mark. The game even has the deceptive charm of being measurable. Replies to coupon ads can be tabulated; the conversion of replies into sales can likewise be measured; offers which fail these statistical tests can be dropped and others substituted.

Then, the tiny percentages required for a successful operation look deeply encouraging. Get 1.5% response to a properly designed mail shot, and you cover your costs. Get 2.5%, and you have a real business on your hands. Get 4% and you can start counting the cash.

Unfortunately, a selling method is no substitute for what is actually being sold. The frenzied efforts of American publishers to boost sales of magazines hurt by television succeeded all too well. The circulation of *Life* shot up from 6 million to 8 million, but since the sales were being serviced for substantially more money than the new, expensively purchased subscribers actually paid, the operation merely brought forward, instead of warding off, the evil day.

In Britain, which has less doorbells to ring than America, a series of door-to-door appliance millionaires have lost their millions through the same basic cause. The number of easy marks who will buy a vacuum cleaner or washing machine over the doorstep is always finite. To maintain sales, the promoter must move on to the harder prospects—and in his efforts to woo these, John Bloom, whose Rolls Razor crash was the most comprehensive of any postwar British growth stock, succeeded in giving away more in premium gifts, advertising, and salesmen's commissions than he received from the marks.

One of Bloom's imitators, a trained economist trading higher up the market, used his professional knowledge and a computer to match advertising and sales, thus avoiding this particular trap. Alas, the system worked only with minor fluctuations in sales. The logic, if sales plunge, is to stop promoting altogether—in other words, to wind up the business. When the economist proved unable to accept this dictate, exactly the same sad fate as Bloom's overtook him.

The doorstep drawback reflects the fundamental fact that using individual salesmen on commission to sell small individual items to individuals is inherently expensive and wasteful. The problem has been overcome only on a long-term basis by the agency and the catalogue (which can be combined for best effect). The agent can even be an amateur, like the 450,000 Avon ladies ("independent businesswomen," according to the company) who helped to make their employer the most profitable company in the whole United States. From 1961 to 1970 the eighty-seven-year-old Avon increased sales by nineteen percent annually, earnings by nineteen percent, and dividends by 464%. By 1973 its stock was so avidly desired by the big institutional investors that, at $7.9 billion, this cosmetic firm was worth more in the stock market than the entire US steel industry.

The psychology of women selling to women in the highly conditioned and conditioning atmosphere of the home is only part of the Avon deal. From a salesmanship angle, the advantage is the low cost of displaying a low-priced article—safely removed from the odious business of price comparison in the shops. Avon and Tupperware are rare birds in the annals of modern selling. Their success isn't easy to emulate, and their version of the agency gambit is specialized in its application.

Door-to-door either needs cheap agents and little or no advertising costs, or indecently large profit margins—like those earned on life insurance or encyclopedias. In contrast, straight mail order, which gets by beautifully on small margins and costly catalogues, has produced more than its fair share of millionaires outside the United States, where the colossal shadow of Sears Roebuck hangs over all. The business built by Julius Rosenwald now turns over more than $30 million every day: an amount many rich retail businesses would be glad to generate in a year.

The idea of mail order selling to ordinary town and suburb dwellers who like shopping from a catalogue, with or without the help of Avon-style neighbors, has made many millions in Britain alone for, among others, the Wolfsons, the Ramptons, and the Fattorinis (two separate branches thereof). The high degree of family ownership implies correctly that mail order doesn't demand much capital, turns over stock rapidly, is highly controllable, and doesn't let the proprietor in for nasty retail necessities like loss leaders, freehold sites, and clearance sales.

The neatest variant on mail order is the trading stamp. This is simply catalogue selling to captive customers, whose money has first been converted into stamps which can be cashed in only for the stamp company's goods. Sperry & Hutchinson, the world's stamping giant, is the pride and joy of the Beinecke family, who must be contemplating with some gloom the dismal decadence of the trading stamp age in the US. In Britain S & H barely got its pink stamps started, because of the combined attentions of Lord Sainsbury and Richard Granville Tompkins. The former, combining ownership of his family grocery chain with active Labour politics, organized a boycott of S & H's biggest outlet: the Fine Fare supermarket empire built up by Canadian Garfield Weston.

Weston's misfortune was that he also sold flour and bread to Sainsbury and his retail allies. After a spirited attempt to sell himself out of trouble, Weston surrendered—in what is possibly the last example of a full-bore restraint of trade that Anglo-American business will ever see. As for Tompkins and his Green Shield company, he had a boycott-proof supermarketeer, Jack Cohen of Tesco, taking his stamps: a business which was one hundred percent in the hands of its proprietor.

In fourteen years Tompkins has built up a £42 million turnover and £45 million profit with no visible sign of either financial strain or undue effort. As for his insistence on keeping this handsome possession, along with a nationwide discount chain and a public furniture business, entirely within his own bosom, that's one of the eccentricities to which self-made millionaires are prone—provided always that going public offers them nothing except an extra capital gain. If your posttax income is high enough (Tompkins paid himself £289,834 in 1972, and collected an estimated £1.4 million of dividends, which is presumably the taxable tip of his particular iceberg), who needs more capital?

High-intensity sellers often fall into this colorful category—especially if they are in a position to conceal from everybody, including the tax collector, just how much they are paid. Hence the self-evident, but secretive, profits of those in the ancient trade known as export-import. The little-known private fortunes often cluster round this admirable activity—not only the Bunge y Born commodity trading empire, but those of Anton Besse, who made enough out of import-export in Aden, the most God-forsaken spot in the British Empire, to found his own postgraduate Atlantic College in Britain: or of Juan March, who made one of Europe's largest piles by bringing tobacco into Franco's Spain; or of a former egg dealer's son, Count Volpi, whose father's tobacco beat was the trade between the Balkans and the Middle East.

The Count, Mussolini's "financial wizard," was crowned with enormous estates in Libya by his patron, and ended up with a hotel chain, a power company, shipping, resorts in Venice (of which he became uncrowned doge), and a Palladian villa, equipped with priceless frescos by Veronese, not far from Bassano. The exporter-importer buys in one place and ultimately sells in another, often far removed in time and space, and after a series of barters and other deals which totally obscure (except in his computer-like brain) precisely where the profit was made—and there usually is a profit.

Since the exporter-importer seeks to buy where his commodity is in surplus and sell where it is short, the profits may well be high beyond the dreams of usury. But so long as he stays in line with prices prevailing locally, nobody is likely to notice, still less care. It's the position into which every salesman hopes to maneuver—selling where supply is demanded but questions aren't asked. Obviously this happiness is hard to achieve in a less exotic trade than Balkan tobacco. But the transparently simple device of charging enormous, nonnegotiable prices, and making that fact part of your sales appeal, can bring the pleasures of the export-import equation to High Street or Main Street.

This particular pitch is the key to the rich specialty shop, the Tiffany or Cartier: the pitchman need only ensure that, like Duveen, he has the best that money can buy. Harry Winston evolved from son of a small New York jeweler to purveyor of million dollar diamonds to the new aristocracy (the Burtons and such Texans as Mrs. Robert Windfohr) by this well-trodden route. At one point or another he owned the Hope, Jonker, and Vargas diamonds; the latter was sold to Mrs. Windfohr, who couldn't even bend her finger with it on. "Harry says," she would remark, "it's the third greatest rock in the world."

The technique reached its most stupendous manifestation in Neiman-Marcus, possibly the only general department store in the world which regularly stocks million dollar bijoux. Long before it found fame by putting His and Her private airplanes in a Christmas catalogue, its ambition was simply the praiseworthy idea of dressing a whole community beautifully. It was started in 1907 in a two-story building by Mrs. Carrie Marcus Neiman and her brother Herbert Marcus; by Christmas 1960 it could afford to lose $5 million, almost entirely in stock, in one fire.

In the process of providing beautiful dressing, the Neiman-Marcus duo discovered that people with an inexhaustible supply of money required an equally endless supply of goods on which to spend it. One vitally important corollary is that the more expensive the goods, the greater the amount of the money supply that can be absorbed. The second corollary is that the more guaranteed the intrinsic virtue of the expensive goods, the less their well-provided purchases will care about the expense.

As Stanley Marcus once explained to an interviewer, in their start "many of these millionaires never had the money to buy fine clothes . . . to provide comfortable, gracious decor . . . But because there was a recognizable authority in the form of a store a hundred miles away,

they were able to avoid many of the pitfalls of the rich."
It's a selling pitch that never misses. In fact, nobody would
regard the Marcus clan, or the lineal descendants of Mr.
Fortnum and Mr. Mason, or their equally exclusive counterparts in France, Germany, and Italy, as salesmen, as
pitchmen, but that they plainly are.

The suave, forceful expertise of purveyors to the rich,
however, has had far less effect on the reputation of selling
than the slick, aggressive confidence tricks of those salesmen who are actually selling an inferior article. Paradoxically, their task is relatively easy: if the sucker doesn't
recognize the shoddiness of the goods, he'll fall for anything. By its nature, however, this nefarious branch of the
trade is self-liquidating: the shoddy seller runs out of suckers, and must move on to a different pitch.

The inferior breed are unfortunately hard to distinguish
from hard sellers in general (since the techniques of per-
suasion are identical), and from cheap sellers in particular,
although the latter are not only respectable, but social benefactors. The sell-it-cheap merchants are another method
of cracking the monopoly of established retailers.

The supermarket chains began as price cutters; the discount stores turned cutting into a religion. Eugene M. Ferkauf, whose very name means "sell," deserves immortality
for the concept which created E. J. Korvette and a personal fortune of $50 million for its boss by the age of
forty-one. The idea of a department store without frills,
from which the customers carted away their own purchases, made high-speed mileage until it fell foul of two
predictable developments. On one hand, the frilly department stores began to compete in price in the area where
the discount stores really hurt, on big-ticket appliances; on
the other hand, the discounters began to get ideas above
their station, and above their management ability.

Ferkauf's management consisted mostly of former high
school friends from Brooklyn, who practiced techniques of
a certain basic simplicity—like marking up all appliances
at $10 over cost, irrespective of that cost. As Korvette
spread, so did its administrative problems and costs; it became harder and harder to maintain the low, low prices.

Much the same thing happened, earlier and more disas-
trously, to Ferkauf's imitators. Before many of them realized what had happened, they were running full-scale
department stores at substandard profit margins. The sub-

sequent spate of setbacks and crashes rubs in the same old lesson: a seller makes his living from the difference between his costs and his prices, and if the prices are low, the pressure on his economics must be high.

The only point at which this rule does not apply is in the type of selling into which every salesman is forced: selling himself. In a sense most supersellers who float their companies do two distinct selling operations: the basic one which creates the business, and the ancillary self-selling, the one which off-loads the business, in part or in whole, on the public, and thus creates the capital wealth.

Nor need these operators be members of the Bernie Cornfeld breed. Wall Street's reputable salesmen-practitioners of the hot-shot era included none hotter than Gerald M. Tsai, the Chinese-American whose success with the Fidelity funds was a legend of the day. On the strength of name alone, Tsai pulled in $247 million of funds; the investing public was so heavily sold on him that it thereby made it impossible for his Manhattan Fund to produce the stock market performance which investors fondly imagined they were buying. Tsai's fund hardly performed at all—but still gave Tsai a million dollar gross income from the beginning. He finally sold out for $30 million in the days when mutual fund management companies were still allowed to cash in their chips for their own benefit. The good soft sell always has hard results.

SCENE 3

The Merit of Manufacture

——————————————— or ———————————————

Money in the Making

Making things is difficult: making them well, that is. Down the centuries the master craftsman has always been able to name his own price. But the Benvenuto Cellinis, the Thomas Sheratons, the Paul Lameries, made only one artifact at a time. The task of achieving their standards of excellence over and over again, with each product identical to and as satisfactory as its twin, triplet, sextuplet, and million-uplet, is of an excruciatingly hard order.

A mass culture demands mass products, and the great manufacturing fortunes have gone, as they still go, to the masters of mass-producing not Cellini cups, Sheraton chairs, or Lamerie silverware, but products that, made in the millions, satisfy the multitude. The greatest fortune ever assembled, after all, was that of Henry Ford, a mint put together, appropriately enough, from being the greatest assembler of all time. Without counting the immense millions piled up in income over the years (at the top of the Model A's earning power, Henry pocketed $13 million in one year and his son Edsel another $8 million), the Ford Motor Company fortune comes to $11.6 billion in assets and $6 billion in stockholders' equity, all valued in the market at $8 billion at the start of 1973.

Ford emerged from the welter of competing car firms at the turn of the century not merely because the Model T offered the best value for money, but because it was designed for mass manufacture by Ford's own mass method. Every manufacturing millionaire has exploited the same basic formula: $vfm + cn + dfm = m^s$, where vfm equals value for money, cn equals consumer need, dfm equals designed for manufacture; m, of course, stands for the inevitable financial reward, even in an industry where, as in cars, the competition is intense and potent.

The product can be widely manufactured by firms in every industrialized state—and still millions are there to be made, simply by making it better. Take the record changer. Supposedly no local British manufacturer can possibly compete with the Germans, the Japanese, and the Americans, and all three of those nationalities have been notably active in recorded music. Yet the world's largest maker of changers is British.

The company, BSR, was started from scratch by an inventive Scots medico called Dr. Daniel McDonald, who founded the business on a design that was simpler and cheaper to make than any of his hard-working competitors could contrive. Bored with his success, McDonald retired to Switzerland with a cash fortune; getting even more bored with retirement, he started all over again, opposite his old works, with a vacuum cleaner, attacking a market which Hoover had dominated, with apparently efficient production and design, for decades.

The gambit of making cheaper to sell more cheaply is by no means the only approach: there is also making things more expensively to sell at a higher price. Thus Johnson Wax once proposed to bring out a car polish for sixty-nine cents. It was persuaded by the ad agency that the price was simply too low for so passionately protective an activity as polishing the beloved car. So the company added some expensive ingredients and marketed the wax, with much heavier advertising, at $1.47. The cynics might wonder why the Johnson boys bothered to alter anything about the mix except its price; but there is a curious morality in your true manufacturer. It was, after all, Henry Ford who promised his customers a cash rebate if sales climbed above 300,000; they did, by many thousands, which cost the old boy $13 million.

The Peugeot business in France, possibly even to the surprise of the Peugeots themselves, became the most profitable carmaker in Europe in the early 1970s by the paradoxical device of extravagance. They would spend far more on a component than their American rivals. The end result, however, was a level of quality, which earned Peugeot a premium price and a consistently rising demand. A Detroit mogul found it all too much to take. "How can you waste money like that?" he demanded, after watching the pains taken on the assembly line. "In Detroit, we run them all straight through and scrap the defective ones at the end."

Good quality is the most moral gimmick in the world: it accounted for the prime position of Zenith, brain child of a differently spelled Macdonald, in an American TV market in which every major electrical company, most backed by far greater resources, was throwing its weight about. The bigger firms suffered from the attendant illness of their healthy bank balances. The latter reflected the edifying cash flow that springs from a multiplicity of businesses: quality, as we have seen, tends to be found in the concentration camps of commerce, where one product or group of products receives the undying attention of every layer of management.

Those who want to play the quality gambit are ill-advised to toy with diversification. It diverts not only management's attention, but that of the buying public. The customer may accept that the most acoustically refined hi-fi comes from the same stable as the most chromatic color TV. But you will confuse the poor fellow if you offer him the best jet engine, toaster, and nuclear power station to boot.

Every market usually contains a premium product, commanding a rich extra in price, manufactured to better specifications and with more consistent performance than any other; and made by, in most cases, a smaller specialist competing with gross generalists. In theory, the generals, with their big battalions behind them, should win. In practice, the specialist is protected by his special weapon: in an industry where percentage margins or mark-ups are by and large the same, the higher price must yield the higher profit per sale. This law applies not only to the manufacturer (which makes him rich), but to the retailer (who therefore pushes that product to the fore, which makes the manufacturer richer still).

At the retail level, Rolls-Royce has to sell 2,000 cars to match the turnover earned on 20,000 Volkswagen Beetles. Admittedly, there won't be many more than 2,000 people in any given year who can afford £12,500 for a Rolls: but the Beetle has to go far beyond 20,000 before it can start to pull ahead: the factory break-even point is numbered in the hundreds of thousands. The enormous weight of capital investment behind a cheap mass-produced item, as VW found to its *Angst* when the Beetle got slightly squashed by more up-to-date competition, rapidly turns profit to loss.

The specialist can cover his fixed costs by lower factory turnover at the price of a higher labor content. It's a far more flexible arrangement, and the equation explains why, in a car industry dominated by dinosaurs, new entrants have continually defied the laws of economics of scale. Contestants as far apart in range as BMW and Lotus have made rapid millions by aiming at a specialized sector in an individualistic way, buying themselves into a high stake game with cut-price counters.

Colin Chapman, the Lotus leader, even survived a crisis that would have crucified any volume manufacturer: the company went on cheerfully producing cars which nobody had ordered. Chapman pulled out of that spin, and in 1972 made a profit of £1.1 million (taking the market value of the company to £6.9 million), in a year when the Vauxhall subsidiary of General Motors contrived to lose some £4 million.

The specialist has to pick his market sector accurately. He will misfire if the product flops in service, but most specialists (like Chapman or Enzo Ferrari) are more conspicuously fond of their machines than their markets. This old-fangled product orientation is despised by the big corporations, and it's their contempt which makes them unable to compete against the inspired specialist. The image of the founder-millionaire wearing overalls, tinkering with some mechanical marvel in workshop or lab, is often reality: that's where Soichiro Honda made his multimillions, where Ken Olsen of Digital Equipment is happiest.

A born manufacturer loves to have his office at the plant; it's the professional managers who fly to the skyscraper eyries of the Big City, where they can forget about nuts and bolts. But plant orientation can work economic miracles fully as startling as those created by the passion for production. Love that plant, and it will grow.

Sir Jules Thorn exemplified the simple rules. One, the vital factor is cost: if a change will bring down the cost of production, change. Two, cost is a function of modernity: if a new machine will improve efficiency and lower cost, buy it. One of Thorn's associates, recalling the early days, said that Sir Jules "did certain things that absolutely shocked me." He bought the key machine for fluorescent lighting tubes "before we had the volume to support it."

That leads on to Rule Three: Unless you can get a suitable build-up of sales, expenditure on the latest million dollar wonder gadget is the way to bankruptcy. That rule in turn leads to the Vertical Gambit. A big enough market at the far end of the line opens up subsidiary markets all the way back to the raw embryo. This perspective is all the more beguiling to the truly acquisitive tycoon, because going vertical promises to transfer to him all the profits made by his suppliers—profits which he tends to resent.

The true productioneer never believes that anybody else can manufacture a component more cheaply than he can himself. If he doesn't like a supplier's quality or price, he simply makes his own. If the end market isn't enormous enough to support his ambitions, he buys somebody else's end market share. Big corporations try the same popular trick, but lacking the entrepreneur's exclusive interest in ultimate profit, they mess up the formula. They are decentralized into product groups and divisions, each with its own target for profit, and each expected to charge prices, even to other divisions in the same group, that will hit the profit bull's-eye in the center.

At each level of the corporate chain of production a profit gets taken, which in turn is compounded into the price and profit of the next link of the chain; until, at the end of the line, when the product actually escapes into the hands of the customer, the final price carries an accumulated profit that is vastly greater than the selling division's final margin. That compounding chain produces a final price that a truly integrated entrepreneur can knock to hell.

This helps to explain how a textile maverick like Kaye Metrebian could produce an uncomplicated product like a nylon sheet for ninety-nine pence when the nearest competition was £1.65. As one of Metrebian's sidekicks remarked of his rivals, "It may be one company, but the yarn is spun in Leigh, woven in Wigan, and finished in Glossop. Here, bales come in at one end, and the finished sheets go out at the other."

The make-it-yourself field is littered with explosive mines, however, as one of the richest families in Europe has learned to its cost. The Philips kin of the Netherlands owe their wealth to the genius of Anton Philips and his technical brother Gerard. Their original specialty is still reflected in the absurd name of the fourth largest industrial group outside the US: Philips Incandescent Lamp Works. Their father, a banker, had invested 75,000 florins in the original lamp factory at Eindhoven, a village which possessed virtually no other industrial resources.

This deficiency forced the Philips brothers to integrate backward into all the supplies lacking in their surroundings—a necessity that, in the nature of institutional history, became a way of life. Back in the simple days of Eindhoven, this presented no problems. But in the complex era of a multinational colossus, tortures can result. For instance, suppose a company's demand for its own internally manufactured supplies falls below capacity. The logical response of that supply's manager, under pressure to meet his own targets, is to seek external customers. Eventually, however, internal demand picks up so strongly that the new and hungry external customers can't be satisfied without new investment. What started out as a simple exercise to meet the company's own needs ends up as a complex operation that competes with the group's other suppliers, supplies the group's own competitors, and charges internally the same price that its customers could get outside.

If outside prices fall, therefore, so do the internal ones, with catastrophic impact on profits. Between 1962 and 1971, Philips more than trebled its sales, but profits (after some helpful juggling with the accounting principles) came out at exactly the same level after a decade of assiduous effort. In two years the fortunes of the Philips family, along with that of every other shareholder, halved in value. Vertical integration was not the sole explanation, but it always will misfire if the integrator ever forgets that his main purpose is not to make gadgets for their own sake.

The aim (as Thorn's Thorn and BSR's McDonald knew well) is to make parts more cheaply, so as to lower the price or raise the profits on the gadgets into which the parts disappear. The true return, the real money, lies in the saving over the lowest available bought-in cost; it's the achieving of lower cost by submanufacture, not the notional profit on selling the submanufactured part to their own companies, from which the vertical fortunes are made.

Verticalism, moreover, is never found alone. There are always other approaches to the production or marketing mix, unaccountably overlooked by the established entities in the game, even if they have been established since the days of Noah. This dating is roughly true of the furniture industry. Its methods have advanced further since Biblical times than, say, printing has since the age of Caxton. But most furniture-makers have not considered their game susceptible to mass production.

It took an immigrant to prove to the British that the impossible was feasible: an outsider is often needed to cut through tradition. The British furniture industry was changed by a Polish-born shoemaker's son, Chaim Schreiber, who came to England in 1939 and, like many other Jewish emigrés, gravitated to cabinetmaking in the East End. By 1969 Schreiber had a well-dovetailed turnover of £8 million a year. But his Big Push came by abandoning older methods of joining pieces of wood in favor of modern adhesives.

Within four years sales were up to £22 million, as Schreiber exploited his production flow to give rapid delivery. He thus pressed the same button as the Levitz furniture supermarkets in the US. Precisely what fortunes the Levitz brothers developed by marketing furniture straight from stock has at times been hard even for a number-crushing computer to figure out. The shares in 1972, for example, bounced about like the magic flying rubber dreamed up in the Disney studios. Sales in 1972-73, however, rose by seventy-one percent to $326.3 million—which in an industry like furniture, even allowing for the Levitz fraternity's accountancy, demonstrates the force of Schreiber's Law: that the ripe time for new aggressors is when existing firms make customers wait. For Schreiber, a one-time architecture student, the law meant profits of £1.5 million at the crest of his wave in 1971-72 and a family paper fortune at that point of around £20 million.

Simple attention to making things, as opposed to marketing them, has distinguished the two most durable economic miracles of the postwar world: those of West Germany and Japan. Millions of customers bought the Beetle (the single most important ingredient of Germany's great recovery, and Adolf Hitler's only lasting claim to fame) not because it was cheaper, smarter, more economical, or more comfortable than the opposition (it was none of those things), but because it didn't, unlike competitive cars, fall apart in the driver's hands (even if, in Ralph Nader's hands, it tended to roll over easily).

The Japanese, possibly because they started by imitating other people's products, founded what are probably the most staggering postwar fortunes by finding better ways to make and design the identical products. They achieved impossible feats, such as making better Leicas than Leitz, before proceeding to advances in design that left Leitz behind. In the dawn of new, genuinely Japanese technology, the insistence on quality and efficient manufacture remained in the risen sun.

The results for such as Konosuke Matsushita have been dazzling to behold—on a par with the creations of wealth in the second American Industrial Revolution, after what Aldous Huxley called the Year of Our Ford. In chalking up his series of world record incomes, Matsushita ran far ahead not only of American salaries, but also of the nearest Japanese; for instance, in 1962, when Matsushita earned £440,000, the runner-up was a £246,000-a-year gentleman whose job, obviously a nice number, was baldly described by the taxman as "son of the President of the Kondo Textile Company."

Small wonder that Matsushita is author of *The Words*

of Peace and Happiness Through Prosperity. His own prosperity stemmed from apprenticeship to a maker of charcoal braziers, to meter reading for the Osaka electrical system, to starting his own electrical firm in 1917. He made electric lamp sockets in the proverbial one room on 200 yen of capital.

In 1971 Matsushita controlled the twenty-fourth largest firm outside the US, with assets of over $2.5 billion, and sported (which is almost unheard of in Japan) both high profits and a decently sized shareholders' equity. Most Japanese companies are in hock to their eyebrows and only minimally in profit. Matsushita sat in 1971 on over $1 billion of stockholders' equity and by far the most exalted profits in Japan, at $165.7 million. His personal five percent stake in this combine is one of the East's largest fortunes, a long, long way from 200 yen.

Matsushita is perhaps the easiest Japanese entrepreneur for a Westerner to understand; he even adopted, down to the last form, the Philips control system, but made it far more effective by applying rigid personal supervision. According to one story, each division had to telephone its results in *every day,* so that Matsushita had them on his desk next morning.

The title of "the Oriental Henry Ford I" belongs not to Matsushita, but to a blacksmith's son Soichiro Honda, a man who baffles even Japanese business journalists. "Mr. Honda," said one, "is a management executive who always wears red shirts and tells naughty stories when drinking." Honda learned the importance of efficient production quality when, out of fifty piston rings tested from a batch of 30,000, only three passed. That was his first manufacturing venture, which understandably led nowhere.

In 1947 he started to make motorized bicycles, with two-stroke engines adapted to run on pine-root extract. Five years later, however, Honda came of technological age. With the Japanese market in recession, Honda spent £300,000 on German, Swiss, and American tools, for the sound reason that they were the best in the world. He then began to take apart the European bikes he was copying— and discovered that their best was not good enough.

European manufacturers believed it was impossible to run motorcycle engines at 15,000 rpm, with even faster bursts. Honda not only proved that you could, but started to win Grand Prix races all over the world. Once again, the superdesign went with superefficiency in production engineering. At Honda's motorcycle plants not a single storeroom existed for parts, raw materials, or finished machines; deliveries went in at one end, up to one every seven seconds, finished bikes moved straight on to double-decker trucks at the other.

Building up a billion-dollar company on a motorbike is not only a prime economic achievement. It's one that, before Honda demonstrated the technique, would have been disbelieved, especially by the established British companies, bearing once proud names like Norton, Matchless, and BSA. In the Honda era, they merely completed their sad decline by adopting the exact reverse of the true manufacturer's formula: their own decline and fall ended pathetically with the workers at the once-famous Triumph factory defying the management's efforts to close the works down forever.

But millions from manufacture, more than most other seven-figure breeds, are closely linked with personalities. It's the aura, drive, and design passion of the resident Our Ford which provides the impetus and maintains the edge. Remove that presence, replace it with mere mortal men, and the manufacturing operation runs the risk of losing its inspiration and becoming merely routine. That's when, if the product has been selling on a quality reputation, the public begins to notice that the quality differential no longer exists; and when, if the product has been living off inspired design, the competition begins to overtake it. This process overtook the Beetle—the bugged bug—in the US at the end of an era dominated by the personality of the late Heinz Nordhoff.

Brilliant manufacture is a highly creative activity; and those who don't make millions at it fail because they approach this act of creation with all the imaginative flair of a cop testing doorknobs.

SCENE 4

The Flights of Fashion
or
A Taste of Money

The mighty corporations devote as much time to future tastes as to the expensive search for technological novelty. Their success ratio is equally miserable. A survey in the British grocery market showed that, out of 3,087 new products introduced in 1959-66, sixty-three percent had disappeared without trace by 1970—and of the surviving thirty-seven percent, many must have earned exiguous profits.

The insensitivity to trends in taste is what distinguishes the common or garden manager from the inspired entrepreneur, and the mature corporation from its origins. All consumer goods companies spring from fertile anticipation or understanding of customer desire. Back in time there truly was a Dr. Clarence Birdseye, whose deep-freeze innovation foreran and facilitated the explosion in convenience foods. Back in these mists, too, a Dr. John H. Kellogg, running a sanatorium in Battle Creek, Michigan, in 1894 invented the health faddist's bread substitute that his Seventh Day Adventist brother, William K., a dozen years later began turning into a world cornflakes neo-monopoly.

Ask the successors of John H. and William K. to parade their own innovations, and the comparison is meager. The Kellogg companies are now in their seventh decade of making millions from a public taste successfully identified while Queen Victoria was still eating her morning porridge. Public taste changes far more reluctantly than the marketing apostles have persuaded businessmen to believe. Hence the latters' penchant for churning out unwanted new products in the hope that they will create their own demand.

The entrepreneur of true taste rarely makes this error.

He recognizes a demand which is apparent or latent. Take the saga of the family which gave its name to another invented foodstuff: broccoli.

The inventor created one new taste. He also created a son who invented another: Cubby Broccoli, the collaborator of Harry Salzmann in putting James Bond on film. It took neither genius nor impeccable taste to see that Bond had screen appeal. The vogue for Ian Fleming's books had gathered momentum long before *Dr. No* appeared. Broccoli and Salzmann sensed, though, how the market should be exploited, which was in the most obvious manner. The laconic style, the exotic gadgetry, the Punch and Judy violence, the sexless sex, the cardboard villains, the artificial luxury—all the ingredients of the Bond package were clearly visible in other pop entertainments of the TV era. The genius of the film-makers was to glimpse the obvious, to roll all the titillating bits into one professional package, and to continue on an ascending scale of expense, special effects, and gimmickry. From *Dr. No* via *Goldfinger* to *Diamonds Are Forever* the costs and the take soared upward in step. By 1973 the combined take of all Bond movies was $600 million.

That's better than broccoli any day. Often in these lucrative satisfactions of taste, the can has been waiting around for somebody to open. Although the opener needs courage and initiative, he needs above all to share the taste: self-identification usually gives the entrepreneur his instinctive appreciation of the market's hungers—as in the hunger for sublimated sex, for transmogrified cheesecake, which existed in full, nubile glory before Hugh Hefner burst into gate-fold view.

In *Esquire,* the combination of good masculine living, pinups, jesting sexual innuendo, sexual frankness, sugared with excellent prose, had worked successfully for decades. But *Esquire's* come-on girls, originally only painted, had a defect: however languorous their poses, their pudenda and nipples were more or (mostly) less covered. Hefner used the basic *Esquire* formula, plus techniques of nude photography no more advanced than those which naked calendar experts had employed for years, and published wholly nude nudes by the yard. He took *Esquire's* sexual themes and suggestiveness and handled them with heavy-handed frankness.

Hefner added one special ingredient to this borrowed, improved concoction: an orgiastic, populist philosophy every man his own Casanova, that bound the soup together. It's useless to argue that no man lives as *Playboy* suggests: Hefner does. With his philosophical outpourings, accessible maidservants, pluperfect pads, personal Bunnified jet, round bed, and millions, Hefner is the Playboy King made manifest.

Just as Henry Luce was the quintessential reader of *Time* and *Life,* so Hefner acts out the role of his own public. His achievement, in strictly business terms, ranks with Luce's triple hit of *Time, Fortune,* and *Life.* At a time when publishers like *Life*'s were giving away subscriptions in their forlorn effort to attract advertising, Hefner founded a mass circulation magazine that made money from subscriptions alone, and then proceeded to establish a prime medium among advertisers who once would not have been seen dead in the company of non-breathing nudes.

The magazine cashed in on the sexual Walter Mitty in every man, pushing up circulation from nothing to a peak of seven million in twenty years, and making Hefner worth the best part of $50 million. The Playboy Clubs gave middle-class Babbitts the key to a door of private enjoyment that had previously been reserved for the rich. The whole operation is, of course, a tease, another come-on: perfect for customers who fundamentally prefer teasing to reality.

Hefner's dreamworld left room to his left for harder-nosed practitioners like Bob Guccione of *Penthouse,* whose customers like to drink their vicarious sex neat, and whose personal life-style dutifully reflects that preference. Both men long ago passed the millionaire stage in a magazine market that many had given up for dead. Helen Gurley Brown performed the same sex trick for a publication which truly was on its deathbed: *Cosmopolitan.*

The necessary skills to syndicate sex probably existed in defunct houses like Curtis Publishing. But the respectable magazine establishment missed, because of its respectability, the blatant information that human beings, male and female, are passionately interested in sex and that, for the best part of two decades, they have become less and less inhibited about expressing that interest, from Hanover to

Grand Rapids, and from Oswego to Yokohama.

The obvious, because of their preconditioning, is what Establishments miss. George Romney, a semifailed politician, succeeded as an auto-maker in the late 1950s by following abundant evidence of a switch in tastes: the $250 million collapse of the Edsel, and the sharp rise in sales of small imported cars, dismissed by Romney's rivals as a passing whim.

Possibly necessity was Romney's virtue, since American Motors had very few shots, and little cash, left in its locker at the time. Nonetheless, his assault, verbal and physical, on the "gas-guzzling dinosaurs" turned out by GM, Ford, and Chrysler utterly transformed AMC's market position and Romney's own finances. Had AMC ever produced a series of excellent compact cars, miracles might have happened. As things turned out, Romney's company was precursor rather than beneficiary of a compact, subcompact, and imported revolution that has greatly changed Detroit.

The attack on the gas-guzzlers undoubtedly sprang from deep Mormon convictions in Romney's own healthy-mind-in-healthy-body, up-at-six-to-play-golf philosophy. In much the same way, the heavy cocktail of sex, schmaltz, patriotic Americanism, violence, melodrama, and wisecracks which poured forth from Hollywood in its golden age mirrored the tastes of the tycoons who gave birth to the industry and presided over its Arabian Nights accumulations of wealth, including their own. The whole history of mass exploitation revolves around four ancient appetites—sex, food, drink, escape.

Of the four, drink has probably been the most reliable, a staple flood of riches through several family generations, and an easy opening for brand-new talent. People need to eat more than they need alcohol. But the price competition in booze is less intense than in food, the need (real or apparent) to generate new products is less pressing, and the outlets are happily more various.

Produce a new breakfast cereal, and you are stuck with the supermarkets and their avaricious, price-cutting monopoly buyers. In contrast, booze flows in bars, clubs, homes, restaurants, trains, planes—and in consequence it takes a rare genius, like that of the wizards who ruined Rheingold, to go bust in booze. The longevity of Britain's brewing aristocracy, or the "beerage," proves the point.

It's a source of eternal wonder, given the small evidence of management skill shown by most beerage barons this century. The continuity of their American counterparts suffered severe interruption from Prohibition, although the leading legitimate (so to speak) bootleggers of that era were still up among the leading lights of hard liquor after World War II.

Muscling in on these long-running acts is no joke—but not impossible. Two Scotch whiskies cracked the critical US market open, stealing first and second places from the Distillers Company Ltd. (itself an amalgam of old Scotch families), entirely by emphasizing an attribute of taste.

Drinking palates worldwide were moving to lightness and dryness. But nobody had ever thought of blended Scotch whisky as something heavy until some unsung hero started the idea of the "light" Scotch. Whether those who flocked to Cutty Sark and J & B Rare could tell the difference, blindfold, from any other Scotch is in grave doubt. But the magnificent results make the question and the doubt irrelevant.

The value of a successful brand of the hard stuff can be seen from, say, Arthur Bell, which owns a big whisky seller in Scotland and has made rapid headway in England. In 1973 the company turned in a profit of £3.5 million, which the stock market dutifully magnified into a value of £27 million. That gives some small idea of the wealth created by Cutty Sark for its proprietors, including two families which were selling wine in St. James's two hundred years ago; and by J & B, which gets its initials from an equally ancient St. James' establishment, Justerini and Brooks.

The J & B family took the common step long ago of merging into another booze brigade, which merged into yet another, which was merged forcibly into a brewery, which was merged forcibly into a hotel and catering group. A curtailed version of this typical modern commercial saga removed the separateness of another invader of the booze families' secure world. A cider house, Showerings, of some antiquity itself, modernized its profits with a drink, unpleasing to all except its unaccountable millions of purchasers, which filled the gap between beer and spirits for those who wanted a short drink that was neither too strong nor too weak.

This champagne perry, sold as Babycham, suited barroom tastes so admirably that the Showering family made rapid millions. The personal stakes of three Showerings in Allied Breweries, the giant which originally bought them out, were worth some £8 million at the 1973 peak, with another £3 million in trusts. Purists can seek consolation from a cider firm which stuck to its apples, H. P. Bulmer; the vigorous life within its ancient vats, treated with management revitalization and marketing razzmatazz, lifted Bulmer's 1972 profits to £1.25 million, at which point the family company was worth £10 million.

A profitable clue lies in the renaissance of cider. If thousands, hundreds of thousands, or millions of people insist on buying some product, or attending some entertainment, there must be a fortune lying in that old taste mine waiting to be picked up. For example, the film box-office smashes of all time have poured forth black ink at the very moment when the last rites were being uttered over the cinema, and have done so all over the world: in Hong Kong one Run Run Shaw and his brother make Eastern westerns and, says Run Run, "have hundreds of millions, Hong Kong or US dollars—it doesn't matter."

The products (like *Love Story*) which create mass taste breakthroughs are often mysterious to more sophisticated palates. Sophisticates can't understand the worldwide enthusiasm for a sweetish, fizzy pink wine from Portugal called Mateus Rosé; they deplore the rush to view another saccharine cinematic confection like *Sound of Music*, which cost $7.6 million to make and made $72 million in the US alone; they shudder at the names of Irving Wallace, Harold Robbins, and Arthur Hailey (whose millions, and those of their publishers, have been made from another supposedly unlucrative art form, the novel).

Possibly this explains why most mass tastes have been created by American men of the people, often from the populist South or Midwest, in sagas like that of Kentucky Fried Chicken. The secret recipe of Colonel Harland D. Sanders enabled John Y. Brown, thirty-nine, to turn twenty of his executives into millionaires; his secretary made $3 million; Brown collected $35 million when he sold out, immortalizing his decision in the words, "One day I asked myself: is this all you're put on Earth for? To be a chicken man." (So, among other things, he promptly became a hamburger man instead.)

Coke, tomato ketchup, cornflakes, hamburgers, instant coffee, standardized hotels, standardized restaurants, other franchised eating chains like Kentucky Fried Chicken—all these inventions have crossed America and then the world on the simple strength of a mass taste simply satisfied on a simple formula with simple economics. But all of these invaluable simplicities, that of down-market taste comes first, and it is desperately hard for the up-market mind to master.

There is no other logical explanation for one major mystery of British commerce: the supermarket conundrum. Would-be millionaires on the right-hand side of the Atlantic have one advantage over the Americans on the left: the Europeans can copy American developments, whereas the Americans have to invent their own gold bricks. Most US manifestations in mass marketing have crossed the ocean in force, none more comprehensively than the supermarket. Its economics were intrinsically superior to those of the individual grocery store, and the British in particular had been flocking into standardized chain stores of all kinds, from Woolworths downward, for years.

The supermarket is part of an on-going social revolution which has endless financial ramifications. At first, supermarkets merely supplied staple goods at lower prices; but they rapidly moved on to the trade-up, which has been the most basic modern evolution in taste and spending. Even Babycham, with its overtones (or undertones) of champagne, belongs in the game of making luxury tastes, in reality or in appearance, available to a panting public. Trading-up, fed by education and travel, feeds them in turn. Sometimes the elevation is vicarious: humdrum sex lives trading up mentally to Hefner's playgirls or Penthouse Pets. Sometimes the process is real: like the broiler revolution, changing roast and grilled chicken from middle-class treat to proletarian protein.

Old-line money has been among all these golden eggs: the Rockefellers, for example, have a big stake in the broiler business. But, as usual, new men have been more tastefully conspicuous. British John Eastwood is worth some £6 million, representing the proceeds of 900,000 broilers a week, plus 4.5 million laying hens; he claims that this total makes him the largest producer of protein on two feet, not excluding the beef barons of Texas and the lords of the Argentine pampas.

Those who fail to trade up, by and large, slip slowly down. A decade ago F. W. Woolworth, whose British chain is the main source of its profits, did a third more turnover than Marks & Spencer. The latter increased its quality, prices, and range, and repeated in food the process of integrated retailing and production began in textiles. In contrast, the Woolworth chain remained solidly, stolidly, and stupidly stuck down-market. After ten years of this inertia, Woolworth's relative turnover had fallen to two-thirds of its British rival's.

The fact of social change is as obvious as the eternal determinants of taste: trading-up has been as clear as the fact that human beings have a continuing yen for sex. The evidence moreover, is omnipresent, blasted out in the pop culture of the day. And it's from the pop pastures that taste changes are picked up, pocketed, and turned into quick cash by the left-hand men and women of all modern business, the advertising agents.

When Mary Wells put Braniff airliners into coats of many colors, she reflected at some removes the fact that people now use color and notice color far more freely. The pre-Braniff sameness of air travel reflected the sameness of the tough, self-made flying men who built the big airlines and stamped their marks all over them: aviation pioneers like C. R. Smith of American Airlines or Juan Trippe of Pan American. In the Mary Wells era, the tastes of these old men, like their management styles, were obsolescent; like so many prop-driven airliners.

When Bill Bernbach, in his campaigns for Volkswagen and Avis, plugged the underdog theme, he consciously or subconsciously reflected another social change: the death of the leadership idea, the realization that you don't have to try to be first; it's a matter of choice. The ad-makers have an advantage in spotting trends. They live in a world of words, pictures, music, and media, and they automatically pick up its coloration: instantaneously the new images and hard-won visions of artists get stolen for the artwork used in ads; pop artists, in fact, sometimes seemed to be in a race with their own material.

The sharper pencils on Madison Avenue or its European equivalents are quick enough in all conscience. But the ad men are still appreciably slower than those who earn their bread in pop itself. Every member of the Beatles ranks as a millionaire not on the strength of past earnings, but from the future income of a group that hasn't performed together since 1969. This calculation doesn't count their loot as individuals, before and since parting.

The possibility of making a pop mint has waxed exponentially with the international market in records and tapes, which has long since passed $3 billion a year. The astute singer or promoter need only corner one-thousandth of that to be Beatle-rich: a ten-thousandth has him or her well on the way. The odds in the pop star's favor are actually better than that long shot. One in twenty-five records has a chance of survival; if one out of twenty-five survivors hits some kind of jackpot, the odds become one in 625. Clearly, this is one of those ideal scenes where taste plus initiative can equal a million without the uncomfortable extra ingredient of capital.

Accumulations worthy of a major industrialist have always dignified the pop scene, from Rudy Vallee via Crosby and Sinatra to Presley. In the mid-1960s Elvis was earning a hot $5 million a year, and sending teenagers into screaming hysteria from pole to pole. In the 1970s, however, the number of Elvis-style fortunes has plainly expanded; expansion was inevitable, since pop singers have developed an irresistible tendency to come in multiples.

There have been hit groups before. But the Inkspots and the Andrews sisters never had it so rich as the Beatles, Stones, Slade, even the wholly synthetic Monkees, and their various, numerous Svengalis. Fragmentation has been facilitated by an enormously enlarged market. Consequently the big music companies, while fat enough by most criteria, have lost any advantage over the small man; and the latter has been quick to seize his golden discs.

Lou Adler, former manager of the Mamas and the Papas, who sold one record company to ABC for $3 million, founded another whose assets include an album which made $5 million on a $400,000 investment. Adler also earned, from *Time* magazine, an oddly uplifting accolade: "Lincolnesque in bearing and probity." Since Adler had houses in Malibu, Bel Air, and Jamaica, Britt Eklund, bell-bottoms, and Jesus sandals, things have plainly changed since Abe was a boy.

Another measurable take is that of Ahmet Ertegun, who sold Atlantic Records for $18 million. Ertegun has to his credit Sonny and Cher, Otis Redding, Roberta Flack, Aretha Franklin, and all four of the Crosby, Stills, Nash, and

Young combine. He rejoices in the title of Pop Sultan and, like Abraham Lincoln Adler, collects residences: a Long Island estate, and a Manhattan town house that boasts a floor apiece for the bedroom and living room.

Society reserves special favors for those who put cherries in its cocktails. Pop entertainment wins these cash prizes because of the magnitude of its audiences. In the higher reaches of faddery, although various priests and priestesses of fashion, from Dior to Quant, have borne plentiful financial fruit, their deployment of taste has lower turnover attached: the mass markets, as Helena Rubinstein knew, make more money by making less tasteful sales.

But the same rules apply both high and low. First follow your own taste: that applies anywhere. Second, choose a soft spot where demand is already heavy or where existing suppliers are panting behind the pace of unmistakeable change. Third, always aim for a sector of heavy spending: Wham-O Manufacturing, the hula-hoop hot shop, or Botany Industries, which sold $15 million of its FuzzyFoot fun rugs, needed only a tiny proportion of toy or floor covering expenditure to make fortunes. But if you are selling golden eagles instead of goldfish, you need the whole world market to make a living; and any such effort shows extremely poor taste—financially speaking.

EPILOGUE

The Rewards of Virtue

or

If You Can't Be Careful, Be Good

There are no golden rules for achieving the seven-digit nirvana, but there are golden rules, guiding principles, for use on the way up, while on top; and, if the best comes to the worst, on the way down. Like every set of rules compiled since the Ten Commandments, every item isn't relevant on every occasion or to every worshipper: the man or woman who covets his or her neighbor's ox (or Boeing 727) may have no interest whatsoever in adultery.

But the charm of rules is that they can be broken, every single one of them, and the breaker can still win. Making money, after all, is a competitive sport; and success in competition doesn't depend on your observation of precept—it depends on whether you outscore the competition.

It may help to achieve this result by sandbagging the poor fellow, putting anti-pep dope in his tea, taking pep dope yourself, lining his track shoes with lead, tripping him, and so forth. But cheating isn't necessary, even if many millions have been made by cheats. The rich in fact divide into three categories: those who would trample over their grandmothers on any pretext, because that is their horrible nature; those who, faced with the choice of losing money or grandma, would kiss the old lady a tender good-bye; those who would honor their grandmother in any circumstances, no matter what the cost.

The general view of economic history is that most millionaires fit into the middle category: they behave decently, or no more indecently than the mass of mortals, unless pushed, when no holds are barred. A small but significant number are natural grandma tramplers: and a tiny minority are upright, benevolent, and honorable at all times.

Virtue in this sense has nothing to do with good works: all the Rockefeller benefactions can no more wash away the memory of the old boy's sins than the perfumes of Araby could cleanse the hands of Lady Macbeth. Many godly religious sects have been handsomely financed by royal flushes of fortune—notably in Texas—but the common assumption is that these benefactions are more often expiations for past offenses committed in the service of Mammon than expressions of great goodness.

It's the same with noble motives; they do not invariably express noble natures. John Spedan Lewis, a second-generation genius who transformed his family department store inheritance, handed over control of his business to all the employees under a unique partnership scheme. Lewis also gave the staff his Longstock Park mansion, complete with contents, plus a handsome riverside estate for their recreation.

Those bald facts might imply that Lewis was a saint among men, let alone millionaires. In truth, however, for all his partnership ideals, Lewis was a highly autocratic, high-handed ruler who, after surrendering control, tended to regret the surrender. Admonitions to his successors would appear embarrassingly in the *Partnership* magazine, dispatched from his self-style "burrow in Longstock Park"—and in Lewis' version of partnership it has always been clear that, to paraphrase Orwell, some partners are very much more equal than others. Generosity with goods need not equate with a generous attitude to power.

Much the same tale can be told of another great social reformer who was indifferent to personal wealth. Gottlieb Duttweiler, a brave Swiss, spotted that big companies were ganging up on the customer by charging unnecessarily high prices; so Dutti undercut the overchargers by selling first from vans, then from his chain of Migros outlets. Migros was a cooperative, owned by its grateful customers in Switzerland, or so it was supposed by those who had not studied the Migros constitution. The set-up left a controlling interest, special rights, and effective power squarely and unfairly in the hands of Dutti and his family for so long as they cared to exercise it—which in Dutti's case was until death did him part.

There is the case of the greatest banker ever to bounce a check, A. P. Giannini, who steadfastly refused to make his family superrich from his building of the Bank of America, but was equally steadfast about his ideas on running the bank; and there is the tribe of Tatas in India, whose former wealth is vested in charitable foundations, but who still rule the East's biggest private industrial empire with iron rods.

The cynical view (and cynics have a saving habit of being right) is that capital accumulation in the private sector plays the same role as tax in the public sector: it provides the means by which the mighty and their minions exercise their power. Indeed, the millionaire's millions, no less than the Internal Revenue's riches, represent a tax levied involuntarily on the citizenry.

The citizen contemplating a war in Vietnam knows that the finance came from him and his fellows; contemplating the Bar Harbor estate of the Rockefellers. the choice acreages of Europe owned by the Rothschilds, or the whopping incomes of the Japanese industrialists, the citizen never thinks that this money came from exactly the same source as the tax dollar: from a percentage of the earnings of the masses. (Not to dwell on the fact that sometimes the private dollars and the tax dollars are one and the same, transferred to the private sector from the public by the beneficence or corruption of the politicians.)

The rich begin by being exceptional, original, unusual, eccentric in varying degrees and styles. Their differences start them on their way, and the rush of power to their purses accentuates their differentiated traits.

But they split into two classes: those who at any time have a clear and precise ledger in their heads; and those who have a much hazier idea of their fortunes, not even to the nearest million. The precision is indicative of a tight, organized, numerate mind; the haziness indicates a loose, sloppy, instinctive attitude, in which hazard lurks.

But to both classes, one law applies: if they have to count the money, pound by pound, dollar by dollar, something is wrong, somewhere: a clerk in the counting house is running away with the loot, or an investment is hemorrhaging, or Midas himself has mislaid his touch. And the sensation that something, somewhere, is awry must never be ignored; like a pain in the abdomen, it's nature's warning.

The messages of nature are a millionaire's most valuable communications. Few fortunes could have been created without a successful hunch, a display of divine intuition. Hunch is not luck, however lucky a hunch may seem. In fact, the computer in the skull has run through a whole series of complicated routines, operational research sums, market research equations, multiple regression analyses, discounted cash flow calculations, opportunity costings, decision trees complete with probability factors. All these mathematical marvels have sped through the brain's maze of electrochemical circuits with speed so dazzling that the computer's owner himself is unaware of the brilliant series of algebraic assessments that lead him to express a hunch or "gut feeling."

To ignore this highly sophisticated machine is a folly—akin to that of the owners of an actual computer, programmed to play the stock market, who refused to believe the thing when it resolutely refused to buy a single stock. "Computer," said they to it, "there must be something you want to buy." It thought again, and still said no. "Computer," they sadly observed, "you must have made a mistake somewhere. We're going to have to override you." The market promptly went into a flat spin, vindicating the computer and mortifying its masters.

The lesson, which applies to millionaires and nonmillionaires alike, is to heed your computer. It will even obligingly provide extra warnings, physical symptoms: a tightening sensation in the stomach, tingling of the scalp, pulsation of the blood, commotion in the bowels. These messages from inner space mean that your computer has evaluated whatever boundless asininity you propose to undertake and found it bad.

The warnings seldom come from the conscience. Only the moral have moral qualms—the immoral or amoral, like the denizens of Richard Nixon's White House, believe self-righteously that their ends (self-evidently right) justify their means. There's no argument on this point: the virtuous course (like not stabbing some unsuspected partner between the clavicles) is always clear, and virtue should always be pursued, even if it costs money. After all, few sensations are more pleasant or enduring than the odor of true sanctity: it's worth every penny.

As a bonus, bear in mind that although virtue is not its own reward, the wages of sin are sometimes death. Grave misdemeanors (as Bernie Cornfield, *et al.*, must have reflected) frequently have grave consequences. For every Rockefeller I who escapes scot-free with his moral crimes, there is a Krupp III who reaps the harvest of his ancestor's misdeeds. Admittedly, finding a fault-free tycoon appears to be only slightly easier than the hunting of the snark.

Two separate inquiries, into the iniquities of wealth (*The Rich and the Super-Rich* and *America, Inc.*) each came up with only one candidate for goodness and a pelf combined: the same man, T. R. Danforth of Ralston Purina. All that this paucity of saintly candidates means is that, in making money as in most areas of achievement, idols have not feet but entire lower limbs of clay.

Goodness is a private matter. What is known about Danforth is not the whole picture; maybe the entirety would reinforce the good image, maybe not. The good that men do lives after them; the evil is oft interred with their bones. If evil, or quasi-evil, does litter your path, however, the same rule applies as to any other vice: don't carry it to excess. If you must cheat somebody, for instance, don't try to cheat the same man or men again; next time around, they may be ready.

It pays, in any event, to be careful whom you pick to cheat, outbargain, or battle with. Remember the natural law that money flows upward, from the weak to the strong, from the many to the few, from the poor to the rich. It is flying in the face of nature to tangle with a richer tycoon. (A contest with a corporation, as we have seen time and again, is a different matter; the odds are on David's side because, in all probability, he is both richer and craftier than the paid servants of Goliath.) The plain millionaire who seeks advantage from dealing with a fancy multimillionaire needs a large insurance policy.

Not only does the richer man have more resources; the chances are that he arrived at his higher status by deploying greater wiliness and garnering greater bargaining skills along his path. Anyway, he has an inherent advantage. By definition, the sum at stake is more important to the smaller man, which makes him more eager to consummate the deal. In that overeagerness, he is apt to overpay. Far better to stay on the top side.

Keeping the top slice is also highly advisable. Common millionaires derive their wealth from equity interests. Dilution of that equity—that is, reducing the proportion of profits or assets to which it is entitled—is justified only if compensated for by a nourishing increase in capital worth. But the most tempting form of dilution is rarely justified: that's the ancient game of sending bad money after good. If a venture blasts off rapidly and then requires further infusion of capital, the sound course is to raise the money from some friendly neighborhood banker. The return on equity must fall sharply if the millionaire dips into his own resources. Cutting others in on the game for a while is always to be encouraged, so long as that first or top slice grows thicker and fatter as a result.

If you are predominantly interested in the money rather than the business, however, it makes no sense to maintain any stake higher than respectability demands. You can reduce a controlling interest to twenty percent before anybody smells either a rat or a sinking ship. A high stock exchange rating should always be cashed in by a cash addict, for the simple reason that what goes up must come down, and always does.

Recognition of that law of financial gravity demands the virtue of humility, which is the essential element in goodness—and one that goes against the driving urge. So the driven man should propel himself to as lofty a height as possible while the propulsion works; he can then more easily withstand a terrible fall. The megalomaniac John H. Patterson, of National Cash Register, was a loony who insisted on his minions chewing each mouthful thirty-two times, who closed down his Dayton plants entirely to teach the city fathers a lesson, and who absented himself for two years in Europe—all without destroying the cash-generating power of a mighty business. His successors, with not a smidgen of mania between them, made mistakes in computerization and product development that wiped out NCR's profits in 1972; the moral there is that mad inspiration beats dull honesty every time.

For Patterson was also a notable breaker of laws. It's easier for the rich and powerful to offend against statute not only because the legal authorities are more reluctant to proceed against plutocrats than pickpockets, but also because the rich, and the rich company, can afford rich lawyers; and because the laws that the wealthy break are often so complex it takes squads of lawyers several years to work their way through the maze (a tangle made more impenetrable still by the tendency of the rich and their lawyers to complicate the simplest transactions).

After Calouste Gulbenkian's five percent deal with his partners in Iraq's oil fields had been rewritten, one of the lawyers remarked that these contracts could never be the subject of litigation, because nobody would ever be able to understand them. The labyrinth in which financial minotaurs like Bernie Cornfeld lie in wait for their prey similarly appeals to the labyrinthine mind, and is the final defense of the ungodly.

But some brave Theseus will wend his way through in the end. It is a matter of historical fact that, by and large, the criminal millionaire (and the millionaire criminal), although he may die in luxury and honors, often does suffer some blow or fate that punishes his sin: like a Capone imprisoned for tax evasion and dying of syphilis, or a Bugsy Siegel bullet-holed by his pals.

This Calvinist-sounding truth has morals as well as morality on its side. He who already has millions no longer has any excuse for immorality: even the usual badness. He can afford to be good, which doesn't mean donating wealth to charity, still less to tax-dodging charitable foundations. It means following strict standards of decency, but that demands the hardest self-sacrifice of all, for the human leopard to change his spots.

One tycoon, caught in a mess of deceitful accounting by his bright young men, was bewailing his bad luck to a business associate: such a mess had entangled him before, he moaned, referring to a cause célèbre a few years back in which he had been widely castigated as a crook. His version of the old story utterly convinced his hearer: as the tycoon reasonably argued, he was over sixty and was very rich; why on earth would he have engaged in any personal skullduggery?

The true answer was simple. He did it just because he didn't need to. The honest crook, so to speak, lies and cheats because he must, and at the time (let alone in hindsight) can't tell the difference between fact and fiction. In this case, not only had the tycoon, in the first place, been guilty as charged (or not charged—the police stayed clear), but was re-enacting a very similar scenario at the time of his apologia.

Many leopards need a professional spot changer or watcher in their employ. As a generalization, a master is only as good as his best servant; the quality of a man's nearest and dearest associate is an excellent guide to his own true stature.

This is an uncommonly useful fact; so long as the master can maintain objectivity about those around him, he can, by applying this test, derive an objective judgment about himself. Unfortunately, the self-deceptive mechanism comes into play. Surrounded by ninnies, the maestro convinces himself that his staff is made up of every genius known to the business world, proved by the way they hang on his every word and behest.

The ultra-rich can be excused for living in a dream world, since so much of their life story is in itself of dreamlike quality. The billionaire H. L. Hunt once said that "there are times when I wish I would wake up stone-broke. It would be a great adventure to see how good I was, to see if I could create lots of wealth again." This, of course, was wishful thinking of the wooliest kind: the process which took him from fifty bucks in 1921 to a couple of billion three decades later proved nothing about his "goodness" in any context other than oil.

But the story, like all get-rich tales, is a true adventure, and a true-life one. You could excuse the old cuss from saying, in effect, that he wanted to live so rewarding a life all over again. And, in his use of the word "good," he put his oil-stained finger on a vital clue: that, in addition to human decency, the rich can afford high professional standards.

By and large, the millionaire has some professional talent which is incomparably superior to those of his fellows. This talent is the horse he rides to the winning post. To develop this star talent fully, and surround it with the most able supporting cast money can buy, is a relatively dignified pastime; and one which has the concomitant virtue of defending a man's fortune. It's not asking much to demand that the man be good at his job and insist that others be equally proficient at theirs.

In this he will differ from one not untypical monster who, in addition to forcing an audience of one hundred and forty to hear a two-day masterly monologue, would sabotage anybody else's ideas as soon as he heard about them—in order to prove that he was indispensable. Very few fortune-makers are; but even those who are possessed of rare genius must recognize that, if man doesn't dispense with them, God certainly will—at least from this Earth.

Until that event, certain moral precepts will guide the feet more safely to their destination, material as well as spiritual. If you are happy being private, count your blessings: not your hypothetical unmade public millions. If you can't manage by yourself, buy somebody who can. If you've made money by fooling all of the people, stop it before some of them find out. If you're telling lies to others, tell the truth to yourself. If you succeed by doing less badly than others, don't kid yourself that you've triumphed by doing much better. If you must buy other businesses, run the many as carefully as the few or the one. If you maintain a complex structure, for tax, divorce, or other reasons, make sure that at least you understand it. If you diversify, keep your eye on the real ball—and the main chance. If you must bet, pick certainties. If you back others, don't pick a simulacrum of your younger self, or anybody else, if your choice is not governed by expertise and experience.

If you borrow, borrow big—and with security. If you lend, lend proportionately small—and with double security. If you work for a company, remember that feathering the corporate nest is the honest way of feathering your own. If dealing, don't steal. If you start small, preserve your little virtues. If you put your hand in the public purse, do so legitimately; graft is criminal. If you get lucky, ride that luck—and recognize it.

If you are paying too much tax, change your tax adviser. If you have an invention, sell it reluctantly—and dearly. If you are selling, don't cheat. If you can make things better, go on doing it. If you know what people want, give it to them.

If your personal life is complex, put plenty in the piggy bank: two Humble Oil beneficiaries, Mrs. Cecil Blaffer Hudson and Bobo Rockefeller, collected nearly $13 million between them as they competed for the world record divorce settlement.

All these are laws of the obvious. But making gigantic fortunes is mostly nothing but the exploitation of the obvious—an obvious so glaring that nobody else has noticed—or known how to exploit. The discovery must be obvious because, unless the truth is large, it will never yield the gains that will add up to a net worth of suitable size. Countless big fortunes have arisen through standing self-evident propositions, received truths, on their heads—including the ancient saw, "If your idea's so good, why isn't anybody else doing it?"

The answer is that one reason why the idea is so good is exactly because nobody else has caught on. What the financially blind use as an excuse for their lack of vision, the long-sighted employ as a radio telescope. There are, true, examples of fortunes made by indulging in some general, humdrum pastime. All that proves is that making money proves nothing.

That fact adds point to the questions asked down the centuries by religious leaders and philosophers, by political thinkers like Veblen and, above all, Marx: questions that will never go away, because they have no answer. To put them at their simplest, these permanent doubts, partly moral, partly rational, partly egalitarian, can be expressed in one huge query: why does one man possess so much, while another has so little?

Because the unanswerable questions of ownership, inheritance, control, accountability, and so on are never tackled (and perhaps never can be), society is uneasily divided between fascination by fortunes and guilty resentment of the rich. But any student of the wealthy, and of the means by which they acquired their wealth, must conclude that there is no rational relationship between their riches and their achievement; the one is wildly disproportionate to the other. This statement of fact carries inevitable connotations of disapproval. It is also the reason (as a few of the rich have had the grace to recognize) behind the powerful truth that "from him to whom much is given, much shall be required." For it is equally true that, to him to whom much is given, too much is given.

BIBLIOGRAPHY

It would not have been possible to write this book without many sources, including several publications: notably the *Financial Times, Time, Fortune,* the *Wall Street Journal, Management Today, Business Week.* But the following books, to whose authors I am eternally grateful, are indispensable to anybody wishing to research the history of wealth in our times.

FOR THE UNITED STATES, PAST AND PRESENT:

Allen, Frederick Lewis, *Only Yesterday.* Harper & Row Publishers, 1957.

Huber, Richard M., *The American Idea of Success.* McGraw-Hill, 1973.

Josephson, Matthew, *The Robber Barons.* Harcourt Brace Jovanovich, Inc., 1934.

Lundberg, Ferdinand, *The Rich and the Super-Rich.* Lyle Stuart, Inc., 1968.

Mintz, Morton, and Jerry S. Cohen, *America, Inc.* Dial Press, 1972.

Myers, Gustavus, *History of the Great American Fortunes.* Modern Library, 1936.

FOR THE GLORIES OF RECENT BRITISH CAPITALISM:

Bull, George, and Anthony Vice, *Bid for Power.* Elek, 1958.

Ferris, Paul, *Men and Money.* Macmillan, 1969.

Marriott, Oliver, *The Property Boom.* Fernhill House, 1968.

FOR THE INSIDE STORY ON SCANDALS:

McDonald, Forrest, *Insull.* University of Chicago Press, 1962.

Miller, Norman C., *The Great Salad Oil Swindle.* Coward, McCann & Geoghegan, Inc., 1965.

Raw, Charles, Godfrey Hodgson, and Bruce Page, *Do You Sincerely Want to Be Rich?* The Viking Press, Inc., 1971.

Sampson, Anthony, *The Sovereign State of ITT*. Stein & Day Publishers, 1973.

FOR INSIGHT INTO WALL STREET:

Brooks, John, *The Seven Fat Years*. John Magee, Inc., 1969.

Galbraith, J. K. *The Great Crash Nineteen Twenty-Nine*. Houghton Mifflin Company, 1972.

Smith, Adam, *The Money Game*. Random House, Inc., 1968.

Smith, Adam, *Supermoney*. Random House, Inc., 1972.

FOR TALES OF THE RICH:

Bainbridge, John, *The Super-Americans*. Gollancz, 1962.

Behrman, S. N., *Duveen*. Little, Brown and Company, 1972.

Frischauer, Willi, *Onassis*. Bodley Head, 1959.

Gulbenkian, Nubar, *Portrait in Oil*. Simon & Schuster, 1965.

Herndon, Booton, *Ford*. Weybright and Talley, Inc., 1969.

Morton, Frederick, *The Rothschilds*. Atheneum, 1962.

Rodgers, William, *Think: A Biography of the Watsons—IBM*. Stein & Day Publishers, 1969.

Saarinen, Aline B., *The Proud Possessors*. Random House, Inc., 1958.

FOR HINTS ON THE DISPOSAL OF LOOT:

Beebe, Lucius, *The Big Spenders*. Doubleday & Company, Inc., 1966.

Wykes, Alan, *Complete Illustrated Guide to Gambling*. Doubleday & Company, Inc., 1968.

FOR GENERAL ENLIGHTENMENT:

Fehrenbach, T. R., *Swiss Bank*. McGraw-Hill, 1965.

Getty, J. Paul, *How to Be a Successful Executive*. Playboy Press, 1971.

Jewkes, J., J. Sawers, and R. Stillerman, *The Sources of Invention*. W. W. Norton & Company, Inc., 1970.

Townsend, Robert, *Up the Organization*. Alfred A. Knopf, Inc., 1970.

INDEX

BESTSELLERS
FROM DELL

fiction

DECEMBER 11, 1944 . . . U.S.S. *Candlefish*, submarine on wartime patrol, mysteriously lost at Latitude 30 in the Pacific. All hands perish, except for one survivor.

OCTOBER 5, 1974 . . . Six hundred miles northwest of Pearl Harbor, a submarine surfaces in front of a Japanese freighter. It is the *Candlefish*, in perfect working order fully outfitted down to steaks in the freezer yet without a trace of life aboard.

In Washington, D.C., a naval intelligence officer is convinced that the *Candlefish* was the victim of another Devil's Triangle, and convinces his superiors to send it on a voyage retracing her route of thirty years before in the hope of uncovering whatever fearful force lies in wait at Latitude 30.

Only when the sub is well out to sea, with no turning back, do he and the rest of the crew begin to suspect why the *Candlefish* has come back from a watery grave, and what that means to every living soul aboard.

GHOSTBOAT

by George E. Simpson and Neal R. Burger